JESUS AND TEMPLE

JESUS AND TEMPLE

TEXTUAL AND ARCHAEOLOGICAL EXPLORATIONS

JAMES H. CHARLESWORTH, EDITOR

Fortress Press

Minneapolis

JESUS AND TEMPLE

Textual and Archaeological Explorations

Cover design: Tory Herman

Cover image © Erich Lessing / Art Resource, NY

Library of Congress Cataloging-in-Publication Data is available

Print ISBN: 978-1-4514-8036-8

eBook ISBN: 978-1-4514-8180-8

The paper used in this publication meets the minimum requirements of American National Standard for Information Sciences — Permanence of Paper for Printed Library Materials, ANSI Z329.48-1984.

Manufactured in the U.S.A.

This book was produced using PressBooks.com, and PDF rendering was done by PrinceXML.

Dedicated to
Michal and Doron Mendels
Wilbur and Frances Freedman
Emile Puech
Ada Yardeni
Richard Bauckham
James Davila
and
John Painter

CONTENTS

Contributors

Harold W. Attridge, Sterling Professor of Divinity at Yale Divinity School, is the author of numerous books on Hellenistic Judaism, including *Hebrews* (Hermeneia).

Mordecai Aviam, Director of the Institute for Galilean Archaeology at Kinneret Academic College, Israel, is the former District Archaeologist of the Western Galilee for the Israel Antiquities Authority.

Dan Bahat, associate professor, faculty of theology, University of St. Michael's College, University of Toronto, was previously District Archaeologist of Jerusalem in the Israel Department of Antiquities. He is the author of *Carta's Atlas of Jerusalem* (1980) and *The Illustrated Atlas of Jerusalem* (1990).

James H. Charlesworth, George L. Collard Professor of New Testament Languages and Literature at Princeton Theological Seminary, is the Chief Editor of the Princeton Dead Sea Scrolls Project and the author of numerous articles and books.

Gary Rendsburg, Blanche and Irving Laurie Professsor of Jewish History, Rutgers University, is the author of numerous books and articles including, as co-author with Cyrus Gordon, *The Bible and the Ancient Near East* (1990).

Leen Ritmeyer, archaeologist, architect, and founder of *Ritmeyer Archaeological Design,* is chief architect on a number of projects, including the Herodian Villas in Jerusalem and the Temple Mount. His doctorate is from the University of Manchester, England.

Lawrence H. Schiffman, Vice Provost for Undergraduate Education, Yeshiva University, is the former chair of New York University's Skirball Dept. of Hebrew and Judaic Studies and past president of the Association for Jewish Studies. He is the author of *Reclaiming the Dead Sea Scrolls* and other landmark works in second-temple halakah.

George T. Zervos is associate professor of philosophy and religion at University of North Carolina, Wilmington.

Preface: Herod the Great, Hillel, Jesus, and Their Temple

The following chapters are the proceedings of a symposium in Boca Raton, Florida, in December 2011. The symposium's purpose was to introduce and discuss before a large audience the new archaeological and historical discoveries focused on the Jerusalem Temple, especially since 1968, and also to examine the often heard assertions that Jesus and his disciples considered the Temple forsaken by God and needing to be replaced. Do such claims represent an accurate assessment of the historical Jesus and of his Jewish disciples? Other related questions follow. How soon after Jesus' death did the Palestinian Jesus Movement become a predominantly Gentile movement? If this happened before the revolt in 66 CE, Gentiles in the movement could not have entered the Holy Temple, since a balustrade had been erected, long before Jesus, to warn non-Jews not to proceed further for fear of being killed by the Jewish Temple guards. Thus, if the Palestinian Jesus Movement became a Gentile movement shortly after 30 CE, the time of Jesus' crucifixion, then many of Jesus' followers would not have been able to enter the Temple to worship there.

Numerous publications open up new vistas in which it is possible to see pre-70 CE religious life in Jerusalem more clearly and reflect on popular contemporary readings of the biblical and apocryphal documents. Among such major publications on the Temple are the following (see also the selected bibliography):

> In 1975, Benjamin Mazar, then dean of archaeologists in Israel and the former president of Hebrew University, published a book that resolved many enigmas about first-century Jerusalem. He exposed, with stunning images, the world in which Jews went up to God's House to worship. As many specialists have observed, his *The Mountain of the Lord: Excavating in Jerusalem* revised what we had imagined was the "atlas" of Herod's Jerusalem and Temple.

In 1983, Nahman Avigad published *Discovery Jerusalem*, after more than ten years of archaeological painstaking labor in the Jewish Quarter of Jerusalem. The book allowed readers to feel his excitement as he and his fellow archaeologists and workmen discovered ancient Jerusalem, sometimes after five thousand years of darkness. A house in Upper Jerusalem—the "Burnt House"—was excavated, and Avigad described the intense reaction of workers who discovered in its basement the remains of a woman who had apparently died in the Roman assault on the city in September of 70 CE. A household weight, from the home of a high priestly family, was discovered nearby, where it had fallen during the city's destruction. Avigad's *Discovery Jerusalem* was rightly hailed by Frank Cross of Harvard as a "masterpiece."

In 1985, Meir Ben-Dov, field director of the excavations in Jerusalem, published a popular book that reported the sensational discoveries surrounding the Temple Mount. (The site of the Temple Mount is today the Haram esh-Sharif, the Noble Sanctuary, revered by Muslims as the site from which Muhammed ascended to heaven on a horse.) In his *In the Shadow of the Temple: The Discovery of Ancient Jerusalem*, Ben-Dov described the monumental enterprise of King Herod, including the remains around the Temple Mount, such as first-century walls, shops, sewers, gates, and "the first overpass in history" (the elevated corridor from the Upper City into the Temple).

In 2007, John Day, Professor of Old Testament Studies at Oxford, edited the proceedings of the Oxford Old Testament Seminar in *Temple and Worship in Biblical Israel*. The book contains reflections by twenty-three experts who improve our understanding of the Temple and worship in Israel from the tenth century BCE (the time of David and Solomon) to 150 CE (the close of the canonical New Testament).

In 2011, Eilat Mazar, distinguished archaeologist, head of the Shalem Center's Institute of Archaeology at the Hebrew University, and granddaughter of Benjamin Mazar, published the definitive study of research upon and recent discoveries of the Temple walls. Her two volumes of *The Walls of the Temple Mount* are a treasure trove of discovery and reflection from the time of Edward Robinson (1794–1863) to the present. It is the most comprehensive and precise documentation of the Temple's walls; the charts and images are invaluable. Mazar shares a valid reflection on the Temple and the massive retaining walls: "The desire to inspire awe and demonstrate power must have been a chief concern of Herod, who sought to make it 'the most notable of all the things achieved by him' (*Ant.* I, 380; XV, 11)" (p. 13). Josephus was writing from Rome. Now we know that the Temple in Jerusalem surpassed any temple in Rome.

Studying these books, which include an *inclusio* from Benjamin Mazar to his granddaughter, Eilat, we may come closer to Jesus and his disciples, one of whom marveled at the Temple grandeur: "Teacher, look, what wonderful stones and what wonderful buildings!" (Mark 13:1). Perhaps, they were looking at the arch that now bears the name of Robinson.

Why is so much research now being devoted to the Jerusalem Temple and its symbolism? First, scholars are now finally recognizing just how Jewish were Jesus and his earliest followers. Second, after 1967, Jews again had unrestricted access to the eastern portions of Old Jerusalem in which the Temple was located, more than in the preceding two thousand years. Excavations from 1968 to the present have revealed, quite surprisingly, that Josephus' description of the Temple was not simple hyperbole. Third, scholars have returned to familiar and to recently published documents, contemplating how they should revise previous estimates of Jesus' relation to the Temple and those of his followers who lived before 70 CE. Further discoveries continue to occur frequently in and around Jerusalem; the full story evolves in new collections and reflections. The distinguished scholars who participated in the Boca Raton symposium and whose papers appear in this volume intend to add to our comprehension of the best reconstruction.

Thus, not only have archaeological discoveries focused on the walls of the Temple Mount and the area surrounding it opened our eyes to some misunderstandings, but we also have much more evidence to explore than is provided in Josephus and the New Testament, and are beginning to regard some of it with new appreciation. For example, an ancient Greek text is significant; it is a lost gospel of Synoptic type (see ch. 7). Most scholars disregard the possibility that it preserves any historical data because it is apocryphal, late, and contains anti-Jewish rhetoric. The document is *Oxyrhynchus Papyrus* 840, a fourth or fifth-century papyrus found at Oxyrhynchus (= Behnesa), Egypt, in 1905. The work preserves one leaf of a miniature book (only 8.5 x 7 cm) from an ancient gospel that is now otherwise lost. Of singular importance is the reference to Jesus and the Temple; the account is not found in our canonical New Testament.

In this work, Jesus, "along with the disciples," enters the holy court of the Temple. They walk "about the Temple." The text describes the Temple as the "place of purification," which contains "holy vessels." To enter this "pure place," one must wash himself and change his clothes. We hear that to enter the Temple one must first enter a certain pool, which is obviously a *mikveh,* one of the first-century Jewish ritual baths that have now been discovered south, west, and north of the Temple Mount. Only recently, archaeologists have learned that the first-century *mikvaot,* for example at Qumran, Jericho, and Jerusalem, have divisions so that one who goes down into the *mikveh* on the right ascends on the left, and is thus protected from another who begins to enter the *mikveh* impure. The one who has immersed himself continues on steps on the other side of a raised area in the plaster. Such architecture helps us understand the concern over becoming polluted by someone who has not been ritually cleansed; the one who has immersed and become purified may now enter the Temple area (or, in Galilee, a synagogue or another sacred place of study to read God's Word).

It is somewhat startling that this highly edited and anti-Jewish text offers us one of the best literary sources for this practice. A certain Pharisee, named Levi, reports to Jesus in the Temple that he had washed himself in a certain *mikveh:* "having descended by one set of steps I ascended by another. And I put on white and clean clothes, and then I came and looked upon these holy vessels." Jesus mentions that the water in the *mikveh* is "running water," which translates back into Hebrew as "living water." Only running water, living water, not transported by human means, makes a *mikveh* a ritual bath for purification (cf. Mishnah *Miqvaot* 5:1-4). The text is an ancient witness not only to the practices we now know were operative in the Temple area, but it signifies that Jesus and his disciples were expected to follow such regulations so as to enter "the holy court."

The following chapters are composed by leading experts on the archaeology of Jerusalem, the Psalms that were chanted in the Temple, and the evolution of the Palestinian Jesus Movement that became eventually the "Christian church." After the destruction of the Temple in 70 CE, many Christians replaced the significance of the Temple with the concept of the Church; Jews replaced sacrifice with halakot (rules for living lives faithful to the Covenant) and the study of Torah and Mishnah.

Two main questions help focus the following explorations: Was the Temple as monumental as Josephus claims or was he exaggerating its grandeur to defend his religion against those who burned the Temple? Before 70 CE, when the Temple service defined life in Jerusalem, did Jesus and his disciples revere the Temple and worship there, or were they offended by what they regarded as the desecration of what had been God's holy house? I am most grateful to Dr. John Hoffmann for organizing the Boca Symposium and helping me edit some of these chapters. Blake Jurgens and Ebb Hagan assisted me as I polished them for publication. I am deeply grateful to each of those who have helped to make the proceedings of the Boca Symposium a gift to world culture, as we explore how we (especially Jews and Christians) are defined by traditions and texts.

J.H. Charlesworth
Easter and Passover 2013
Princeton

Introduction: Devotion to and Worship in Jerusalem's Temple

James H. Charlesworth

A few brief reflections will help readers comprehend the following chapters. The Temple was indeed the center of worship for Jews both within and outside the Holy Land, but it was much more than the center for worship.[1] In Hebrew, Aramaic, and Greek, the three primary biblical languages, the verb "ascend" defines one's approach to the Holy City and the House of God, the Temple. While the final journey sometimes was downward topographically, the journey had always been considered upward and the overriding concept was always to ascend to the hill of the Lord. In his chapter, Leen Ritmeyer helps us imagine the Temple known to Jews before 70 CE when it was burned by Roman soldiers at the end of the first great Jewish revolt against Rome (66–74). Ritmeyer has also helped many visualize the Temple in Jesus' day in many publications in which his drawings have appeared, and in his attractively illustrated *The Quest: Revealing the Temple Mount in Jerusalem*.[2]

A superb study of the Temple Hillel that Jesus knew is "The Rebuilding of the Second Temple and Its Precinct," by the masterful Ehud Netzer, who finds that Herod the Great was not the only one who built the Temple, as Josephus says, as "the most glorious of all his" building projects (*Ant* 15.380), but a king who was a gifted architect who became involved in his works.[3] Josephus (c. 37–100 CE) supplies a description of the Temple, and we know assuredly he was an eyewitness (but no eyewitness can be unbiased). Josephus was not only from a priestly family but an Aaronite (a descendant of Aaron) who officiated in the

---

1. See C.T.R. Hayward, *The Jewish Temple: A Non-Biblical Source Book* (London: Routledge, 1996).

2. Leen Ritmeyer, *The Quest: Revealing the Temple Mount in Jerusalem* (Jerusalem: Carta, 2006). One of the best guides to Jerusalem today, in light of archaeology and biblical sources, is the 1266-page work by Max Küchler, *Jerusalem: Ein Handbuch und Studienreiseführer zur Heiligen Stadt*, Orte und Lanschaften der Bibel 4.2 (Göttingen: Vandenhoeck & Ruprecht, 2007).

3. Ehud Netzer, "The Rebuilding of the Second Temple and Its Precinct," in *The Architecture of Herod the Great Builder* (Grand Rapids, MI: BakerAcademic, 2008), 137–78.

Temple. He describes the Temple in his *War* 5.184-227, *Antiquities* 15.410-20, and *Against Apion* 2.102-109.[4]

Thus, in many ways Josephus's works are the most important sources. The other three sources are the New Testament writings (which are clearly confessional), archaeology (but the Temples of Solomon and of Herod were razed to the ground by conquering armies),[5] and Mishnah *Middot* (which may in places be based on an eyewitness's memory).[6] Martin Goodman's "The Temple in First-Century CE Judaism" is a masterful and succinct survey of the Temple and its importance from the time of Herod the Great, through the time of the apostate Julian, who wished to rebuild the Temple in 362 CE, to Nahmanides.[7]

CENTER OF THE WORLD

Not far from Jerusalem, and especially from the Mount of Olives on the east, pilgrimages could see the dominating presence of the Temple Mount (*Har Habayit*). The presence of the Sanctuary and especially the Temple was signaled by large pillars of smoke rising from the sacrifices during the day and plumes of fire during the evening and night. The mystical sight was remembered by an eyewitness, Josephus:

> Now the outward face of the Temple in its front . . . was covered
> all over with plates of gold of great weight. Thus, at the first rising
> of the sun, it reflected back a very fiery splendor, causing those who

4. See Lee I. Levine, "Josephus' Description of the Jerusalem Temple," in *Josephus and the History of the Greco-Roman Period: Essay in Memory of Morton Smith*, ed. F. Parente and J. Sievers, Studia Post-Biblica 41 (Leiden: Brill, 1994), 233–46. Also see R. Bauckham, "Josephus' Account of the Temple in *Contra Apionem* 2.102-109," in *Studies in Josephus' Contra Apionem*, ed. L.H. Feldman and J.R. Levison (Leiden: Brill, 1996), 327–47.

5. Still valuable is N. Avigad, *Discovering Jerusalem* (Oxford: Basil Blackwell, 1984). For those who read modern Hebrew, Joseph Patrich's work is invaluable: *Hidushim ba-arkhe'ologyah shel Yerushalayim u-sevivoteha: Kovets mehkarim* (Jerusalem: Rashut ha'atikot, Merhav Yerushalayim, 2007).

6. Alfred Edersheim (1825–1889) wrote an erudite description of worship in the Herodian Temple. The massive 828-page volume is full of important information but much needs correcting in light of archaeological discoveries and the more conservative estimate of the reliability of oral traditions preserved in the Mishnah over one hundred years after the burning of the Temple in 70 CE. See Edersheim, *The Temple: Its Ministry and Services as they were at the Time of Jesus Christ* (London: Religious Tract Society, 1874). As the title indicates, Edersheim was born a Jew and became convinced that Jesus from Nazareth was the Messiah; many critics may imagine this conversion may have influenced some pages in his work.

7. Martin Goodman, "The Temple in First Century CE Judaism," in *Temple and Worship in Biblical Israel*, ed. John Day (New York: T&T Clark, 2007), 459–68.

forced themselves to look upon it to turn their eyes away, just as they would have done at the sun's own (blinding) rays. But this Temple appeared to strangers, when they were at a distance, like a mountain covered with snow. For, as to those parts of it that were not gilt, they were exceedingly white. On its top it had spikes with sharp points, to prevent any pollution of it by birds sitting upon it. (*War* 5.222-23)[8]

During the centuries from the Exile in Babylon in the sixth century BCE to the first century CE, Jews lauded the Holy City and declared Jerusalem to be the center of the earth. Such claims and perceptions loom prominently in Ezekiel 38:12, *1 Enoch* 26:1, and *Jubilees* 8:19. They evolve from earlier poetic visions, notably Psalm 87:

> On the holy mount stands the city he founded;
> the LORD loves the gates of Zion
> more than all the dwellings of Jacob.
> Glorious things are spoken of you,
> O city of God. (Ps 87:1-3 NRSV)

PILGRIMAGE

The Torah, God's Word, demanded that every Jew make a pilgrimage to the Temple. Three pilgrimages were required each year to the Holy City (Deut. 16:16-17, Exod. 23:14).[9] Faithful Jews must travel to the Holy City to worship in the Temple at Pesach (Passover), fifty days later at Shavuot (Pentecost or Feast of Weeks), and in the autumn at Sukkot (Tabernacles or the Festival of Booths). During the time of Jesus, the regulation was liberalized. Those in the Diaspora should make the pilgrimage once in a lifetime. Philo traveled, at least once, from Alexandria to Jerusalem to fulfill this law. Jews living in Galilee or far away from the Temple should make the pilgrimage once a year. In his chapter, Mordechai Aviam clarifies how and in what ways Galilean Judaism was linked socially and symbolically with the Temple. Pilgrims clearly affected the economy of Jerusalem.[10]

---

8. William Whiston, *The Works of Josephus* (Peabody, MA: Hendrickson, 1996), 707–08. This most popular of translations of Josephus's books was translated long ago; Whiston lived from 1667 to 1752. I have capitalized "temple" in Whiston's translation and adapted his archaic English for modern readers.

9. See Charlesworth and D.T. Olson, "Prayers for Festivals (1Q34-1Q34bis; 4Q507-509)," in the Princeton Theological Seminary Dead Sea Scroll Project Series, vol. 4A, pp. 46–105.

10. See Martin Goodman, "The Pilgrimage Economy of Jerusalem in the Second Temple Period," in *Jerusalem: Its Sanctity and Centrality to Judaism, Christianity and Islam*, ed. Lee I. Levine (New York:

BANKING FUNCTIONS

The Treasury in the Temple also performed banking functions, receiving donations as well as the required taxes and tithes. The Temple Tax of a half-shekel demanded of each male every year insured that money flowed into the Temple treasury from all over the known world, from Adiabene in the east to Spain in the west. Other gifts insured outstanding wealth within the Temple, including Herod the Great's lavish edifices and spoils of many wars (*Ant* 15.402). The fee for entering the Temple increased the deposits in the bank and demanded moneychangers made so famous by the Gospels.[11] Other gifts include the Nicanor Gate and the Golden Menorah (Lamp) given by Queen Helena of Adiabene (probably about a decade after Jesus' death). The Sanctuary was richly endowed; for example, except for the Nicanor Gate, all gates were covered with gold and the bronzes "shone like gold" (m*Middot* 2:3).

ARCHITECTURE

The Temple Mount, the walls of the Sanctuary, the gates, the stoas, and the monumental structures within the Sanctuary, especially the Temple, were Herod the Great's "most glorious" achievement (*Ant* 15.380). One Jew, who lived more than a century before Herod, imagined an eschatological Temple that would be, even more than Solomon's edifice, "great and spacious," indeed "a lofty building" (1 *En.* 89:50). One tradition would never change; it was established by Solomon when he dedicated the First Temple:

> [W]hen a foreigner comes and prays toward this house,
> then hear in heaven your dwelling place,
> and do according to all that the foreigner calls to you,
> so that all the peoples of the earth may know your name and fear you,
> as do your people Israel,
> and so that they may know
> that your name has been invoked

Continuum, 1999), 69–76. Also see S. Safrai, *Pilgrimage at the Time of the Second Temple*, 2nd ed. (Jerusalem: Akademon, 1985) [in Hebrew].

11. The abuse of the moneychangers in the Temple is supported by warnings in Rabbinics about the abuses of the high priestly families and Josephus's report that the High Priest Ananias sent his slaves to confiscate the tithes reserved for the priests; they were so successful that some of the priests starved to death (*Ant* 20.205-07). See the helpful discussion by Randall Buth and Brian Kvasnica, "Temple Authorities and Tithe Evasion," in *Jesus' Last Week*, ed. R. Steven Notley et al., Jewish and Christian Perspectives Series 11 (Leiden: Brill, 2006), 53–80.

on this house that I have built.
(1 Kings 8:42-43 NRSV [my arrangement])

Beginning in the tenth century BCE and continuing until at least 70 CE, Israelites and Jews confessed that God dwells on earth in the Jerusalem Temple, "the House of the Lord."

Herod began his expansion of the Temple by preparing one thousand wagons and ten thousand skilled artisans, and one thousand priestly garments to be worn by priests who were taught masonry, carpentry, and related crafts (*Ant* 15.390). He first removed the old foundations of the Temple Mount, as we know from Josephus (*Ant* 15.391) and from excavations to the west and south of the Temple Walls. The Temple doors extended to the roof and were adorned with embroidered veils, flowers of purple, and elegantly chiseled pillars. Herod built massive cloisters on all sides of the interior of the Sanctuary. The most elaborate is the Royal Stoa inside the southern wall. Note the description by Josephus, who spent many years in the Sanctuary:

> This cloister had pillars that stood in four rows one over against the other all along, for the fourth row was interwoven into the wall, which [also was built of stone]; and the thickness of each pillar was such, that three men might, with their arms extended, fathom it round, and join their hands again, while its length was twenty-seven feet, with a double spiral at its basis; and the number of all the pillars [in that court] was an hundred and sixty-two. The capitals of the columns were sculptured after the Corinthian style,[12] and caused amazement [to the spectators], by reason of the grandeur of the whole. (*Ant* 15.413-14; W. Whitson's translation)

Inside the cloisters or porticoes, the Sanctuary constituted many areas. Strict barriers portioned off the sections of the Sanctuary so that as one moved from the Outer Courtyard in the south northwards into the Inner Courtyard (which was 500 cubits square; see Ezek. 42:20 and m*Middot* 2:1), through the Court of Women and towards the Temple, the level of sanctity increased significantly. Finally, the Jewish worshipper could see the area in which the High Priest alone could enter and only on the Day of Atonement.

Artists, engineers, masons, carpenters, wood and metal artisans, and gifted workmen frequented the Temple, especially during its massive rebuilding and

---

12. My rendering of Whitson's translation: "The chapters were made with sculptures after the Corinthian order . . ."

expansion under Herod the Great and his descendants. Herod extended the Sanctuary southward and westward and perhaps northward. Most likely, most artisans were Jews from many areas of the world. The architecture of the Temple was both elegant and monumental; it was almost always a political statement: We are Jews. We are important. We were chosen by the one and only God.

The Sanctuary had many divisions. Proceeding inward, purified Jews passed through the outer court or the Court of the Gentiles to the Temple. A balustrade warned Gentiles not to proceed further; after that was a raised partition called "Soreg." Within the Temple were more divisions: the Court of the Women, then further inside, the Court of the Men of Israel, and the Court of the Priests. In this sacred area were the altar of incense, the golden lampstand, the table for bread offering, and the place for slaughtering animals. Above this courtyard to the west was the Porch or Ulam (אולם); it separated the Court of the Priests from the Heikal (היכל), the interior of the sacred area. The Holy of Holies, or Debir (דביר), was the most sacred area. In this area, the Ark of the Covenant once stood.

Eupolemus (ca. second century BCE) wrote a description of the Temple and claimed the monumental work had been done by Solomon. It is possible that Eupolemus's description helps us comprehend the architectural magnificence of the Sanctuary and Temple in Jesus' day. On the one hand, Herod's builders may have been influenced by Eupolemus's account. On the other hand, his account may have been altered by eyewitnesses of Herod's Temple. His description was transmitted through Alexander Polyhistor's *On the Jews* (first century BCE), to Eusebius (c. 260–340). Note how Eupolemus's account of the Sanctuary and Temple harmonizes with, but also adds details not found in, Josephus's works:

> He also made two bronze pillars and overlaid them with pure gold, a finger in thickness. The pillars were as tall as the sanctuary, and each pillar was ten cubits in circumference. He stood them one on the right of the House (i.e. the Temple) and one on the left. He also made ten golden lampstands, each weighing ten talents; he took as a model the lampstand placed by Moses in the tent of witnessing. He stood them on each side of the sacred enclosure, some on the right, some on the left. He also made seventy golden lamps so that seven might burn upon each lampstand. He also built the gates of the Temple and adorned them with gold and silver and covered them with coffered work of cedar and cypress. He also made a portico on the northern side of the Temple, and supported it with forty-eight bronze pillars.

He also fashioned a bronze laver, twenty cubits in length, twenty cubits in width, and five cubits in height. He also made a brim upon it, which extended outward one cubit over the base for the priests to stand upon and bathe their feet and wash their hands. He also made the twelve legs of the laver of cast metal and of the height of a man; and he stood them at the back end under the laver, at the right of the altar of sacrifice. He also made a bronze platform two cubits in height near the laver for the king to stand upon whenever he prays so that he might be visible to the Jewish people. He also built the altar of sacrifice twenty cubits by twenty cubits and twelve cubits in height. He also made two bronze rings wrought like chains and stood them upon stands, which were twenty cubits in height above the sanctuary, and they cast a shadow over the entire Temple. He hung upon each network four hundred bronze bells, a talent in weight, and he made all the networks in order to ring the bells and scare away the birds that they might not settle upon the Temple or build a nest upon the coffered works of the gates and porticoes and defile the Temple with their excrement. (*apud* Eusebius, *Praeparatio Evangelica* 9.26.1. *Old Testament Pseudepigrapha* 2.869–70; translated by F. Fallon)

Eupolemus's account does not suit Solomon's Temple; it also does not apply to the Hasmonean, or pre-Herodian, Temple. Thus, F. Fallon rightly suggests that Eupolemus's description "may derive from the Second Temple," that is, the Herodian Temple (*OTP* 2.869 note m). Some descriptions may derive from the Hebrew Bible, but other traditions seem to be enriched by eyewitnesses of Herod's Temple. Eupolemus's information must no longer be ignored in discerning the Temple Jesus knew; of course, the accounts in the Mishnah and apocryphal works are not to be taken without careful evaluation, either. The most important rabbinic work regarding the Temple is Mishnah *Middot*. This tractate preserves the dimensions and descriptions of the Temple but is not found in the Tosephta (the "Supplement" to the Mishnah).

The recent astounding archaeological discoveries are outside the Sanctuary and part of the Temple Mount.[13] The massive stones that Roman soldiers pushed from the top of the Sanctuary to their present location during the destruction of 70 CE can be seen today where they fell.[14] These relics demonstrate the fact that nothing of Herod's Temple itself remains. Evident

13. See plate 20 in Ehud Netzer, *The Architecture of Herod the Great Builder* (Grand Rapids, MI: BakerAcademic, 2008).

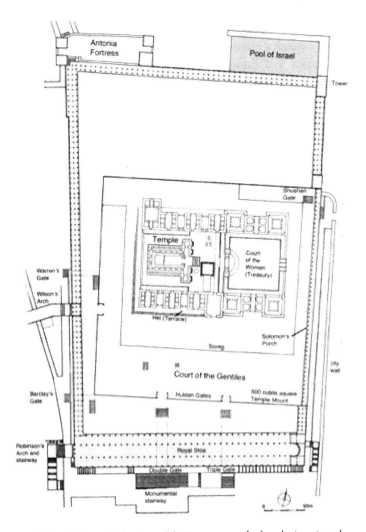

Fig. 0.1. Leen Ritmeyer's drawing of the Sanctuary and where he imagines the Shushan Gate was located. Reprinted with the courtesy of Leen Ritmeyer.

are many *miqva'ot* (ritual immersion baths) near the entrances and beneath the houses to the Western Wall, including the massive *miqva'ot* in Bethzatha to the north and the Pool of Siloam much farther to the south of the Sanctuary.

14. The author of *Pseudo-Philo* (*LAB*) describes the stones, the altar, and the offerings. It is precarious to use his descriptions for the Temple Jesus knew because he is imagining Kenaz and Solomon; see D. J. Harrington, "Pseudo-Philo 26" in *OTP* 2.336–41.

Still visible are the outlines of gates on the walls of the Temple Mount, but only in the south and west.[15] They can be seen, or imagined, as one walks clockwise from the eastern section of the southern wall. They are the triple gate, the eastern edge of the double gate (that some think is "the Beautiful Gate"),[16] Robinson's Gate that can be only imagined above Robinson's Arch, Barclay's Gate, a gate above Wilson's Arch that is no longer visible (priests would walk into the Sanctuary on this bridge from the Upper City), Warren's Gate, the Tadi Gate and the Sheep Gate on the north (exact locations are debated), and the Shushan Gate (mentioned in the Mishnah but there is now no evidence of it).[17] Most of these gates do not bear the original names; they bear the name of the nineteenth-century Europeans who discovered them.

The compilers of the Mishnah in *Middot* 1:3 name five Temple gates: the two Hulda Gates in the south, the Qiponos Gate on the west, the Tadi Gate on the north, and the Eastern Gate (Shushan Gate, through which the High Priest leads the red heifer to the Mount of Olives). The Mishnah was codified after 200 CE and should not be taken literally, even though there is intermittently reliable oral tradition preserved, since it conflicts both with the descriptions of Josephus, who knew the Temple intimately, and archaeological discoveries. Most likely, the Mishnah preserves descriptions of the pre-Herodian Temple, and this hypothesis makes sense since Mishnah *Middot* often parallels, and even quotes, the descriptions of the Temple in the Pentateuch, Kings, Ezekiel, Isaiah, and Chronicles.[18]

Especially impressive today are the massive retaining walls, including the Western Wall (also called the "Wailing Wall"), with its beautifully chiseled and embossed Herodian ashlars (polished stones with an elegant border). These

---

15. See the definitive publication by Eilat Mazar, *The Walls of the Temple Mount* (Jerusalem: Shoham Academic Research and Publication, 2011). As Netzer warned, the gates into the Temple Mount are "clear with regard to the southern and western sides but somewhat hazy with regard to the northern and eastern ones." See Netzer, *The Architecture of Herod the Great Builder*, 171. I am deeply indebted to Ehud for years of discussing our shared passion of understanding Herod and the massive buildings and cities he created.

16. See the claims and more especially the elaborate drawings and photographs of the Double Gate in figs. 36, 39, 40, and 41 in Roger Liebi, *The Messiah in the Temple*, trans. Timothy Capes (Düsseldorf: Christlicher Medien Vertrieb, 2012). This volume will be unattractive to some specialists because of its faith-based discussions.

17. For images of Robinson's Arch, Wilson's Arch, Warren's Gate, and Barclay's Gate, see Liebi, *The Messiah in the Temple*, 54–59. For the Shushan Gate, see Netzer, *The Architecture of Herod the Great Builder*, 175.

18. See the professional drawing of the Pre-Herodian Square Temple Mount by Leen Ritmeyer in *The Quest: Revealing the Temple Mount in Jerusalem* (Jerusalem: Carta, 2006), 185.

archaeological discoveries often prove that Josephus's descriptions of Jerusalem and the Temple before 70 CE are not mere hyperbole; sometimes they are astoundingly accurate. One stone in the western retaining wall weighs approximately 570 tons and is 13.7 meters long, 3.5 meters high, and about 4.5 meters wide.[19]

TEMPLE POLICE

The thousands of priests and the treasures demanded a Temple police. They also controlled the crowds that could become mobs during the festivals, especially Pesach (Passover), when Jerusalem frequently tripled in size. As we know from the history of Jesus, charismatics were attracted to the Temple cult; and these free-thinking, powerful individuals clashed with any institutional group, such as priests. The Temple police not only guarded the High Priest but they guided many who needed to know where to go within the Sanctuary. Most likely, they also monitored those who entered the Sanctuary, not permitting Gentiles to cross the balustrade or "latticed railing" (mMiddot 2:3), and prohibited Jews from continuing further into the Sanctuary if they were a *mamzer* (someone who could not prove full and authentic Jewish lineage), or not healthy, or had not entered a *miqveh* (a ritual immersion bath for purifications of Jews), or had been in too close contact with Gentiles, treated the priests without honor, or wore inappropriate garb. These guards protected the purity of the Sanctuary from the danger of pollution from any who were not well, including especially the blind, the lame, the leper, and the *mamzer*. These guards arrested first Jesus, according to John, and then later Paul, according to Acts. Finally, among their other duties, the Temple guards sought to keep Roman soldiers at a distance.

WORSHIP CENTER

The most important dimension of the Temple was worship. From all parts of the known world, Jews affirmed that Jerusalem's Temple was the only place to worship and was the abode of the LORD God. As Martin Goodman states, the unparalleled importance of the Temple to most Jews around the world is placarded by the willingness of Alexandrians, Galileans, and Judeans to sacrifice themselves, and their children, for its sanctity between 38 and 40 CE.[20] Moreover, King Agrippa I risked losing prestige, power, and even his own

---

19. For a color image of this massive stone, see www.IJCO.org "Image Gallery" [double click on it] and Liebi, *The Messiah in the Temple*, 60.

20. Goodman, "The Temple in First Century CE Judaism," 459.

Fig. 0.2. A large mikveh near the Temple. Reprinted by courtesy of Alexander Schick.

life, when he sought to persuade Gaius Caligula (Emperor from 37–41 CE) to rescind an order in the winter of 39 and 40 to send an army to Jerusalem to erect his effigy in the Temple so he might be declared a god.[21] The resulting calamities were averted by the assassination of the mad emperor on 24 January 41 CE,[22] and the Temple continued its supreme importance. The worldwide solidarity among most Jews was summarized by E. P. Sanders, who signaled the "payment of the temple tax by Diaspora Jews, pilgrimage to the temple from abroad, world-wide alarm at the threat of Gaius to have his statue erected in the temple . . . and many other points."[23]

The Torah demanded that the Jerusalem Temple was the only legitimate place to worship and sacrifice; other rival temples such as that at Leontopolis were insignificant in contrast.[24] The Samaritans, strictly speaking, never had

21. See Philo (*Legatio* 33 [248]) and Josephus (*War* 2.188-92 and *Ant* 18.262).

22. See the scholarly summary of these events in Emil Schürer, *The History of the Jewish People in the Age of Jesus Christ (175 B.C –A.D. 135)*, ed. Geza Vermes, Fergus Millar et al., vol. 1 (Edinburgh: T&T Clark, 1973), 388–96.

23. E.P. Sanders, "Common Judaism and the Temple," in *Judaism: Practice and Belief 63 BCE–66 CE* (London: SCM, 1992), 47.

a "temple"; they sacrificed lambs in a sacred area that was cut out of the ground. Greek and Roman authors often cast aspersions on the idiosyncratic Jewish customs, but they understood and even admired the Jewish fondness for and dedication to the Temple (viz., Tacitus, *Histories* 5.8.1). Martin Goodman rightly points out that thanks to Josephus, who knew "the cult from the inside," and the trustworthy reports or comments in the New Testament, Mishnah, and Tosephta, the Temple and its cult—ascent, music, dance, sacrifice, incense, offerings, and elegance—is "much better known than any other temple system in the ancient world precisely because these later Jews and Christian preserved so much evidence about the way that the Temple operated."[25] The Temple was destroyed in Jerusalem, but no one could destroy its memory or its ability to shape eternal traditions.

The Temple also needed animals for slaughter, including bulls, lambs, and pigeons. The offering of "the first fruits" demanded that produce be brought to the Temple, and that required transportation, roads, and storage facilities. Wood was a necessary commodity for sacrificial fires, and the Temple had rooms reserved for storing the logs. Incense was demanded for reverence and the required offerings. Consecutive stages of holiness demanded upkeep, cleaning, and all requirements of maintenance. (Philo of Alexandria, who made at least one pilgrimage to the Temple, remarked about the impressive cleanliness in the Sanctuary [*Spec. Laws* 1].) The cult created and stimulated special language and an elaborate symbolism.

Imagining Jesus Entering the Temple to Teach and Worship

Many interested readers of the following chapters would benefit from an informed, imaginative journey up and into the Temple by devout Jews, like Hillel and Jesus. Thus, in light of archaeological discoveries and texts, especially the ancient reflections in the Old Testament Pseudepigrapha, Josephus's *Antiquities*, and Mishnah *Middot*, and profiting from conversations with great archaeologists, such as those contributing to this symposium, I boldly share my own imagination of what it was like to climb the sheer steps into the Sanctuary and move toward the interior where the Temple rose majestically.

Almost always, pilgrims approached the Sanctuary from the west or the south. As Ehud Netzer suggested,[26] the main entrance façade of the Temple complex was in the south, with the Hulda Gates (both the triple and double

---

24. The Leontopolis temple was closed by the Roman about 72 CE. (Josephus, *War* 7.420–32).

25. Goodman, "The Temple in First Century CE Judaism," 459.

26. Netzer, *The Architecture of Herod*, 171.

gates were named after this Old Testament prophetess [2 Kgs. 22:14; 2 Chron. 34:22]). Perhaps this desired approach to the Temple was ancient, reflecting the traditions that associated David and Solomon with the Ophel. It was certainly more attractive because of the numerous *mikva'ot in situ* and the large plazas near the southern wall that accommodated the masses as they prepared to ascend into the hill of the Lord.

To better appreciate the chapters that follow, originally presented as public lectures, let us imagine what transpires when Jesus—or Hillel—walks from the southern section of Jerusalem and up into the Sanctuary. According to John 9, Jesus heals a blind man and tells him to go to the Pool of Siloam. Perhaps Jesus also went to that Pool to immerse himself so he could enter the Sanctuary. He most likely puts on more appropriate clothes, conceivably white linen similar to that worn by Essenes and the high priests (m*Middot* 5:4). He then turns around and heads northward to ascend the monumental stairway (the width of which remains uncertain, since a large portion is today hidden beneath houses). Moving through the open plaza, he ascends into the Triple Gate. Then he climbs the interior steep steps, most likely looking up to admire the richly decorated ceilings. Once he passes under the Royal Portico, he enters again into the blinding sunlight.

Fig. 0.3. An artist's rendering of the Pool of Siloam, looking south. Courtesy of Alexander Schick.

He moves northward through the Outer Courtyard (or Court of the Gentiles) and enters the sacred square of the older Sanctuary. He now leaves behind the southern extension of the Temple Mount, designed by Herod, even though the northern portions of it may have been constructed by the Hasmoneans. He passes through the two-foot-ten-inch balustrade[27] that, in Greek (and Latin),[28] warned Gentiles they were "liable to the death penalty" if they proceeded further.[29] Most likely, this warning allowed the Temple priests to deliver the desired punishment.[30] According to a speech by Titus, recorded by Josephus, the Roman governors allowed Jews to put to death anyone who transgressed the balustrade, even a Roman (*War* 6.124-26).

Apparently, there were additional *mikva'ot* within the Outer Courtyard in which Jews could immerse themselves, if they had become inadvertently impure.[31] For the High Priest on the Day of Atonement, a *miqveh* was constructed on the roof of the Salt-Parva Chamber that was north of the altar (m*Middot* 5:3). Any priest who had a nocturnal emission would proceed through a passage below the buildings to "the immersion room" (m*Middot* 1:9).

In the Inner Courtyard, Jesus heads towards his favorite area, Solomon's Portico, which extended along the eastern edge of the Sanctuary. Perhaps he pauses in this elegant portico for some hours, delivering one of the speeches that are located there by John (John 5:2; 10:23; cf. Acts 3:11 and 5:12). Eventually, he heads westward and through the Eastern Gate of the Temple complex and into the Court of the Women, which denoted that women could not proceed further into the Temple. Jesus moves consecutively past the Chamber of Wood on the right and the Chamber of Nazirites on the left (m*Middot* 2:5).

In the center of the Court of the Women is the treasury. Jesus halts and remembers how he had sat nearby and heard a widow drop two small

---

27. The Hebrew name is "Soreg"; see m*Middot* 2:3.

28. Josephus, *War* 5.193-94; 6.124; *Ant* 15.417.

29. See the image of the Greek inscription and discussion of the balustrade in Ritmeyer, *The Quest*, 346–47.

30. On the question of administering the death penalty by Jewish authorities in Jesus' time, including crucifixion that was practiced by Alexander Jannaeus, described in the *Nahum Pesher*, and mirrored in the *Temple Scroll*, see Geza Vermes, "Was Crucifixion a Jewish Penalty?" *Standpoint* (April 2013): 66–69. Vermes affirms that the *Temple Scroll* allowed the Chief Priest the power to crucify someone for serious crimes (cf. *Targum to Ruth*). Many scholars conclude, perhaps under the influence of John 8:31, that the Romans did not allow the Judean leaders to execute Jews. See, for example, Ritmeyer, *The Quest*, 347.

31. See R. Reich, "Two Possible Miqwaot on the Temple Mount," *Israel Exploration Journal* 39 (1989): 63–65. Most likely these *mikvaot* antedated Herod's extension to the south of the Temple Mount and would have been used earlier before one entered the Sanctuary.

coins into the treasury (Mark 12:42). Then, he continues past the northern and southern gates, pausing again, this time to talk with Mary Magdalene and his mother, but only briefly because women and men "should not mingle" (m*Middot* 2:5). Before he passes the Chamber of Lepers (right) and the Chamber of Oil (left), he pauses to admire the many Levites who had gathered on the fifteen semi-circular steps that fronted the Nicanor Gate and led to the Court of the Israelites (m*Middot* 2:5). He appreciates hearing the trumpets, tambourines, and the chanting, accompanied by drums, lyres, cymbals, harps, and other musical instruments (m*Middot* 2:6). Within the Court of the Women, twenty-four young girls dance with joy and swirl, holding aloft brightly colored silk. They are ecstatically entranced by the chanting of the final psalm in the Davidic Psalter by the Levites:[32]

> Praise the LORD!
> Praise God *in his sanctuary*;
> praise him in his mighty firmament!
> Praise him for his mighty deeds;
> praise him according to his surpassing greatness!
> Praise him with *trumpet sound*;
> praise him with *lute and harp*!
> Praise him with *tambourine and dance*;
> praise him with *strings and pipe*!
> Praise him with *clanging cymbals*;
> praise him with *loud clashing cymbals*!
> Let everything that breathes praise the LORD!
> Praise the LORD! (Ps 150 NRSV; my italics]

Hearing and seeing such elevating drama and music, Jesus feels at home in the House of the Lord, and hears an inner voice say: "This is my Father's House."

After this celebration, Jesus continues moving west and ahead, past the Nicanor Gate and into the Court of the Israelites. He leaves behind the pressing crowds that had misinterpreted his teachings and wished to place titles on him. He sees some lurking Sadducees whom he knew were trying to entrap him and claim that he had been born in fornication (John 8:41). He probably knew that

---

32. There are only 150 Davidic Psalms in the Hebrew Bible; thanks to the Qumran Scrolls, the Septuagint, and the Syriac Bible, we now have the texts of Psalms 151 to 155. See Charlesworth and James A. Sanders, "More Psalms of David," in *Old Testament Pseudepigrapha* 2.609-24.

soon these teachers who denied the resurrection would brand him a *mamzer* and prohibit him from entering the Temple (cf. *Some Works of the Torah*).

Fig. 0.4. Leen Ritmeyer's depiction of the Nicanor Gate and the Court of the Women, with Levites on the fifteen steps of the Semi-Circular Steps. Reprinted by courtesy of Leen Ritmeyer.

Jesus pauses before the Duchan Gate that led from the Court of the Israelites to the Court of the Priests; he looks at the altar, which is thirty-two cubits square at the base (mMiddot 3:1). Not too much farther to the west is the porch, the Hêkhal, and finally the Debir (the Holy of Holies). Over the entrance to the inner Temple is a golden vine from which many philanthropists hung gold leaves and clusters (mMiddot 3:8). Only the High Priest could enter into the Holy of Holies, and only on the Day of Atonement. At other times, when repairs were needed, workmen would be lowered into the Debir in boxes from an upper room (mMiddot 4:5). But the boxes were closed on three sides so that the craftsmen "should not feast their eyes on the house of the Holy of Holies" (mMiddot 4:5).[33]

As a devout Jew faithful to Torah, Jesus recites a prayer from a scroll he had memorized:

O LORD, I love the house in which you dwell,
And the place where your glory abides. (Psalm 26:8 NRSV)

33. Translated by J. Neusner, *The Mishnah* (New Haven: Yale University Press, 1988), 881.

CONCLUSION

A prominent lawyer in Los Angeles heard about the preparation of this book and wrote me the following: "I always thought that Jesus was born, lived and died a Jew, and was in Jerusalem to go to the Temple and observe Passover; and that Seder turned out to be 'The Last Supper.' There was matzo on the table of the famous painting [by Leonardo da Vinci]. Are there some scholars that believe otherwise?"[34]

Those who have devoted themselves to produce the erudite chapters that follow share the hope that the unfortunate increase in anti-Semitism will cease, and that more and more people will comprehend that Jesus lived as an observant Jew. It was as an observant Jew that he ascended the Mountain of the Lord at his last Passover, to obey Torah and worship in the Temple. At that time, Jesus ate his last supper with his disciples. Far too often, the institution of the Last Supper is divorced from its setting and grounding in the Torah and the Temple. As Christians observe the Eucharist, they commemorate Jesus' injunction, according to Paul and Luke, to do so "in remembrance of me" (1 Cor. 11:25; Luke 22:19).[35] We who write these chapters hope the symbolic importance of the Temple will also be remembered.

34. This lawyer is a very dear friend; he also loves to chase coyotes (not the animal).

35. Despite the influences from Paul and Luke on the transmission of the Last Supper in Matthew and Mark (conflationism), no scribe (as far as I can detect) added "in remembrance of me" to the first two Gospels. The Fourth Evangelist redacts the tradition so that the Last Supper is not a last supper but a speech following the feeding of the five thousand in the synagogue in Capernaum; Jesus claims he is "the living bread which came down from heaven" (John 6:51). Justin Martyr preserves "in remembrance of me" (*Apol* 1.66.3) but it is not found in the Eucharist traditions in the *Didache* or in the *Gospel of the Ebionites* (*apud* Epiphanius, *Panarion haer.* 30.22.4-5).

1

Imagining the Temple Known to Jesus and to Early Jews

Leen Ritmeyer

There is great value in making reconstruction drawings to imagine the Temple that Jesus and the early Jews knew. First and foremost, the process allows historical and archaeological information about this site, venerated by members of the three major faiths, Judaism, Christianity, and Islam, to be presented in a meaningful way. It also provides a fruitful focal point for collaborative work between those of other disciplines who are trying to understand the site.

However, I also realize how privileged we are when dealing with this particular site as compared to others. When I did my master's degree in Conservation Studies at the Institute of Advanced Architectural Studies at the University of York, one of the axioms I noted from an ICOMOS document (the International Council on Monuments and Sites offers advice to UNESCO on World Heritage Sites) was the following:

> An all-important principle to be observed in restoration, and one which should not be departed from on any pretext whatsoever, is to pay regard to every vestige indicating an architectural arrangement. The architect should not be thoroughly satisfied, nor set his men to work until he has discovered the combination which best and most simply accords with the vestiges of ancient work: To decide on an arrangement a priori, without having gained all the information that should regulate it, is to fall into hypothesis; and in works of restoration nothing is so dangerous as hypothesis.[1]

---

1. Viollet-le-Duc and Eugene Emmanuel, "Appendix 1: On Restoration," in *Our Architectural Heritage: From Consciousness to Conservation* (Paris: Cevat Erder, 1986), 208.

Making reconstruction drawings is not very different from actual restoration or any other form of archaeological reconstruction. In these realms also, hypothesis is the great enemy. But the vestiges of ancient work (and these need not always be physical remains on the ground) are so abundant with the Temple and its mount, that there is no need to fall into hypothesis, and these vestiges are increasing with the years.

Briefly summarizing these remains: we have rich literary sources, which provide detailed architectural descriptions; then we have the results of the daring investigations of explorers of the nineteenth and twentieth centuries. The massive excavations south and west of the Temple Mount, following the Six-Day War in 1967, provided information on the outer frame of the Temple platform; and in the absence of excavations on the mount itself (no one is foolhardy enough to attempt this, as it would start another Middle East war!), recent research into surface traces preserved there has yielded results that add detail and complete the picture.

Before we look at the most up-to-date portrayals, it is instructive to look at how the study of these vestiges has built up over time to give a more accurate picture.

The earliest known representation of Herod's Temple is found on coins of Bar Kochba, the Messianic name given to the Jewish leader Shimon Bar Kosiba, who led the Jewish revolt against the Roman Emperor Hadrian in 132 CE. On the obverse side, these coins depicted the façade of the Temple (Fig. 1.1) that some scholars believe Bar Kochba actually rebuilt, as he also restored the priesthood and began a new calendar system. Although schematic in design, the form of the Temple with a flat roof supported by four columns or half-columns can clearly be seen. We know little of this period as there are no written sources and we rely purely on the numismatic evidence, but it is intriguing to note that in the center of these coins of Bar Kochba is an opening in the Temple façade that allows one to view an object in the recesses of the Temple. This object is covered by a semi-circular cover and rests on four legs or supports. Apparently, there was such hope of the Temple being rebuilt that it was believed that the Ark of the Covenant would be restored to its place inside the Holy of Holies. Helen Rosenau pointed out:

> Whereas Roman coins depicting Roman temples usually record the temples with pediments, Herod's Temple on the Bar Kochba coin is represented with four columns or half-columns and a flat roof, thereby following the reference in Middot 4.6. How far Herod's Temple was inspired by the Solomonic tradition must remain

Fig. 1.1. The façade of the Temple and the Ark of the Covenant, depicted on a silver tetradrachm of Bar Kochba.

conjectural, but a conscious imitation of the older building, including perhaps the ground plan, seems in keeping with Herod's endeavors to appear as a legitimate and benevolent ruler to his Jewish subjects. At any rate, some novel features which distinguish Herod's Temple from the simple prototype of Solomon's Temple, such as the four columns or half-columns, appear to have been incorporated on the coins and in this manner the earliest extant image of the Temple corresponds with the tradition of the latest building.[2]

The next representation chronologically shows the door of the Temple as closed (see Fig. 1.2). It is found in a painting over the scroll-niche in the Synagogue of Dura-Europos in Syria and was completed c. 245 CE. Here again, the Temple façade is represented as having a flat roof and four columns or half-columns.

2. Helen Rosenau, *Vision of the Temple* (London: Oresko Books, 1979), 21. *Middot* is one of the tractates of the Mishnah, the earliest code of rabbinic law.

Fig. 1.2. The Torah niche in the synagogue at Dura-Europos, third century CE.

Looking at other representations, it appeared that the further away in time one went from the period in which the Temple still stood, the more the details lost their accuracy. The mosaic from the synagogue of Khirbet Susiya, which dates probably from the fourth or fifth century, shows a temple with its doors closed and a gabled roof. [3]

---

3. Zeev Yeivin, "Susiya, Khirbet" in *New Encyclopedia of Archaeological Excavations in the Holy Land* 4:1415–421.

All of these representations were stylized, but there is one tantalizing reference in Helen Rosenau's work[4] to an actual drawing of the Temple by Rashi. The name is an acronym of Rabbi Solomon ben Isaac, who lived between 1040 and 1105 CE and who wrote groundbreaking commentaries on the Bible and Talmud. Rashi wrote to the rabbis of Auxerre in France concerning verses on the Temple in Jeremiah and in Ezekiel that he could not add any more to what he had already explained in a commentary (assumed to be about *Middot* 5.3, which deals with the northern outer chambers) but that he would send an explanatory plan. The plan has been lost to us, but it is fascinating to know that as early as the eleventh century someone was attempting to reconcile the various descriptions of the Temple.

There are, however, actual drawings of the Temple after the sources extant from the twelfth century. These can be found particularly in the works of Maimonides (also called Rambam), the foremost Jewish philosopher of the medieval period, who lived from 1135 to 1204. In his Mishnah Commentary, which he began at the age of twenty-three, he includes drawings of the Temple made either by himself or close associates.[5] These diagrams, which include plans of the Temple itself and other details, have Hebrew captions and are surprisingly complete and accurate, if somewhat sketch-like. The drawing in his Mishnah Torah, a codification of Jewish Law, is more finely drawn and is clearly an interpretation of *Middot*, showing a plan of the Temple that includes the Chamber of Hewn Stone and the four rooms in the Chamber of the Hearth.

In the main, the drawings of Christian artists in the medieval period, by contrast, ignored specifications available in the Hebrew Bible and in the Mishnah and gave their imagination free rein. For instance, before the literary sources were translated or explorers had ventured underground on or near the Temple Mount, visions of the first-century Temple were based on one of three different types. These depicted the Temple as a structure similar to: (a) the Dome of the Rock (see Fig. 1.3), (b) a church-type building (see Fig. 1.4), or c) an oriental-type structure.[6]

---

4. Rosenau, *Vision*, 35.

5. The manuscript is held at the Bodleian Library; the drawing may be seen at http://www.bodleian.ox.ac.uk/whatson/whats-on/online/crossing-borders/temple.

6. An example of the second category is the depiction of the Temple in Petrus Cosmestor's *Historia Scholastica* (thirteenth century) in Rosenau, *Vision*, 54. See http://images.bridgemanart.com/cgi-bin/bridgemanImage.cgi/400wm.AIS.5705920.7055475/291896.jpg.

Fig. 1.3. The Marriage of the Virgin, by Raphael (1504).

With the coming of the Reformation, however, scholars and artists went back to biblical sources. There is a remarkably accurate drawing of the Temple of Solomon in the Latin Estienne Bible, which was published in Paris in 1540. This drawing was made, as the book's acknowledgement states, "following" Franciscus Vatablus, Professor of Hebrew at the Royal College in Paris, a renowned scholar of ancient languages. Because both the roof and front are left out of the drawing, almost the whole interior of the Temple is made visible with its laver, lampstands and incense altar, and even the Holy of Holies with its crowned ark and cherubim. The three levels of chambers *(tselaot)*,

Fig. 1.4. Scenes from the Passion of Christ, by Flemish painter Hans Memling (1470).

gradually stepping in, are faithfully shown. Another drawing, after Vatablus, shows the Temple with its courts while the sacrifices are proceeding. This is most interesting, as the Holy of Holies is clearly shown to be located on the highest part of the mountain on which the Temple is depicted. These, of course, showed the Temple of Solomon and not that of Herod. Nevertheless they exerted a great influence, notably on the architect Claude Perrault, who illustrated the Latin edition of Maimonides, *Mishneh Torah* As the latter work was based on an original source, one would expect it to be accurate, but these two drawings (Rosenau, Ill. 85 and 86) are so accurate, particularly in the detail of the five cedar beams of graduated length that lay over the Temple lintel, that they could almost be used today to illustrate a book on the subject (Fig.1.5).

A Jewish scholar who made such a notable contribution to the understanding of how the Temple worked that he was given the name "Templo" was Rabbi Jacob Judah (Aryeh) Leon (c. 1603–1675). Rosenau writes of him that he "appears to have been the first Jew to build models for historical consideration."[7] In fact, his model of the Temple appears to have been brought to England from Holland, according to a letter that has been found addressed to Sir Christopher Wren,[8] although its whereabouts are now unknown. His drawings, however, are extant and show a temple placed asymmetrically on

7. Ibid., 133.
8. Ibid., 135, 141n4.

the platform, according to the Jewish sources, with six large buttresses on the eastern side.

Fig. 1.5 Entrance to the Holy of Holies.

The first truly realistic drawing, which shows Herod's Temple somewhat as we know it now after our study of the sources and the archaeological remains, is that of French diplomat and scholar Marquis Charles Melchior de Vogüé. In 1864, he produced a magnificently illustrated book on the Jerusalem Temple that today is a collector's item. His concept of the Temple was clearly based on the sources and the topography with which he was intimately familiar, having made a few exploratory journeys to Jerusalem. One could indeed say that his drawing[9] was the precursor for the reconstruction drawings that came out of the excavations one hundred years later (Fig. 1.6). It shows a Temple with an elevated porch placed asymmetrically on the Temple platform according to *Middot*. The various courts, such as the Court of the Priests and the Court of the Women, are all represented. The Huldah Gates are shown with paths leading up to them and the passageways that begin at these gates exit just beyond the Royal Stoa on the Temple platform. The Antonia stands at the northwest corner and

---

9. Melchior de Vogüé, *Le Temple de Jérusalem. Monographie du Haram ech-cherif, suivie d'un essai sur la topographie de la Ville Sainte* (Paris: Noblet & Baudry, 1864), plate 16.

a causeway leads over the Tyropoeon to the gate over Robinson's Arch (which, of course, had not yet been given that name). Apart from fine details, de Vogüé only gets two major items wrong. He omitted the magnificent steps leading up to the Huldah Gates (which de Vogüé could not have known lay under the hill of Ophel, which was green in his day) and the stairway that led down from the southwestern gate into the Tyropoeon Valley (the find most associated with the Temple Mount Excavations team, arrived at by a process of much trial and error).

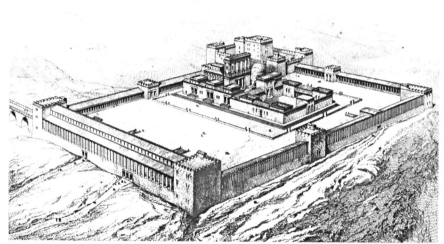

Fig. 1.6 Drawing of the Temple Mount of "Herod's temple", from Volz Paul, Die biblischen Altertümer (Antiquités bibliques). 1914, Page 51, Plate 8.

Prior to the Temple Mount Excavations, Professor Michael Avi Yonah's model (which used to be located in the grounds of the Holyland Hotel in Jerusalem, and is now in the Israel Museum) came as close as was possible to determining what the sacred complex looked like during the period in question.

Following on from this, there were a number of reconstructions made after the excavations but before recent research into the architectural development of the Temple Mount carried out by the author.

My original reconstruction drawing of Herod's Temple Mount (Fig. 1.7), made in 1977,[10] which has been published in many books and numerous

10. This drawing was first published in: Leen Ritmeyer and Kathleen Ritmeyer, "Reconstructing Herod's Temple Mount," *Biblical Archaeology Review* 15, no. 6 (1989): 3–42. See also Leen Ritmeyer, *The Quest: Revealing the Temple Mount in Jerusalem* (Jerusalem: Carta, 2006), 19.

periodicals, was based on the results of the excavations combined with the evidence of the ancient sources.

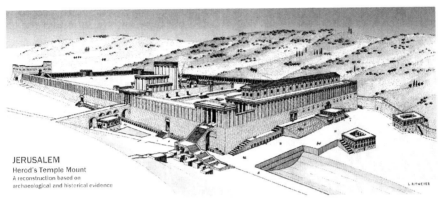

Fig. 1.7. Herod's Temple Mount, copyright © Leen Ritmeyer, 1977.

This design was the logical outcome of my work as site architect on the Temple Mount Excavations and a necessary foundation to what followed after. The perspective used in the drawing conveniently discounted any need to depict the Herodian Temple in any detail. However, it was a joint study with Professor Benjamin Mazar (who directed the Temple Mount Excavations), undertaken a few years after excavations had ceased, that gave the impetus to proceeding further with the research into the historical development of the Temple Mount. The result of this study was based on the analysis of archaeological remains on the Temple Mount that belonged to a pre–Herodian platform, 500 cubits square. In 1984, Mazar published the preliminary results of our research into the location of the original, square Temple Mount.[11] Using this as a basis, I went on to devote myself to an intensive inquiry into how the Temple Mount had developed and particularly into its appearance during the first century.

Other portrayals of the Herodian Temple have been based on the results of my research into the location of Herod's Temple and the surrounding courts. These include: a model built by the late Alec Garrard at Moat Farm, Fressingfield, near Ely in Suffolk (partly designed with help of the author, see Fig. 1.8), a model commissioned by the late Ben Adelman (Chairman of the American Friends of the Israel Exploration Society) of Washington, DC, and designed by the author (Fig.1.9). That design also forms a large part of a digital 3D reconstruction of first-century Jerusalem made in Poland by a

11. Benjamin Mazar, "The Temple Mount," in *Biblical Archaeology Today, Proceedings of the International Congress on Biblical Archaeology, Jerusalem, April 1984*, ed. Avraham Biran (Jerusalem: Israel Exploration Society, 1985) 463–68.

company called Sephirot, and of a computer-generated portrayal made by a Swiss foundation, called "Messiah in the Temple." None of these depictions, including my own reconstructions, can be an exact reproduction of the structure that existed in Jerusalem in the time of Christ but are a picture of probability.

Fig. 1.8

This chapter will briefly examine, in turn, each of the vestiges (remains) of the Temple in the time of Christ and then work our way inwards from the outer walls of the platform to the Temple proper. Basically, I would like to demonstrate how reconstructions work and on what my drawings are based. Firstly, here is a compendium of the main historical sources.

The most well-drawn description of the Temple and its mount is to be found in the pages of the Tractate *Middot* of the Mishnah.[12] Compiled within a century after the destruction of the Temple, it is based on the teachings of Eliezer Ben Jacob, who witnessed the ritual of the Sanctuary prior to 70 CE. There is much information on Jewish religious practice of the time contained in other of the Mishnah's tractates, but it is *Middot* (which means "Measurements") that is specifically dedicated to detailing the Temple and its dimensions. It had been dismissed as irreconcilable with our other main source, that of Josephus, as

---

12. The quotations in this article are from H. Danby, *The Mishnah* (Oxford: Clarendon, 1933).

Fig. 1.9

it describes the Temple court as a square of 500 cubits (861 ft.). The writings of the first-century Jewish historian, by contrast, portray a court with a perimeter that is twice as long. However, my research into the location of the 500-square-cubit Temple Mount described in *Middot* convinced me that this description related to a large court inside what is known as the Herodian Temple Mount (see my drawing, Fig. 1.10). Historically, this square area constituted the Temple Mount after it was restored by the exiles returning from Babylon in the sixth century BCE.[13] As the returnees had very few resources, they would have been unable to do much more than repair the original structure, so the configuration would, of necessity, have been much the same as that of the First Temple. My research showed that in 19 BCE, Herod preserved this original square in the rebuilding of the Second Temple, as it was the only area considered holy. As the new additions constructed by Herod were probably considered profane by the religious authorities of the time, they only referred to what was contained inside the original square, and it is this that is described

13. Ritmeyer, *The Quest*, 322.

in *Middot*, written after the destruction of Herod's Temple in 70 CE. However, if we take into consideration that the outer courts added by Herod are ignored in *Middot*, the information provided is of tremendous value and can be used to complement that of Josephus, who described the mount as it had been enlarged by Herod.

With this understanding, we realize that the gates described in *Middot* must refer to the earlier, square Temple Mount. So, the five gates described in the tractate as leading to the Temple Mount were not those whose remnants we see preserved in the present-day outer walls of the platform but must have been further inside. For instance, by contrast to the one gate assigned to the Western Wall in *Middot*, Josephus gives four. *Middot* mentions a railing or low barrier, called *soreg*, with inscriptions placed at intervals forbidding Gentiles to proceed further, that would be encountered before entering the holy precincts. The tractate goes on to describe seven gates that led to the Temple Court and then the chambers that lay around the Temple and their functions. It is here, in the description of the Temple and its courts, that, essaying to record its appearance with loving accuracy, the tractate comes into its own. Additional material on the ritual of the Temple is provided in other tractates of the Mishnah, particularly in the second division, *Moed* (Set Feasts), and in the fifth division, *Kodashim* (Hallowed Things), which contains *Middot*. We shall see later on that a vivid picture can be built up from the Mishnaic record.

The record of Flavius Josephus is vital for its description of the outer part of the Temple Mount, which Herod the Great doubled in size, creating a vast esplanade. The surpassing beauty of Herod's Temple is proverbial. That the megalomaniac Herod intended the building of the Temple to be the crowning glory of all his architectural creations is clear from the words of Josephus: "For he believed that the accomplishment of this task would be the most notable of all the things achieved by him, as indeed it was and would be great enough to assure his eternal remembrance" (*Ant*.15.380) Because of the sensitivity of his Jewish subjects, however, the originally Edomite King Herod was not permitted to make any substantial changes in the Temple building, apart from doubling the height of the Porch to bring it into line with the dimensions of the First Temple built by Solomon. Although Josephus was an eyewitness of the Temple, some scholars consider his account to be unreliable. And his measurements, in comparison to the carefully recorded measurements of *Middot*, can sometimes be misleading and prone to exaggeration, as he was trying to defend Judaism to pagan readers of his works.

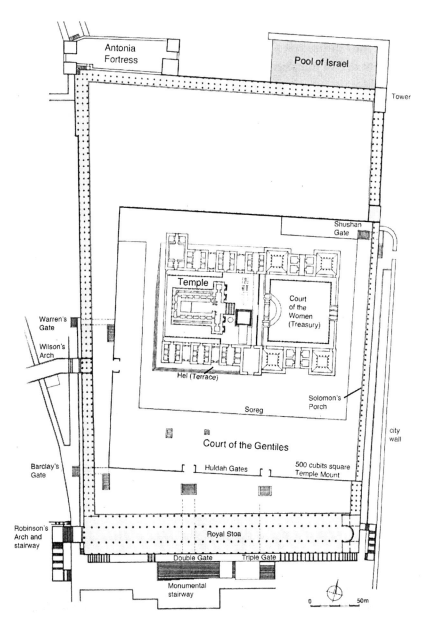

Fig. 1.10

The two main descriptions of the Temple by Josephus appear in *War* 5.184–226 and *Ant* 15.410-25, but even these records do not always agree with one another. In *Ant* 15.380, Josephus states that Herod commenced construction of the Temple in the eighteenth year of his reign (20–19 BCE), whereas in *War* 1.401, he gives the construction date as Herod's fifteenth regal year (23–22 BCE). In *Ant* 15.420-21, he tells us that the inner courts were completed in a year and a half, but that construction of the porticoes and outer courts took eight years. However, construction related to the Temple project went on until the reign of Agrippa, and Josephus records that the work was halted in 64 CE, with eighteen thousand workmen being put out of work *(Ant* 20.219 -23). This continuing construction of the Sanctuary has recently been confirmed by excavations at the foot of the Western Wall below Robinson's Arch.[14]

Josephus tells us that Herod expanded the Temple platform on three sides *(War* 5.187), to the north, west, and south, and erected porticoes inside these new walls. The depth of the Kidron Valley precluded any extension to the east, so that the eastern portico followed the same line as that of the earlier mount. Josephus tells us that the western wall had four entrances *(Ant* 15.410), all of which have now been found and named after the explorers who discovered them. The southern wall had two entranceways, known as the Double and Triple Gates. These led into passageways that led northwards, exiting in front of the ancient double gates that were known according to *Middot* 1.3 as the Huldah Gates. There was also one gate in the Eastern Wall and possibly another gate in the Northern Wall.

In *Against Apion* 2.103-109, he describes the four surrounding courts of the Temple. The outer court could be accessed by all, including foreigners, but excluding menstruating women. The second court admitted all Jews and non-menstruating Jewish women. Male Jews only were allowed into the third court, while priests in proper priestly attire were allowed into the fourth. The inner sanctuary was restricted to the High Priest, clad in his high priestly garments. This is similar to the degrees of holiness stipulated in Mishnah *Kelim* 1.6-9.

The New Testament provides invaluable traditions that add detail to the information provided in the other two main sources. For instance, John 2:20 tells us that the Jewish leaders said to Jesus: "This temple has been under construction for forty-six years, and will you raise it up in three days?" (NRSV). "This adds to the information given in Josephus about the length of time it took to build the Temple. Luke 1:5-22 records an angel appearing to Zechariah in the Temple announcing the birth of the John the Baptist, who would herald the coming of the Messiah. And the scene of the purification of Mary, the mother of Jesus, and the presentation of the child Jesus presumably took place in the

---

14. An announcement by the Israel Antiquities Authority on Nov. 23, 2011 revealed that the Western Wall below Robinson's Arch could not have been built before 17–18 CE.

Court of the Women (Luke 2:22-39). It was probably on the Temple Terrace or *ḥel,* in the company of the scribes and teachers, that Jesus was found by his parents on his visit to Jerusalem for Passover at the age of twelve (Luke 2:46). Matthew 4:5 records the temptation of Christ at the "pinnacle of the temple," early in his ministry. This has been identified as the southwest corner of the Temple Mount. There are frequent references to the Temple as a backdrop to the work of Christ (e.g. Matt. 21:14, Luke 19:47, 21:38, John 7:14, John 18:20). The eschatological prophecy of Matt. 24, Mark 13, and Luke 21 has as its springboard the stones of the Temple, with Jesus prophesying, "there shall not be left one stone upon another that shall not be thrown down."

Now to the explorers; the advent of the science of archaeology to Jerusalem in the nineteenth century transformed understanding of the Temple Mount. Throughout the Ottoman period, the Muslim authorities forbade access to the mount to non-Muslims. A handful of westerners did manage to disguise themselves as Muslims and gain entrance. One of the first plans of the Temple platform was made in 1833 by a team of three Englishmen, led by Frederick Catherwood, who disguised themselves as Egyptian army officers. In 1838, Edward Robinson, the American biblical scholar known as the "Father of Biblical Geography," carried out a meticulous topographical survey of the city. Restricting himself to an examination of the exterior walls of the Temple Mount walls, he was the first to suggest that the stones jutting out from the wall near the southwest corner were the remains of an original entranceway. Robinson's Arch, as it was called after him, was assumed to be the first of a series of arches supporting a bridge that spanned the Tyropoeon Valley. This was the way these remains were understood up until the Temple Mount Excavations that followed the Six-Day War.

In the early 1850s, Edward Barclay, an American missionary, gained access to the Temple Mount when he was appointed assistant to a Turkish architect doing repair work on the Dome of the Rock. He discovered the gate that was later named after him, from inside the platform. Part of the lintel of this gate is still visible in the southern part of the Herodian wall at the Western Wall Plaza.

The first real scientific research done on the mount was by de Vogüé. His 1864 publication, which contained the surprisingly accurate reconstruction drawing of the Temple Mount, has been mentioned above.

The following year, in 1865, the British engineer Captain Charles Wilson mapped the Temple Mount for the first time as part of the Ordnance Survey of

Jerusalem.[15] This is still the most widely reproduced plan of the Temple Mount today.

At that time, he publicized the finding of a complete arch that sprang out of the Western Wall, north of Robinson's Arch, that was identified as part of the bridge that led from the Temple Mount to the Upper City. Although it may have been a Swiss scholar named Titus Tobler who originally discovered it, it has retained the name of Wilson's Arch. The foundation of the Palestine Exploration Fund in 1865 by a group of academics and clergymen was the major impetus to scientific investigation of the Temple Mount. It was under their auspices that Wilson's colleague, Captain Charles Warren, carried out landmark explorations around the mount for three years, from 1867 to 1870. Forbidden to dig inside the platform, Warren cut deep shafts alongside the wall, joining them up so that he could trace the bedrock contours of the Temple Mount and the subterranean courses of the Herodian walls. The plans resulting from these daring investigations and published in 1884[16] were some of the most treasured objects in the office of the Temple Mount Excavations.

Another highlight in the history of Temple Mount research was a discovery by the French epigrapher and diplomat Charles Clermont-Ganneau. In 1871, he found a Greek inscription prohibiting the entrance of Gentiles into the Temple court. In the 1911 Parker Mission, a misguided English aristocrat caused havoc by searching for Temple treasures on the mount; his lack of diplomacy caused the Muslim authorities to ban any further scientific exploration on the Temple Mount.

Beginning in 1961, when Jerusalem was under Jordanian rule, until the Six-Day War, Dame Kathleen Kenyon of the British School of Archaeology excavated in the city. As part of her investigations, she carried out limited excavations to the south of the Temple Mount. However, most of her work was concentrated on the City of David.

Excavations of the area south and west of the Temple Mount began in earnest in 1968, under the direction of the late Prof. Benjamin Mazar, on behalf of the Israel Exploration Society and the Hebrew University of Jerusalem. Meir Ben-Dov was his assistant and the dig continued without a break until 1978. Work commenced under Robinson's Arch and eventually took in a wide area from the Mughrabi Gate to the southeast corner of the Temple Mount.

As the dig progressed, each wall and stone was surveyed and each architectural element examined and recorded until a complete plan of the multi-

15. Charles Wilson, *Ordinance Survey of Jerusalem* (London, 1865).

16. Charles Warren, *Plans, Elevations, Sections, etc., Showing the Results of the Excavations at Jerusalem, 1867–1870, Executed for the Committee of the Palestine Exploration Fund.* (London, 1884).

period site was achieved. To make the accompanying reconstruction drawing of Herod's Temple Mount, the Herodian elements were separated from the rest, the ancient sources were searched again for illumination, and parallels were made with other monumental Hellenistic buildings, such as the Tomb of the Patriarchs in Hebron, the Temples of Baalbek, Damascus, and Palmyra, and the decorated Herodian tombs in Jerusalem. The plans made by Charles Warren, recording in great detail his underground survey of the Temple Mount walls, were, needless to say, invaluable and consulted on almost a daily basis. We will first examine the outer walls and access points of the vast esplanade of the Temple Mount and then examine the actual remains on which the reconstruction drawing is based.[17]

We have mentioned Josephus' record of there being four gates in the Western Wall of the Temple Mount. *Antiquities* 15.410 tells us that "The first led to the [Hasmonean] palace by a passage over the intervening ravine, two others led to the suburb, and the last led to the other part of the city, from which it was separated by many steps going down to the ravine and from here up again to the hill." Archaeological explorations have proved that this description is correct. The ravine is the Tyropoeon Valley and the gates are respectively those over Wilson's Arch, Warren's and Barclay's Gates, and that over Robinson's Arch. The street that went "up again to the [western] hill" was found adjacent to Robinson's Arch (Fig. 1.11).

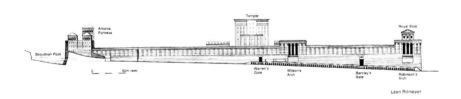

Fig. 1.11 Side View of the Tyropoeon Valley.

The Western Wall plaza is perhaps the most well-known part of the Temple area and a suitable place to begin looking at the architectural remains of this huge complex. The stones in the seven lowest courses visible in the 1590-foot-long Western Wall are Herodian and belong to the 15-foot-wide retaining wall that Herod commenced building in 19 BCE. An additional twenty-one stone

17. A more extensive description of the Temple Mount walls is found in Ritmeyer, "The Herodian Temple Mount Walls," *The Quest*, 15–135.

courses lie beneath the level of the present-day plaza. Here the wall's foundation course is, as elsewhere, built on the rock, which is seventy feet below the pavement.

To the left of the plaza is an underground area where Wilson's Arch is located. This arch appears to be an early Islamic restoration of the first of a series of arches built to support the bridge that spanned the Tyropoeon Valley, linking the Temple Mount with the Upper City to the west. The pier on which Wilson's Arch rests, however, is still the original Herodian one. Above this arch was one of the four aforementioned gates that gave access to the Temple Mount from the west, the side on which the city was located.

The northernmost gate in the Western Wall, Warren's Gate, is situated in the tunnel that has been excavated along the Western Wall to the north of Wilson's Arch.

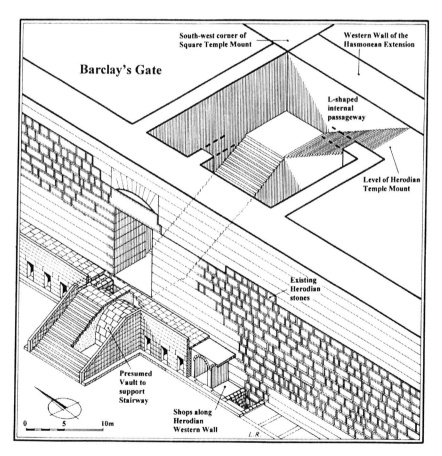

Fig. 1.12 Isometric Reconstruction Drawing of Barclay's Gate. Copyright Leen Ritmeyer.

Immediately to the south of Warren's Gate, the largest ashlars used in the Herodian Temple Mount walls have been found. There are four stones that are approximately twelve-feet high and the largest of them is forty-five feet long.

Returning to the plaza, we see the massive lintel of Barclay's Gate in that part of the area reserved for women's worship, below the ramp that leads up to the Temple Mount. Behind this lintel, parts of the original Herodian L-shaped stepped passageway have been preserved. Below the sill of the gate, Warren discovered the spring of an arch, which presumably supported a stairway leading up from the main street to the gate (Fig. 1.12).

Inside the Temple Mount Excavations, the Herodian street is visible alongside the Western wall. The huge paving slabs are part of the main street that began in the north at the present-day Damascus Gate and, going down through the Tyropoeon Valley, passing by the Western Wall, terminated at the southern city gate near the Pool of Siloam.

The foundations of shops, which were built against the Western Wall and on the opposite side of the street, gave this major north-south thoroughfare the distinctive character of a market street.

Fig. 1.13 Model of Robinson's Arch. Copyright Leen Ritmeyer.

Robinson's Arch provided the southernmost point of access to the Temple Mount from the west. In the excavations, a series of equidistant arches of graduated height were revealed, ascending from the south and then turning eastwards over Robinson's Arch. These are the remains of a monumental stairway, which led down from the Royal Portico to the street in the Tyropoeon Valley (Fig. 1.13).

Fig. 1.14 Photograph of the Inscription upon the Trumpeting Stone. Courtesy Leen Ritmeyer.

On the pavement near the southwestern corner, a corner parapet fragment was found, bearing an inscription above a recess. The Hebrew inscription "*l'bet hatqia l'hakh ...*" is incomplete (Fig. 1.14). Various readings have been suggested, but the correct meaning is probably "To the place of trumpeting to [announce]." Apparently from the top of this corner of the Temple Mount, a priest used to announce the beginning or end of the Sabbath with a trumpet blast (Fig. 1.15). This would explain a passage in Josephus (*War* 4.582) that states that above the roof of the priests' chambers at the southwest corner there was a "point where it was the custom for one of the priests to stand and give notice, by sound of trumpet, in the afternoon of the approach, and on the following evening of the close, of every seventh day, announcing to the people the respective hours for ceasing work and for resuming their labours."

לבית התקיעה להכ רז

Fig. 1.15 Reconstructed drawing of the Trumpeting Stone and Inscription. Copyright Leen Ritmeyer.

It would appear that the inscription was not on view once the Temple Mount was completed. Traces of white plaster were found on the stone, suggesting that the niche and the inscription also were covered over with plaster. The inscription may therefore only have been an indicator to the builders where to place this stone, as hundreds of other similar stones must have been made to complete the parapet all around the roofs of the towers and porticoes that surrounded the Temple Mount.

A narrow street was found adjacent to the northern part of the pier that supported Robinson's Arch and led up to the Upper City. This ascending street is referred to in the above quotation of Josephus (*Ant* 15.410), which indicates that from the last gate in the Western Wall, one could go "from here up again to the hill."

The design of the upper parts of the Temple Mount walls was different from that of the lower parts. In the destruction layers, pilaster stones were found, similar to those that have been preserved intact at another Herodian structure, the Tomb of the Patriarchs, in Hebron. Remains of pilasters have also been found at the enclosure of nearby Mamre, where Herodian masonry is also in evidence. In both cases, the pilaster construction began at the level of the inner court. From these parallels, we deduce that the walls of the Temple Mount were of a similar construction.

The 912-foot-long Southern Wall of the Temple Mount had two gates, the Double Gate and the Triple Gate (Fig. 1.16). From west to east we see a row of shops built against the Southern Wall, which carried a narrow street over its roofs. These shops were burned by the Romans in 70 CE, leaving the darkened outline of their vaulted ceilings in the wall. Measuring these burnt imprints, we were able to reconstruct this narrow street, with its shops below, to a high degree of accuracy.

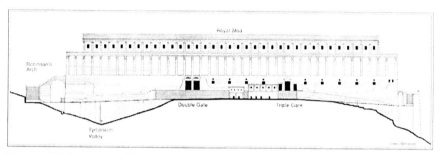

Fig. 1.16 The Southern Wall. Copyright Leen Ritmeyer.

The Double Gate is the westernmost of the two gates in the Southern Wall. From the outside, only the blocked part of one gate can be seen. The other gate is open, but obscured from view by the large Crusader tower built in front of it.

The original lintel of the gate can be seen behind the decorative arch that was applied on the exterior in the early Islamic period. The gate led into a long passageway that ascended northwards, giving access to the Temple Court above (Fig. 1.17). In the southern part of this passageway, four exquisitely decorated Herodian domes have been preserved. The decoration of each dome is different, although the design is always based on floral and geometric patterns. The beautiful design of this passageway has led some to suggest that this may have been the Beautiful Gate, mentioned in Acts 3:2,10, as the place where the lame man sat begging and was healed by Peter and John. After he was healed, he entered into the Temple Courts, from which he may previously have been barred, and went to Solomon's Porch (v. 11).

Leading up to the Double Gate, the remains of an originally 210-foot-wide stepped approach is the grandest of all the approaches to the Temple gates, indicating that this was the gate most used by the multitudes to go up to the Temple Mount. The eastern part of the stairway, which was discovered in the excavations, and which was partly cut out of the bedrock, has been restored.

Fig. 1.17 Copyright Leen Ritmeyer.

In front of this stairway, the remains of a large paved plaza were found. From the point of view of town planning, such an expanse was necessary as a place of assembly for the many visitors to the Temple.

From this plaza today, one looks up to the black, leaden dome of the El Aqsa Mosque. During the Herodian period, the Royal Stoa graced the whole length of the Southern Wall. This structure was built in the shape of a basilica, with four rows of forty columns each, creating a central nave and two side aisles. The central apse was the place of meeting for the Sanhedrin, the supreme Jewish Council.

It has been suggested that it was here that the scene of Jesus overturning the tables of the moneychangers and those that sold doves was enacted (Matt. 21:1-16). However, as this was not part of the ancient sacred area, it is likely that these activities must, on that occasion, have spilled over into what (as we have seen) the Mishnah regarded as the hallowed area of the Temple Mount. Such desecration of the holiness of the Sanctuary would certainly have provoked Jesus.

Of the Triple Gate, only one Herodian stone has been preserved. This is a part of the western doorjamb, which we can see at the base of the left arch of this gate. The present-day arched gate dates from the early Islamic period. However, its width reflects the original dimensions of the Herodian gate, which gave access to an underground passageway that led up to the Temple Mount. In the western wall of the underground passageway, a Herodian pilaster, which supported the Royal Stoa above, has survived the Roman destruction of 70 CE. The Triple Gate also gave access to huge underground structures, which are known (erroneously, as they date from a later period) as Solomon's Stables. During the Herodian period, large subterranean rooms were located here at the southeast corner of the Temple Mount. Some have suggested that they were used to store materials needed for the Temple ritual. A complete window frame was found in the Temple Mount Excavations in this area; it had grooves for metal bars to allow light and air into these underground structures.

In the excavations to the south of the Triple Gate, a bedrock-cut vault, designed to support a staircase leading up to the gate, can be seen.

In between the monumental stairway of the Double Gate and the Triple Gate, several *mikva'ot* (ritual baths) and reservoirs have been cut into the bedrock. The building to which these baths belonged was used for ritual purification, suitably located next to one of the main entrances to the Temple Mount.

A complex of rock-cut Herodian chambers has been found just east of the bathhouse and west of the Triple Gate. It has been suggested that these belong to one of the three council-houses mentioned in Mishnah *Sanhedrin* 11.2: "One used to sit at *the gate of the Temple Mount*, one used to sit at the gate of the Temple court, and one used to sit in the Chamber of Hewn Stone."

In the southern part of the 1530-foot-long Eastern Wall of the Temple Mount, the remains of a Herodian arch can be seen below a blocked double entrance. This small gate, which gave access to the vaulted area now known as Solomon's Stables, stood at the top of an ascending staircase, similar to that of Robinson's Arch, although constructed on a smaller scale.

Apart from this small entrance, the Golden Gate is the only large gate located in the Eastern Wall of the Temple Mount. Although most of the building dates from the Umayyad period, it was in fact built at the location of a much earlier gate. Two massive gateposts that can be seen inside the gate predate this construction.[18] The tradition that the Golden Gate stood in the original location of the Shushan Gate, "the Eastern Gate on which was portrayed the palace of Shushan" (*Middot* 1.3), is probably correct (Fig. 1.18). On the Day of Atonement (*Yom Kippur*), both the red heifer (for the purification ritual described in Num. 9:2-13) and the scapegoat (Lev. 16:8-10) were led out through this gate to the Mount of Olives.

Fig. 1.18 Upper View of the Eastern Gate. Courtesy Leen Ritmeyer.

At the northeast corner of the Temple Mount, a substantial part of the original Herodian tower can be seen. Eleven stone courses have been preserved at the northern corner above ground, while another seventeen courses exist below ground. The northern face of this tower has also been partially preserved. This

18. Ibid., 109.

face was badly damaged during the Roman siege of 70 CE and many small stones have been used to patch up the wall.

The Northern Wall of the Temple Mount is 1038-foot-long. At its northwest corner, a huge rock scarp supported the Antonia Fortress that, according to Josephus, was a "guard to the Temple." It was surrounded by a rock-cut moat. The Antonia Fortress itself (Fig. 1.19) had four towers, three of which were 50 cubits high (86 ft.), while that on the southeast was 70 cubits high (120 ft.). The latter tower was so high that it "commanded a view of the whole area of the Temple" (*War* 5.242). The view from this tower must have been spectacular. The towers undoubtedly had shooting holes for arrows and larger windows for dropping heavy objects on any assailants.

Fig. 1.19 Reconstruction of the Antonia Fortress. Courtesy Leen Ritmeyer.

In the corner, where the porticoes met, a staircase led up to the level of the roofs of the porticoes, and from there the Antonia could be entered. At the point where the staircase came up, near the southwest tower, the southern wall of the fortress is set back a little, providing ample space for this staircase. The apostle Paul was probably led on these stairs to the Antonia Fortress as mentioned in Acts 21:37. The roof at the junction of the western and northern porticoes was the most suitable place from which he could have addressed the people that were assembled below (Acts 21:40).

After Herod extended the Temple Mount on three sides, he built porticoes along the newly built walls. They had double rows of columns supporting beautifully carved ceilings. Josephus, in *War* 5.190-92, gives a glowing description of these porticoes:

> The porticoes, all in double rows, were supported by columns five and twenty cubits high—each single block of the purest white marble—and ceiled with panels of cedar. The natural magnificence of these columns, their excellent polish and fine adjustment presented a striking spectacle, without any adventitious embellishment of painting or sculpture. The porticoes were thirty cubits broad, and the complete circuit of them, embracing the Antonia, measured six furlongs. The open court was from end to end variegated with paving of all manner of stone.

The location of these columns would have corresponded with the pilasters that were built in the outer walls.

Having now completed our brief survey of the walls of the Temple Mount, which have a total circumference of 5073 feet or approximately one mile, we turn our attention to the interior layout of the Temple Mount.

We have mentioned earlier the inscription found by Clermont-Ganneau in 1871. This confirmed the presence of the low-latticed screen (*soreg*—see the plan in Fig. 10), which marked the separation between the Court of the Gentiles and the sacred area. Strangers were forbidden on penalty of death to proceed any further into the Temple complex. Attached to this screen at regular intervals were plaques with inscriptions in Greek and Latin warning of this prohibition (*Ant* 15.41).

After the location of the Mishnaic square Temple Mount was established, the location of the Temple itself could be determined. We have already noted that according to Josephus's account, the Temple was built on the summit of the mountain. The top of Mount Moriah is visible inside the Dome of the Rock. According to *Middot*, the Temple was located inside the Temple Court, which measured 187 by 135 cubits. From additional measurements, the location of the Temple inside its court can be calculated exactly. *Middot* 2.1 further informs us concerning the sizes of the courts that surrounded this Temple Court: "The Temple Mount measured five hundred cubits by five hundred cubits. Its largest [open] space was to the south, the next largest to the east, the third largest to the north, and its smallest [open space] was to the west; the place where its measure was greatest was where its use was greatest."

Based on this information we concluded that the Holy of Holies was located over the Sakhra, the rock mass inside the Dome of the Rock.[19] The length of the courts turned out to be, going counter-clockwise from south to west, 250, 213, 115, and 100 cubits respectively.

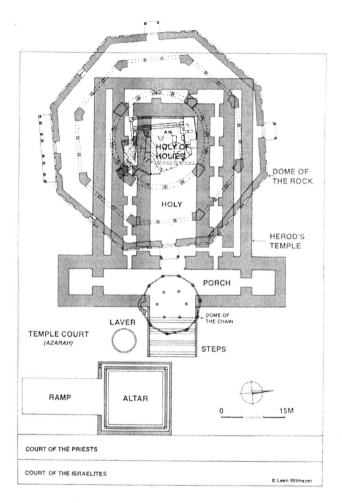

Fig. 1.20 Copyright Leen Ritmeyer.

According to *Middot* 5.1, the Temple Court, that is, the space where the actual Temple building and the Altar were located, was 187 cubits (322 ft.) long and 135 cubits (232 ft., 6 inches) wide (Fig. 1.20). Next, we read that the length, from east to west, was divided as follows: the Court of the Israelites and the Court of the Priests, both 11 cubits deep, then a space for the Altar of 32 cubits,[20]

19. Ibid., 241–77.

the space between the Altar and the Porch was 22 cubits, while the Sanctuary measured 100 cubits with a space behind it of 11 cubits.

The distance of 135 cubits from south to north was divided as follows: the Ramp; 30 cubits, the base of the Altar; 32 cubits, the space between Altar and rings; 8 cubits, the area of the Rings; 24 cubits, the space between the Rings and the Tables; 4 cubits, the space between the Tables and the small pillars; 4 cubits, the space to the north of the small pillars; 8 cubits and the remainder (between the Ramp, the wall, and the small pillars); 25 cubits (Fig. 1.21).

From these measurements it is possible to draw up a plan of the Temple, its courts, gates and other buildings that surrounded the Temple courtyard (Fig. 1.22). According to *Middot* 1.4, there were three gates in the north, three in the south, and one in the east. In the south were, beginning in the west, the Kindling Gate, then the Gate of the Firstlings, and next to it the Water Gate. The Nicanor Gate, which had two side entrances, was in the east. In the north, from east to west, were the Gate of the Flame, the Gate of the Offering, and the Chamber of the Hearth, which also had a gate.

Fig. 1.21 Courtesy Leen Ritmeyer.

20. Josephus gives 50 cubits square for the Altar, but this figure is too large, as it would not leave enough space for the twelve steps leading up to the Porch. Assuming that the Sanctuary was placed symmetrically in the Temple Court, and following *Middot* 4.5, which says that the Sanctuary measured 100 by 100 [cubits], we see that the spaces on either side of the Porch measured 17.5 cubits (30 feet 2 inches). The back part of the Sanctuary was 70 cubits (120 feet 6 inches) wide.

In *Middot* 2.6, however, we read about nine gates, the upper gate being added in the southwest, while the gates in the north are called, from west to east, the Gate of Jeconiah, the Gate of the Offering, the Gate of the Women, and the Gate of the Singers. As these gates had many chambers in which different activities took place, the same gate may have been referred to by different names. In the west there were two apparently nameless gates (*Middot* 2.6). It has also been suggested, however, that the southern one of the two may have been the upper gate and the other that of Jeconiah, mentioned in the same paragraph.

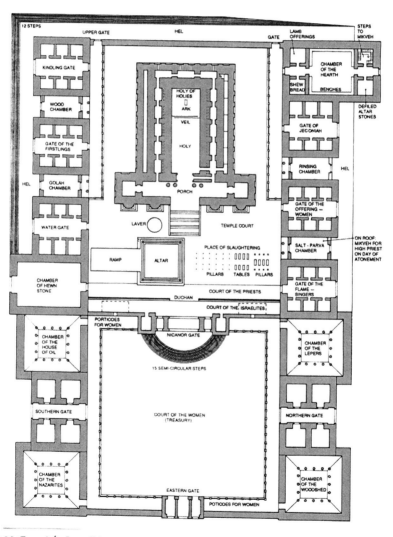

Fig. 1.22 Copyright Leen Ritmeyer.

Middot 5.3 mentions three offices in the north, one for the salt that was put on the offerings, one for the conservation of hides by salting (Parva Chamber), and one for the rinsing of the intestines of the sacrificial animals (Rinsing Chamber). From the Parva Chamber, a passage went up to a chamber where the High Priest immersed himself on the Day of Atonement. This room was located above the middle office. These rooms were probably located between the two spaces left between the three gates. One may have been positioned above the other. The salt chamber must, of course, have been located close to the chamber where they prepared the hides, where salt would be in constant demand.

The next paragraph in *Middot* mentions a Wood Chamber in the south, an office for the Exile (Golah Chamber), and the Chamber of Hewn Stone. In the Chamber of the Golah was a wheel whereby water was drawn from a cistern, most likely the one called the Cistern of the Golah (Cistern no. 5), mentioned in *Erubin* 10.14. The easternmost gate (i.e. the Water Gate) was probably built adjacent to the Chamber of Hewn Stone. In this proposal, the present wellhead of Cistern 5 falls exactly between the Water Gate and that of the Firstlings. The Chamber of the Golah must therefore have been located here, while the Wood Chamber was located on the other side of the Kindling Gate. It is indeed thrilling to see this wellhead preserved up to the present day. Standing beside it, one can imagine the great wheel that once was built here to draw water for the altar services. The eastern gate referred to is the Nicanor Gate (*Middot* 2.3), which corresponds to the Corinthian Gate mentioned in *War* 5.201. In front of this gate was a staircase with fifteen semi-circular steps. *Middot* 2.5 states that these are "corresponding to the fifteen Songs of Ascents in the Psalms, and upon them the Levites used to sing. They were not four-square, but rounded like the half of a round threshing-floor" (*Middot* 2.5).

Some of the names of the offices are related to the names of the gates. This indicates that these gates were not mere openings in a wall, but gatehouses with upper chambers, each one apparently having a different function, which may account for the many offices mentioned in *Middot*, *Tamid*, and elsewhere.

According to Josephus (*War* 5.203), the inner measurements of these gates were 30 cubits square and 40 high. Although in general we do not find the measurements given by him very reliable, in this case we have to give him the benefit of the doubt, in the absence of any other specifications.

Apart from the three gatehouses on the north and south, two important buildings are referred to, the Chamber of the Hearth and the Chamber of Hewn Stone. The latter was located near the southeast corner of the Temple Court and the former near the northwest corner. In making a plan of these gates and chambers, we have to remember that the walls of the Temple Court must have a thickness (e.g. of about five cubits) in order to fit in with the rest of the proportions. In front of the gates was a terrace (*hel*) of 10 cubits wide, which was reached by a flight of twelve steps of half a cubit high and deep. Assuming that the Chamber of Hewn Stone was not a gate building, but a larger construction, like the Chamber of the Hearth, we have drawn it on the plan, having its southern wall in line with the bottom step of the aforementioned staircase. It is interesting to note that, at this very place, the present southeast corner of the raised platform is located. Although tentatively, we suggest that this corner is the remaining southeast corner of the Chamber of Hewn Stone.

The Chamber of the Hearth was located at the northwest corner of the Temple Court. It had four rooms. The one in the northeast had steps leading down to an underground *mikveh*. This room, together with a corresponding one to the east, was located outside the holy area, (i.e. outside the *hel*). The place where the holy area began was indicated inside the building by a row of stones. According to our plan, this building is located above Cistern 3, which was explored by both Wilson and Warren. The cistern has several chambers, one or more of which apparently contained facilities for ritual bathing. A passage continues to the north, but this section was not excavated. If excavation had continued a few more meters, the steps from the Chamber of the Hearth would probably have been found, as Cistern 3 and the passageway are completely rock-cut. Again we see that the connection between the historical sources and the archaeological remains on the Temple Mount has been preserved.

The Altar and the Laver stood in the Temple Court *(azarah)*, with the Laver positioned between the Altar and the Porch of the Temple. The Laver was made of brass and there are a few references in the Mishnah to a special wooden device for the Laver made by a person called Ben Katin *(Yoma* 3.10; *Tamid* 1.4, 3.8). It was apparently designed to divert its water to a well, so that it "would not be rendered unfit by remaining overnight." The working of this device could be heard as far as Jericho, according to ancient traditions. The sound of the machinery and the water inaugurated the day's service in the Temple.

Middot 3.1 describes the Altar of Burnt Sacrifice as being four-square, originally 32 cubits by 32 cubits but records alterations that were made to its size following the exile. It does not give its height. Josephus gives the dimensions as 50 cubits by 50 cubits with a height of 15 cubits. These measurements, however, are too large. A ledge for the priests to walk around the Altar while they tended the sacrifices was known as the "circuit." A scarlet line was placed along the sides of the Altar according to traditions that stipulated where the blood was sprinkled, with clear distinctions as to those sacrifices where the blood was sprinkled above or below the red line. *Middot* 3.2 also describes the outlet of "two holes like two narrow nostrils" at the southwest corner of the base of the altar where the remainder of the blood was sometimes poured, to go down a water channel into the Kedron Valley.

During the Feast of Tabernacles *(sukkot)*, a special ceremony involving the Altar was performed. Each morning of the feast, a procession went down to the Pool of Siloam where a priest filled a golden vessel with water. Back in the Temple, the priest would perform the water libation ritual by pouring out the water into a silver bowl, while another priest poured wine into an adjacent bowl. In the Fourth Gospel, it was during the last day of this ceremony that Jesus said, "Let anyone who is thirsty come to me, and let the one who believes in me drink. As the scripture has said, 'Out of the believer's heart shall flow rivers of living water'" (John 7:37-39 NRSV). According to John, Jesus apparently respected these ceremonies.

Sacrificial animals were slain to the north of the Altar. The Place of Slaughter *(beit ha-mitbachim)* consisted of twenty-four rings, arranged in rows, into which the heads of the sacrificial animals were placed. Next to these rings were eight short pillars upon which rested blocks of cedar that held iron hooks in which the slaughtered animals were hung. Marble tables stood between the pillars and were used to flay the sacrifices.

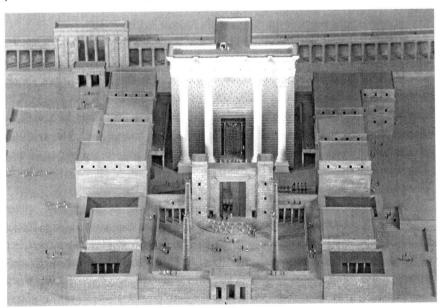

Fig. 1.23 Courtesy Leen Ritmeyer.

In between the Court of the Levites and the Court of the Israelites was a special platform (*duchan*) on which the daily Psalms were sung. One can conjecture that the music of the Temple was as splendid as its wealth. It included both vocal and instrumental music with the real service of praise in the Temple being only with the voice. Instrumental music was for accompaniment only. The vocal music consisted of extracts from the Psalms and other poetic sections from the Hebrew Bible.

The Nicanor Gate stood between the Temple Court and the Court of the Women (Fig. 1.23). Josephus gives a glowing description of this gate, which he calls the Corinthian Gate *(War* 5.201-206). It was fifty cubits high and the doors were forty cubits high. The doors of the gate were of "Corinthian bronze, and far exceeded in value those plated with silver and set in gold." The gate had a large central opening with two smaller side gates. These gates were usually kept open so that worshipers in the lower Court of the Women could follow the proceedings in the Temple Court.

Fig. 1.24 Courtesy Leen Ritmeyer.

To the east of the Temple and the Nicanor Gate was the Court of the Women (Fig. 1.24). The name indicates that this was the farthest women were allowed to proceed into the Temple. This court, which measured 135 cubits square, had raised galleries on all sides. *Middot* 2.5 states that "beforetime the Court of the Women was free of buildings, and afterward they surrounded it with a gallery, so that the women should behold from above and the men from below and that they should not mingle together."

These galleries or porticoes are also mentioned in the Mishnaic Tractate *Sukkah* 5.2, which deals with the laws concerning the Feast of Tabernacles *(sukkot)*. Here also we find explained the significance of the four great lampstands that stood in the Court of the Women. Each of these towering lampstands carried four bowls that were filled by young members of priestly families during the Feast of Tabernacles. The light from these sixteen bowls illuminated the whole city, according to *Sukkah* 5.3: "there was not a courtyard in Jerusalem that did not reflect the light of the Beth ha-She'ubah." It is possible that Jesus had this ceremony in mind when he said, "I am the light of the world" (John 8:12).

This court is also called the Treasury, because of the thirteen trumpet-shaped boxes for monetary offerings that were placed under the colonnades that ran round the Court of the Women. This court can almost certainly be identified as the Treasury mentioned in Luke 21:1-4, where Jesus observed "a poor widow put in two small copper coins" (NRSV).

Another of the Mishnaic tractates called *Shekalim*, which deals with the Shekel dues, records that each of the thirteen chests *(shopharot)* carried an inscription that indicated the object of the offering. There were receptacles for "New Shekel Dues," "Old Shekel Dues," "Bird Offerings," "Young birds for the whole-offering," "Wood," "Frankincense," and "Gold for the Mercy-seat." The remaining six were for "Freewill-offerings". One of these latter chests would have received the gift from the widow to which Jesus called attention: "she out of her poverty has put in everything she had, all she had to live on" (Mark 12:44 NRSV).

At the corners of the Court of the Women were four unroofed chambers. The chamber on the southeast was the Chamber of the Nazirites and it was here that those who had taken the vow of the Nazirite cooked their peace offerings, cut off their hair that had grown for the duration of their vow, and threw it on the fire under a pot. Going clockwise, the next chamber was the Chamber of the House of Oil, where oil and wine for the drink-offerings was stored. On the northwest of the Court of the Women was the Chamber of the Lepers, where those who were healed of leprosy came to be immersed, before presenting themselves before the priest. After Jesus had healed a leper (Matt. 8:2-4), he told him: "[G]o, show yourself to the priest, and offer the gift that Moses commanded, as a testimony to them" (NRSV). According to Mishnah *Negaim* 14, such a person would have to be confined for one week. On the seventh day, he had to bathe in the Chamber of the Lepers and then present himself before a priest standing in the Nicanor Gate, after having brought specific sacrifices.. He was at liberty to participate in worship again once the priest had pronounced him clean. The Nicanor Gate was also the location where women coming for purification presented themselves to the priests and there, too, the "water of bitterness"] was given to the wife suspected of adultery (Num. 5:24).

The chamber on the northeast was known as the Chamber of the Woodshed. Here, priests who because of some blemish could take no part in the sacrificial service of the Temple, examined the wood that was destined for use on the Altar.

To the east of the Court of the Women was the Eastern Wall of the Temple Mount, which was not extended by Herod by reason of the steep eastern slope of Mount Moriah. It carried a portico that therefore predated the time of Herod. This is most likely the portico called Solomon's Porch in the New Testament.

John 10:22-23 records that "at that time the festival of the Dedication took place in Jerusalem. It was winter" and "Jesus was walking in the temple, in the portico of Solomon" (NRSV). (Original was in KJV). The Feast of Dedication, called *Hanukkah* in Hebrew, commemorated the rededication of the Temple in 164 BCE after the desecration by Antiochus Epiphanes IV. In winter, the colonnade would have provided shelter against the elements. Later it became a popular meeting place for the followers of Jesus as recorded in Acts 5:12.

The Temple itself was the crowning glory of Herod's architectural achievements. The porch stood to a height of 100 cubits (172 ft.) and was equally wide. A modern-day parallel in terms of size would be an 18-story-high building towering above the surrounding landscape. *Middot* 4.1 records that the whole house was overlaid with gold. In our reconstruction, the façade is ornamented with four columns in the Corinthian style, as depicted on ancient coins.

Combining the descriptions in *Middot* and Josephus, we get a glowing picture. Josephus (*War* 5.222-223) supplies us with the following details: "The exterior of the building wanted nothing that could astound either mind or eye, for being covered on all sides with massive plates of gold, the sun was no sooner up than it radiated so fiery a flash that persons straining to look as it were compelled to avert their eyes, as from the solar rays. To approaching strangers it appeared from a distance like a snow-clad mountain; for all that was not overlaid with gold was of purest white."

The entrance to the porch was 40 cubits (69 ft.) high and 20 cubits (34.4 ft) wide. Above it, five oak beams covered with gold and of graduated length were set in the facade.

Beneath these and framing the entrance into the Sanctuary was a vine made of pure gold. This feature was one of the most remarkable in all the Temple precincts. *Middot* 3.8 records that "A golden vine stood over the entrance to the sanctuary, trained over posts; and whosoever gave a leaf, or a berry, or a cluster as a freewill-offering, he brought it and the priests hung it thereon." Josephus in *War* 5.210 also writes that the Temple entrance had "above it those golden vines from which depended grape-clusters as tall as a man." Jesus may have been alluding to this feature of the Temple when he said, "I am the true vine" (John 15:1).

A parapet of golden spikes was placed along the rooftop, the purpose of which was to stop birds from soiling the Temple walls.

The Temple itself was only 70 cubits (120 ft.) wide and 78 cubits (134 ft.) long. Three stories of small chambers surrounded the Temple proper, which was divided into the Holy Place and the Holy of Holies. This description makes it possible to appreciate the description of the Temple in *Middot* 4.7 as "like to a lion," "narrow behind and wide in front," a passage that also brings to mind one of the biblical titles of Jerusalem, Ariel, meaning "Lion of God." An Upper Chamber stood above the inner sanctuary, which had a device for lowering baskets into the Holy of Holies for maintenance purposes and a ladder in the form of two cedar beams with steps cut into them, by means of which the upper roof could be reached.

The Holy Place measured 40 cubits (69 ft.) high and 20 cubits (34.4 ft.) wide. It contained the seven-branched Lampstand (*menorah*) in the south; the Table of Showbread in the north; and, closer to the veil that separated the Holy Place from the Holy of Holies, the Altar of Incense.

The Veil in the Second Temple differed from that described in Exod. 26:31-33. Whereas the latter was made of "blue and purple and scarlet and fine twined lined of cunning work" and apparently decorated with cherubim, the Veil in Herod's Temple is described as having the symbols of lions and eagles portrayed on it.

The Mishnaic tractate *Shekalim* 8.5 records that the Veil was "one handbreadth thick and was woven on (a loom having) seventy-two rods, and over each rod were twenty-four threads. Its length was forty cubits and its breadth twenty cubits; it was made by eighty-two young girls and they used to make two in every year."

It is interesting to note that both Josephus and the New Testament refer to one veil. Josephus would have remembered this from the time when he served as a young priest in the Temple. However, the Mishnah (*Yoma* 5.1) mentions that there were two veils separating the sanctuary from the Holy of

Holies with a cubit wide space (*amah traksin*) between them. It is recorded in the Gospels (Matt. 27:51; Mark 15:38; Luke 23:45) that when Jesus died there was an earthquake and the veil of the Temple was torn from top to bottom, making it possible to look into the Holy of Holies. Is it possible that soon after this event, a second veil was added to prevent this from happening again?

There are more details as to the Veil given in the ritual for the Day of Atonement (*Yoma* 5.1). Here, the High Priest entering the Holy of Holies is described as going in via the south side of the outer curtain, which was slightly open, passing between this and an inner curtain and going into the Holy of Holies on the opposite side to which he began, which again was slightly open. The cubit space in between the two curtains was known as *amah traksin.*

The Holy of Holies was a square of 20 cubits (34.4 ft.) and was 40 cubits (69 ft.) high. As recorded in *Yoma* 5. 2, "After the Ark was taken away a stone remained there from the time of the early Prophets, and it was called 'Shetiyah.' It was higher than the ground by three fingerbreadths." This "foundation stone," I believe, is the rocky summit of Mount Moriah, on which the Holy of Holies of Solomon's Temple was built. It was visible inside the Holy of Holies and served as its floor. When King Herod built a six-cubit-high foundation for the Temple, the rocky floor of the Holy of Holies was slightly higher than the floor of the Holy Place. This original stone surface, now known by its Arabic name *Sakhra*, and enshrined within the Islamic shrine of the Dome of the Rock on the Temple Mount, was therefore a link with the original Temple. On the Day of Atonement *(Yom Kippur)*, the High Priest used to place his incense censer or fire-pan in the rectangular depression that marked the original emplacement of the Ark of the Covenant. The walls of the inner sanctuary were decorated with gold sheets with engravings of palmettes.

Such was the Temple with which the life of Jesus and the early Jews were so intimately bound up. Jesus called it "my Father's House" (John 2:16) and lost no opportunity to use its ritual to deepen and elucidate his teaching.

2

The Second Temple in Jerusalem

Dan Bahat

The Temple in Jerusalem has played a central function in the life of the city since the tenth century BCE, when King Solomon built the First Temple on the site of a small, dome-shaped hill named Mount Moriah. It is that hill that has given Jerusalem its meaning and sanctity to this day.

The name Moriah stems from the Hebrew root YRH which means "to found," hence the name of the Summit of the Hill. A British archeologist, Sir Charles Warren (with his team), who surveyed Jerusalem and the Temple Mount in 1867–1870, discovered the size and limits of the hill. It is a dome-shaped hill, the summit of which is protected today (actually since the seventh century CE) by the Dome of the Rock. The rock under the dome is the holy rock (known in Arabic as *as-Sakhra*), on which the Holy of Holies of the Temple was located. Since the days of Herod the Great (37–4 BCE), the entire Moriah Hill has been covered by the Temple Mount platform that Herod built. Archeologists believe that the sanctity of the Hill should be dated somewhere 23–22 BCE, when graves were dug on the summit of the Hill. These graves, because of their shape, probably belonged to dignitaries. Two of these tombs, which were surveyed by Warren (cisterns nos. 2 and 34), today serve as cisterns. Under the holy rock, another tomb is located, to which many traditions were attached, especially by the Muslims. Today, tourists may go down into this cistern while visiting the Dome of the Rock. With the exception of two Muslim praying niches, there is nothing of meaningful value in the cistern today. It is merely a cave.

Of Solomon's Temple, there are no evident remains. During the Judean Monarchy, the Hill included not only the Temple but also the royal palace built by King Solomon, as described in the Book of Kings.[1] Outside of the present Temple Mount were discovered remains of a wall which sets the city's limits, but as no remains have been preserved of that wall; we can only draw the line of the natural topography of Mount Moriah and its limits.

In the later period of the Judean Monarchy (eighth century BCE), the Hill got a new name: "The Temple Mount," or in Hebrew "*Har Ha-Bayit,*" which means the "Mountain of the House (of the Lord)." This name is used for the first time by prophet Micah:

> Therefore, on account of you
> Zion will be plowed as a field,
> Jerusalem will become a heap of ruins,
> And the mountain of the temple will become high places of a forest.
> (3:12 NASB)

The destruction of the First Temple by Nebuchadnezzar, the Chaldean, and the exile to Babylon that followed, left no traces on the Temple Mount. Only the biblical account can be used to describe it.

The Second Temple period begins with Cyrus's declaration in 538 BCE that enabled the Jews who were exiled to Babylon to go back to their homeland. Cyrus is quoted in Ezra 1:2–3:

> Thus says Cyrus king of Persia, "The Lord, the God of heaven, has given me all the kingdoms of the earth and He has appointed me to build Him a house in Jerusalem, which is in Judah. Whoever there is among you of all His people, may his God be with him! Let him go up to Jerusalem which is in Judah and rebuild the house of the Lord, the God of Israel; He is the God who is in Jerusalem."[2]

Several years later, in 515 BCE, the new Temple was consecrated. For exactly seventy years there was no Temple on the Mount. The new Temple was very poor compared to its predecessor. Many of those who remembered the older Temple wept upon seeing the new one (Ezra 2:12-13). But the builders of the new Temple, Zerubbabel, the son of Shaltiel, and Jehoshua, the son of Yehozadak, should not be blamed, since the poverty of the newly repatriated community did not provide for a more extravagant Temple.

In the fifth century BCE, under the outstanding leadership of Nehemiah and Ezra, the Temple began to play an important role in Jerusalem, a role that

---

1. See 1 Kgs. 5–8 for the biblical account of the building of the Temple and the palace by King Solomon.

2. See also 2 Chron. 36:23.

continued for the next five hundred years. Ceremonies and celebrations took place in the Temple's courts. One such ceremony was celebrated when the walls of Jerusalem were consecrated after Nehemiah's efforts to build them after many difficulties. The country underwent many vicissitudes and in 333 BCE it was annexed to Alexander the Great's realm. In Jerusalem, unlike other cities in the country, Hellenistic civilization did not have a great influence on life in the city. Indeed, the culture in Jerusalem would be quite slow in changing.

It is at this point that our story of the Second Temple starts. While studying the Temple, one should take into consideration the fact that no remains have been preserved of this early Temple of Zerubbabel or its precinct. The oldest remains found on the Mount, although quite scant, date from Herod the Great's time. These will be described below. Three main sources describe Herod's Temple: the Mishna, the New Testament, and the writings of Flavius Josephus. Josephus, the contemporary Jewish historian, writing under the auspices of the Roman Emperor Vespasian, was an eyewitness to the Temple. He came from a priestly family and knew the Temple well.

A study of these three sources shows a great discrepancy between Josephus and the New Testament, on the one hand, and the Mishna, on the other. The basic description of the Temple in the Mishna is primarily found in a special tractate named "Measurements," which deals with the measurements of the Temple Mount. It is important to note that the Mishna is dealing with the measurements of the Temple Mount and not the Temple itself. The measurements of the Temple itself are given in 1 Kings 6:2, when Solomon built the Temple and dictated its size as sixty cubits long, twenty cubits wide, and thirty cubits high. Indeed, the Second Temple fell short of some of the measurements required by Solomon's dictations, and this was the excuse of Herod the Great to expand the Temple in order to achieve the measurements required in 1 Kings.

When the Dome of the Rock was built in 691 CE, the soil on the site was stripped down to the natural bedrock. In the 1960s, the floor of the Dome was removed for improvements and an objective archeologist observer drew the underlying bedrock. But no significant archaeological remains of the Temple could be discerned. Therefore, the only indications for understanding the development of the Temple are the historical descriptions. The Book of Maccabees tells us about the cleansing of the Temple from the Hellenistic cult, which was practiced during the beginning of the second century BCE, as well as the rebuilding the walls of the Temple Mount. However, this record does not always agree with the meager description of the Temple given by the repatriates from Babylon. Thus, it is necessary to look for improvements made to the Temple Mount between the period of the rebuilding of the Temple and the Book of Maccabees. During the third century BCE, prior to the Maccabean rule, there was a period of literary prosperity among the Jews of Alexandria, the capital of Hellenistic culture in the entire Mediterranean area. Some of the books written during that time are among the apocryphal and other extra-biblical books. One of these books, an apocryphal source called the *Letter of Aristeas to Philocrates*, describes the course of events that brought about the translation of the Bible into Greek, known as the Septuagint. In the letter, there is a very impressive description of the Temple Mount (*Aristeas* 84-88). According to the description, Aristeas, an official in the court of Ptolemaius II (Philadelphus), was sent by that king to Jerusalem in order to bring back to Egypt seventy sages to translate the Pentateuch into Greek (later the whole Bible was translated).[3] When he came to Jerusalem he was invited to visit the Baris and the Temple. The Baris was the fortress that protected the Temple Mount from the north (*Aristeas* 100-104). In the Greek text, it is named the "Akra," but the name does not refer to the famous Akra that was constructed by the Greeks during the Maccabean revolt in an unknown, different place. Aristeas's description concentrates on the enormous walls of the Temple Mount as well as the water system that supplied water to the Temple by an aqueduct (*Aristeas* 89-91). This description of the Temple Mount contradicts the description of the modest Temple that was built by the repatriates from Babylon, over two hundred years earlier. There is no way to explain it other than understanding that there were great improvement works taking place on the Temple Mount. This assumption is strengthened by another book from Alexandria, the Book of Ben Sira (sometimes referred to as Ecclesiasticus). The date of this book is a matter of dispute, but the most probable date seems to be the first third of the second century BCE. Ben Sira is praising Simon, the son of Jason the high priest, as a builder of the Temple Mount from its very foundation. It is possible that the writer is alluding to the construction work done earlier by Zerubbabal, the son of Shaltiel, and Joshua, the son of Yehozadak.[4] He, like Aristeas, mentions the massive walls of the Temple Mount as well as the water supply to the Temple. Ben Sira's translation into Greek, made by his grandson, adds more information to the Hebrew text. There he says,

> Simon the high priest, the son of Onias, who in his life repaired the house again, and in his days fortified the temple: and by him was

---

3. *Aristeas* 40, 43.

4. *Ben-Sira* 49:11-12; 50:1-4.

built from the foundation the double height, the high fortress of the wall about the temple. In his days the cistern to receive water, being in compass as the sea, was covered with plates of brass. He took care of the temple that it should not fall, and fortified the city against besieging.[5]

Both sources seem to prove that in the third century BCE, or at the latest the beginning of the second century BCE, the Temple Mount was rebuilt and became a real stronghold in the city. Such changes in the Temple Mount were definitely a part of great improvements to the Temple. Therefore we refer to the reconstruction of the Temple Mount as also the reconstruction of the Temple itself. Are these works mentioned in other sources? In the books of 1 and 2 Maccabees, there are descriptions of work carried out on the Temple Mount by the first members of the Hasmonaean (also named Maccabees) family in 140–37 BCE. All of these works can be understood as improvements and repairs on the existing Temple Mount and the Temple after its pagan use during the Hellenistic period in Jerusalem. There are some archaeological finds that may indicate an older source for some of the passages in the *Letter of Aristeas* and Book of Ben Sira. In general, the archeologists and historians who deal with the descriptions in these books agree that when Herod the Great enlarged the Temple Mount, he added area to the northern, western, and southern sides of the older Temple Mount, but because of the steepness of the eastern slope of Mount Moriah, the eastern wall of the pre-Herodian Temple Mount remained as it was. Indeed, the eastern wall of the Mount, unlike the other three walls, is composed of more than one phase of construction. With the exception of the Herodian phase, the dates of this reconstruction cannot be identified with confidence. There is no doubt that the Temple Mount, just described, is the Temple Mount to which the Mishna, Tractate Middoth (= Measurements), refers.

The next phase of the Temple and the Temple Mount occurs in the days of Herod the Great (37–4 BCE). According to Flavius Josephus, Herod decided to build the Temple in 22 or 20 BCE, after completing some of his other important architectural undertakings. As the Temple Mount in Jerusalem is unique in its shape and dimensions, it is impossible to say what his model was for the construction of this enormous structure. There have been attempts to create an architectural model on which Herod based his program for the construction, but all these theories do not take in account the fact that there was already a considerable structure existing on the site. It seems much more

5. *Ben-Sira* 50:1-4.

plausible that he enhanced the size of the Mount based on the principles of the preceding structure. The Mishna describes the pre-Herodian structure in the famous tractate "Middoth" (= Measurements). There the dimensions of the Mount are given as 500 cubits by 500 cubits (approximately 250 x 250 meters). These dimensions may be compared with the dimensions of the Herodian Temple Mount (western wall 488 meters, eastern wall 465 meters, northern wall 320 meters, and southern wall 290 meters). According to most scholars, Herod's expansion of the Temple Mount was in the north, west, and south, leaving the older eastern wall as it was before the Herodian reconstruction. This fact led Flavius Josephus to write that the eastern wall was built by King Solomon (*War* 5:184, *Ant* 20:219). Had it been built by the Maccabeans, he would have known about it, as he had a vast knowledge of their time. The portico above the eastern wall was, therefore, named Solomon's Portico and as such it is mentioned by Josephus and in the New Testament (Acts 5:12). The early Christian community used to assemble there (Acts 3:11; 5:12) and the Gospel of John tell us that Jesus also walked under Solomon's Portico during the Hannukah festivities (10:22-23).[6] From this we can deduce that the older Temple Mount was also surrounded by porticos, as was Herod's Temple Mount. With the enhancement of the Temple Mount, all the other three porticos of the old Temple Mount had to be removed; otherwise, the porticos would have stayed in the middle of the court of the Temple and disturbed the national events on the Mount. Even today, the eastern wall of the Temple Mount is different from the other walls. One can see the "seam" that is the joint between the pre-Herodian masonry of the wall and the Herodian addition to it. All the other three walls of the Mount are made in one style of masonry, an archaeological fact that emphasizes the uniqueness of the eastern wall. The contemplation of the limits of the pre-Herodian Temple Mount uses the eastern wall as a starting point. As the Mishna marks the size of the pre-Herodian Temple Mount in cubits, it seems that the western wall of the pre-Herodian Temple would have been about sixty meters east of the present Western Wall. Had the eastern wall been further west, closer to the present Western Wall, it would have extended the pre-Herodian Temple Mount beyond Mount Moriah—definitely not the wish of its original builders. The excavations along the Western Wall have exposed some remains of the hill that was located north of Mount Moriah. This is another hill of Jerusalem named Antonia Hill. On this hill there are remains of the Baris fortress, which was located just north of the Temple Mount. Between the two hills, that of

6. "At that time the Feast of the Dedication took place at Jerusalem; it was winter, and Jesus was walking in the temple in the portico of Solomon" (John 10:22-23).

Mount Moriah and the Antonia Hill, a small ravine, a tributary of a deep valley named St. Anne's Valley, was located. When Charles Warren surveyed the Temple Mount in 1868, he found the rim of an artificial moat excavated in the bedrock connecting the Tyropoeon (central) Valley with the tributary of St. Anne's Valley. Unfortunately, Warren was ejected from the Mount by the local guards and so we do not have further details about that moat. The northern wall of the pre-Herodian Mount could not have been built north of this moat, and so it becomes another strong consideration in delineating the boundaries of the 500-square-cubit Mount.

There is no doubt that this moat is pre-Herodian, as Herod had to fill it in order to create the large platform of the Mount as we know it today. It must be assumed that the older Temple Mount was limited only to Mount Moriah, and thus, the northern wall of the pre-Herodian Temple Mount can be more or less located. Therefore, we have a full picture of the Mount before Herod decided to extend it on three sides. By his enlargement of the Mount, Herod went beyond Mount Moriah and thus it is possible to infer that the new part of the Mount may have been considered of lesser holiness than the original parts of the Mount. This theory stems from the fact that the Mishna is a legal codex and its interest is not the physical description of the Temple Mount as seen by the contemporary people who visited the Temple and its courts but rather the legal status of the various sites.

The reason for specifying the details of the size of the pre-Herodian Temple Mount stems from the legal system that prevailed regarding the Mount. The strictest law that was observed in the most ardent way was the law of purity. It was not possible to overstate the importance of the laws pertaining to the purity of the Mount. Trespassing was punished by the death penalty. This was the reason why the gentiles, who did not know or observe the laws of purity, were not allowed into the Temple precinct proper (the pre-Herodian Mount). The Mishna, which is the basic book of laws for the Jews, mentions the limits where the gentiles could approach the inner courts. According to the Mishna, the gentiles could enter the Women's Court in the Temple, but, it seems that for the sake of security, they could not get closer to the inner courts than the older Mount. This can be concluded from the following: Flavius Josephus tells us that there was a kind of wall or stone screen (*soreg*) on which inscriptions, Greek and Latin respectively, were installed. They forbade the gentiles to trespass that screen under the penalty of death. Two of these inscriptions have been found, both in Greek (we don't have the Latin version yet). One is exhibited now in the Archeological Museum in Istanbul and the other in the Israel Museum in Jerusalem. Josephus's description of the screen says that the screen was installed above a stairway, leading many scholars to believe that it was above the stairway of the *soreg*. The *soreg* is mentioned as a low wall, which had steps and a narrow pavement that served as a walkway around the Temple's wall. This complex of wall, steps, and walkway is named in the Mishna as the *Hel* (in Hebrew, a "wall"). The surprising thing is that such an important fact as the existence of the inscriptions, with their legal implications, is repeated a few times by Josephus, but not at all in the Mishna. The most probable explanation is that before Herod expanded the Temple Mount, there was no need of the inscriptions. Simply, the gentiles visiting Jerusalem knew that there was a prohibition on them visiting the Temple Mount. As Herod enhanced the size of the Mount, they could visit the Mount, but only within the area that was added by Herod. The pre-Herodian Temple Mount remained inaccessible to the gentiles, as its sanctity was determined before Herod's construction. Only then was there a need to install the inscriptions, as a gentile could, unnoticeably, trespass the limits of the sanctity. A nineteenth-century photo shows a very broad stairway located more or less on the possible southern limit of the pre-Herodian Temple Mount. It is assuredly the case that this stairway is of ancient times, as a medieval stairway was built above it. This could be the stairway where the screen with the inscriptions was installed.

Josephus also tells us that the Temple Mount was originally built by Solomon, who endeavored especially to construct the eastern wall of the precinct. Josephus repeats in both *Antiquities* (20:219) and *War* (5:184) that the eastern wall of the present Temple Mount was constructed in a few phases, the latest of which was the Herodian phase. This may be why, to this day, one can see the two phases in this wall. When Herod built the Holy Precinct, he did not have to build the eastern wall but only had to add extensions in the southern and the northern ends of the wall so that the eastern wall would run the entire length of the present (Herodian) eastern wall. The portico that surrounded the pre-Herodian wall remained as it was before Herod's construction and it was named Solomon's Portico, as it was believed to have been built by King Solomon. Solomon's Portico is of great importance to Christianity, as I have described above. It should not be surprising to us that this important Christian site is not visited by pilgrims today, since after the conquest of Jerusalem in 1187 by Saladin, no Christians were allowed to visit the Temple Mount. Thus, when the Holy Places were created, as they are known to us today, the Temple Mount was forgotten by the Christians who did not have access to the sites on the Mount.

We have been able to locate the eastern wall of the pre-Herodian Temple Mount, the so-called Solomon's Porch, and the southern wall of that Mount that could be located by the steps. It will not be too difficult to locate the other two sides using the measurements of 500 cubits.

The pre-Herodian Temple Mount would have been located more or less in the middle of the Herodian Mount when describing its north-south axis. However, the eastern side would have been the same as the existing Herodian Mount and the present Western Wall, which is worshipped at today by Jews worldwide, would have been outside of the sanctity of the Temple Mount as described in the Mishna. The modern rabbinical literature avoids this conclusion by suggesting a large cubit of 57 centimeters. This would bring the Western Wall into the holy precinct. The shorter cubit (approximately 45 cm), in which we believe, complies well with another factor. When Herod enhanced the size of the Mount, he went beyond the slopes of Moriah and it is, therefore, his area of the extension of the Mount that was not considered holy where the laws of purity had to be observed. Therefore, the Mishna does not refer to the Herodian extension. In order to appease the rabbinical circles, a study of the connection of the Jewish people and the Western Wall did not occur before the sixteenth and seventeenth centuries and thus does not have any implications on the question of the size of the pre-Herodian Mount. The limits of the pre-Herodian Mount and the Herodian one may also be seen in Josephus's description of an Outer Court and Inner Court. The outer refers to the Herodian extension of the Inner Court, which is the pre-Herodian Mount. Furthermore, one may conclude that the non-Jews who were barred from going into the Inner Court had to remain in the Herodian extension which may have been called that the Gentiles Court. This court is described in Acts when Paul came into the Inner Court accompanied by two Greeks, breeching the laws of purity.[7] The terms of outer and inner courts are already mentioned in Ezekiel 40–41, but this may be ascribed to an eschatological vision, just as it appears again in the Dead Sea Scrolls—the *Description of New Jerusalem* (*DNJ*) and the *Temple Scroll*.[8] There are very few remains preserved of the pre-Herodian Temple Mount, the joint between the older and the Herodian eastern wall being the primary remnant. Scholars name this joint the "seam," which is easily visible 32 meters north of the southeast corner of the Temple Mount. There is also the nineteenth century picture of the stairs and possibly also a stairwell south of the Triple Gate in the southern wall of the Temple Mount.

---

7. Acts 21:28.
8. See 11QTemple Scroll.

Another factor which may help us to locate the pre-Herodian Temple Mount on the surface of the present Herodian Temple Mount is the description of the Mishna, according to which, when the Temple stood on the Mount, it left the largest open area between it and the southern precinct wall. The smaller open area was in the east, even less than that in the north, and the narrowest area was in the west. In other words, the Temple did not stand in the center of the Mount. This is due to the natural topography of Mount Moriah. When the Muslims built the Dome of the Rock in the seventh century CE, they were aware and disturbed by this. They then constructed in the center of the Mount a smaller dome named the Dome of the Chain that mistakenly was believed to be a model for the construction of the Dome of the Rock. But it is so different that such a suggestion is out of the question. They built the Dome of the Rock, as they saw it, as the heir of the Jewish Temple that stood on the site. In spite of some other suggestions, there is no question that the Dome of the Rock is standing right on the site of the Holy of Holies (the *debir*) of the Jewish Temple. Since the Dome is the central point for the Mishnaic description, and there is no dispute among scholars about the eastern pre-Herodian precinct wall and the northern wall, then it is possible to delineate the 500 by 500 cubit Temple Mount that complies with the Mishnaic description of the open areas around the Temple.

The Herodian Temple Mount was the greatest architectural achievement of the Greco-Roman world.[9] It took ninety years to build and even so, its northwestern corner was never finished. In order to create the enormous platform that we see today, four retaining walls first had to be built. These walls were built in a very exquisite way. Up to the level of the Mount's surface, it was built of large stones, shaved in a very precise manner that gave them the appearance of marble stones. Each stone had margins that gave the impression of a frame. Sometimes even the central protruding part of the stone also had margins, so that there were two frames one within the other. Above the level of the Mount's surface, the freestanding wall comprised of recesses and pilasters "as the wave of the sea," as it is described in the Jewish sources.[10] The entire wall was built of huge limestone ashlars with no cement used to secure them. The wall was built with hundreds of these massive stones with a slight offset of only a few centimeters, as the stones were placed on top of each other to keep them from leaning outwards. The largest of these stones are larger than the largest stones in the Great Pyramids in Egypt and approximately the size of a city bus![11]

9. It was twice the size of Trajan's Forum in Rome built in the early second century CE.

10. The Mishna.

11. The largest identified stone weighs approximately six hundred tons.

Although only three such pilasters were preserved, we find a good example from Hebron, where Herod built a magnificent monument over the tombs of the Patriarchs, which remained intact for over two thousand years and can still be seen today. Inside the Mount, double porticos rested against the freestanding wall of the Mount. These porticos were connected to the wall pillars and two more rows of columns, thus creating two parallel naves.

The exception was the southern portico, which was a triple portico or, moreover, a basilica form with the central nave having an elevated ceiling over the two lateral naves. Many scholars deliberate about this southern portico, as it was the highlight of Herod's work. It is believed to reflect his personal problems with the Jewish people, as he was not accepted in the Temple proper, so he decided to build a monument where he would be "at home" and which would surpass in beauty and magnificence the Temple itself. Josephus goes out of his way to describe that portico, which must have been a real wonder. All the porticos had gilded capitals, some of which were found in the 1940s and are still standing on the Temple Mount today.

As Herod's construction went beyond Mount Moriah, he had to annex the southern slopes of the Antonia hill lying just north of Mount Moriah and shave the hill to the level of the platform. This work can still be seen in the northwestern angle of the Mount where a high rocky scarp creates the angle of the Mount. A deep ravine that separated Mount Moriah from the Antonia hill had to be filled to the level of the Mount platform. Such works were also carried out in the southwestern corner of the platform where Herod annexed to the Mount a section of Mount Zion, which was separated from Mount Moriah by the Central Valley of Jerusalem (dubbed "Tyropoeon" by Josephus). In order to do that, he filled the valley with a great amount of earth and also filled the immediate vicinity of the Mount so that he could build a horizontal street alongside the western wall. This eliminated the need to go down into the ravine and again up from it.

There were seven entrances to the Temple Mount: four gates in the western wall, two in the southern wall, and one in the eastern wall. The one in the eastern wall, named the Susa Gate in the Mishna, probably dated from the time of the pre-Herodian Temple Mount. Its only use, according to the Mishna, was to take out the red heifer after a certain ceremony in the Temple to the Mount of Olives in order to be sacrificed. The Christian tradition, dating to the Byzantine period (335–638 CE), claims that it was from this gate that Jesus entered Jerusalem on Palm Sunday. But as it had only one use, this Christian tradition about the entry of Jesus is impossible. The traditional gate, named today the Golden Gate, is a seventh-century construction based on tradition and not on any plausible fact.[12] The two southern gates, named the Double and Triple gates, are Herodian. The name "Hulda Gates," which may be found in the literature, is inaccurate, as this was the name given by the Mishna to the two pre-Herodian gates, and there is no certainty whatsoever that this name passed on to the Herodian gates. In the excavations carried out in the area leading to these gates, a very broad stairway was uncovered. It occupies the entire breadth of the two gates as well as the area between them. For various reasons, among which are quotations from the Mishna and the archeological finds, it is almost impossible to escape the conclusion that this is the site where Jesus expounded the law and marveled the Rabbis with his knowledge, being only twelve years old.[13]

In the western wall there were four gates. Today they are named after the scholars who discovered them in the nineteenth century: Robinson, Barclay, Wilson and Warren. Two were on the level of the Temple Mount's platform (Robinson's and Wilson's Gates). In order to reach this level from the street below, the bridge carrying the aqueduct to the Temple was used for passage from the Upper City of Jerusalem (today the Jewish and Armenian quarters) to the Temple. Entry to the gate on Robinson's Arch was gained by an enormous stairway constructed over the arch carrying that stairway. The two other western gates led directly from the street level to the Temple platform, where they entered the esplanade by means of long tunnels that were used from the medieval era as cisterns. Since Josephus does not name them in his description, we still use their modern names.

Upon ascending to the level of the Mount, one could see the enormous paved piazza. At a certain distance, a low wall, named the "stone hedge" by Josephus, was placed, bearing the Greek and Latin inscriptions forbidding the gentiles to trespass into the Inner Court (*War* 5.193-94; 6.124-26).[14] It may be believed that the moneychangers were located in the area outside the Inner Court and so they could be seen south of the screen. The tables were located on the southern open area outside the screen, since on the west the area was too

12. Today the Golden Gate is the only one of the seven gates that is closed. It was closed by the Muslims about eight years after its construction in 630 CE. By tradition, the Jewish Messiah would come through the Eastern Gate from the Mount of Olives. Therefore, it was sealed by the Muslims to keep out the Messiah. It was reopened by the Crusaders twice a year on Palm Sunday and on the 14th of September and finally closed by the nephew of Saladin about 1229 CE. Suleiman the Magnificent added the uppermost part of the gate, but it was not opened in his days.

13. Mark 11:27—12:17.

14. "No Gentile may enter beyond the dividing wall into the court around the Holy Place; whoever is caught will have himself to blame for his subsequent death." See Peretz Segal, ""The Penalty of the Warning Inscription from the Temple of Jerusalem,"" *Israel Exploration Journal* 39 (1989): 79–84.

narrow and on the north there were no gates from which people could enter the Temple Mount and see the moneychangers. After passing this screen, the Jewish pilgrims passed into the Inner Court. Also from Josephus's description, we learn that even the pavement was different in the two courts. The Inner Court, unlike the Outer Court, had a multicolored stone pavement. Another screen, a low wall named the *soreg*, was the next partition to be encountered by the visitors to the Temple. The *soreg* encircled the Temple on all four sides and it also marked another degree of sanctity with more limits on the visitors. From the narrow platform, there were doors leading to the various chambers (the verbatim term for these rooms used in the Mishna is "offices"), the number of which is a matter of question in the Mishna. The number thirteen is the most probable (it should be remembered as mentioned above, the tractate dealing with the description of the Temple was written after the destruction of the Temple and the memory of the writer was not always precise). The main entrance to the Temple was from the east. This gate, named in Hebrew, the "Gate of the East," was the stage for the event, known from Acts, where John and Peter healed the mendicant.[15] The fame of the Gate, because of this event, gave it the name "Beautiful Gate," and although it does not exist today (as nothing of the Temple has remained), the Christian tradition moved the event to the eastern wall of the Temple Mount to the Golden Gate (the gate built in the seventh century CE). Upon entering the real Beautiful (or Eastern) Gate, one arrived at the Women's Court, so named since this was the closest to the sanctuary that women could approach. Women could go only to the balconies that encircled the court whereas men could walk on the ground level.

The Women's Court, measuring 135 by 135 cubits, was not a square, as there were four chambers or offices in each of its corners. One was used as storage for the wood necessary for the altar. Here the priests who could not serve in the Temple because they were not aesthetically suitable (bald, scarred, etc.) examined every piece of wood in order to make sure that there was no impurity (insects and the like), since it was to be used for the fire on the altar. In another room, water was kept and in the other was the Nazarene's (celibates) chamber. In Judaism, celibacy was not allowed, but if somebody vowed to become a celibate, he could perform his vow for one year only. At the end of this year, he had to come to the Temple and bring a sacrifice to the priests. Then he had to come to the chamber dedicated to this purpose and make a fire, using his hair and nails (which during the one year vow were not cut) as burning

15. Acts 3:1–10.

material. He would then cook the sacrificial meat in a cauldron and eat it there. Thus, his vow was paid.

As to the fourth chamber, even the writer of the tractate did not remember its purpose. From the Women's Court, the male Jew could go higher to the Court of the Israelites, so named because this was the closest an ordinary Jew could approach the holiness of the Sanctuary. The passage between the two courts was by a semicircular stairway. Under it, there were on both sides two doors into rooms where the musical instruments used during the various celebrations were stored. At the top of the stairwell, there was the large gate with two bronze doors that shone like gold (they were made of what the Mishna calls Corinthian gold, a material having the appearance of gold but was composed of a certain brass alloy). It was flanked by two smaller posterns. The large gate was named the Gate of Nicanor, who was a rich Alexandrian Jew who donated the two doors. There are many legends that described the way by which the doors were brought to Jerusalem from Alexandria.[16] In the 1930s, a burial cave was uncovered in Jerusalem (on Mt. Scopus) and on the ossuary there was found the inscription, "Nicanor and Alexa of Alexandria, the sons of Nicanor who made the doors." The pride of taking part in the construction of the Temple has its expression also in another ossuary discovered in the 1970s on which the inscription, "Simeon, the Builder of the Temple," was incised. The fact that the Gate of Nicanor had three openings was unusual, as all the entrances to the Temple Mount were either with one or two gates, never with three, as is common in other religions.

The Court of the Israelites was very narrow. It measured only 135 by 10 cubits. It enabled the person who came there to stand and watch the priest take from him the animal he brought for sacrifice. It was slaughtered in the abattoir, which was located to the left of the Sanctuary, and then the butchered meat was taken to the altar that was located to the right and in front of the entrance of the Sanctuary. The abattoir was comprised of stone columns on which the carcass was hung and skinned, and then it was butchered on a marble table of the slaughterhouse. The partition between the Court of the Israelites

16. "When Nicanor went to Alexandria in Egypt to bring the doors, on his return a huge wave threatened to engulf him. Thereupon they took one of the doors and cast it into the sea, but still the sea continued to rage. When they prepared to cast the other one into the sea, Nicanor rose and clung to it, saying, 'Cast me in with it.' The sea immediately became calm. He was, however, deeply grieved about the other door. As they reached the harbor of Acre (present-day Akko in Israel), the door broke the surface and appeared from under the sides of the boat. Subsequently, all the gates of the Temple were changed for golden ones, but the Nicanor gates, which were said to be of bronze, were left because of the miracles wrought with them" (Talmud; *Yoma* 38a).

and the Court of the Priests, which surrounded the Sanctuary, was not a wall or a screen but a large wooden beam. There was also a difference in the level between the two, with the Court of the Priests being higher than that of the Israelites. In the Court of the Priests, there were chambers and a few gates so that on occasions there was direct access from the *Hel* to the court. Also, there were some chambers there, among which the most famous was the Chamber of the Hearth, so named because the priests used to sleep in this chamber during their service of the Temple. On cold winter nights in Jerusalem, the priests used to sleep on stone benches covered with furs while a hearth burned during the night.

It is interesting that from the Chamber of the Hearth there was a shaft with steps leading down to a tunnel that went to the outer court (or outside of the pre-Herodian Temple Mount). This enabled a priest who was contaminated for any reason during his service in the Temple, or because, as the Mishna says, during his sleep possibly by nocturnal emission, to leave the holy area of the Temple and go outside of the holy precinct. It seems that a tunnel, which serves today as a water cistern, named in the nineteenth century "cistern number 1," may be such a tunnel. The northern end of the cistern may indicate the northern line of the pre-Herodian Temple Mount, since the contaminated priest had to be outside of the holy precinct in order to purify himself before returning to his post in the Temple.

Above the Chamber of the Hearth there was a ritual bath in which the high priest on the eve of the Day of Atonement used to purify himself before entering the Sanctuary and the Holy of Holies. The question of how water reached this ritual bath is still an unsolved mystery.

The Sanctuary was a very impressive structure and its dimensions had to comply with the dimensions mentioned in 1 Kings 6, where the dimensions of Solomon's Temple are dictated. The entire Temple of Solomon was a kind of royal chapel, and thus was isolated with no ancillary structure attached to it. Thus, the Solomonic Temple consisted of the sanctuary only. All the other structures, the Women Court, the Court of the Israelites, and the Court of the Priests, did not exist in the First Temple period. Herod added these ancillary structures as he greatly expanded both the size of the Temple and the extravagance of the Temple structure. The entrance was impressive, as it was very high. From the outside, there was not much that one could see; two curtains blocked the vision into the Sanctuary. They were slightly inside the structure, leaving a narrow space between the entrance to the Sanctuary and the curtains. On both sides of the small space were some stores where the sacrificial knives were stored. The front curtain did not reach the northern wall of the Sanctuary and the inner one did not reach its southern wall. This resulted in the famous view of the Day of Atonement, when the high priest entered the Sanctuary and was seen, with great concern, by the people who stood to view the exciting event. The High Priest entered the sanctuary, walking from north to south between the two curtains, then from south to north and then disappearing to the public, because the opacity of the two curtains concealed what was inside.[17] Therefore, even the sages of the time were expounding the problem of how the various object of the Holy of Holies were installed. Were they in an east-west line or were they in a north-south axis? When the Temple was rebuilt in Herod's time, the builders of the walls of the Holy of Holies were not supposed to see what was inside, so they had to build while standing with their back to the Holy of Holies so as not to see anything they were building.

Thus, we have reached the innermost part of the Temple. It should be remembered that we do not have any archeological remains of the Temple. The mosque named the Dome of the Rock is standing on the site of the original Jewish Temple. The only thing that may have belonged to the Temple proper is a small stone vessel measuring about five centimeters on which the inscription "for sacrifice" is incised. A small depiction of a dove is also incised there and it may indicate what sacrifice was offered in this vessel. It is impossible to know for certain, as the vessel is very small.

From all the descriptions (Josephus, the New Testament, and the Mishna), it seems that this complex of the Holy Precinct was very impressive to all visitors. The Temple became the stage for all the events in the country, some of which finally brought the destruction of this wonderful structure. As we have seen, there were four stages in the development of the Temple and its precinct during the two thousand years of its existence: the Solomonic, the post-exilic, the Hellenistic (the pre-Herodian), and finally, the Herodian Temple. Such a long period of the existence of the Temple could not have disappeared without making a major impression on the Jewish people. One should not wonder, therefore, that there is a constant desire to rebuild the Temple. The reason why even the Herodian Temple is dubbed the "Second Temple" is due to the fact that, since the reconstruction of the Temple after the return from Babylon until the destruction of the Temple in 70 CE, the daily rites never ceased (with the exception of a very brief period prior to the Hasmonean revolt in 167 BCE).

---

17. Due to the extreme sanctity of the Holy of Holies (the *debir*), only the High Priest could enter and only once per year on the Day of Atonement. A rope was tied around his leg, since if God were to strike him dead because of some impurity, there would be no way to bring his body out of the Holy Place.

3

The Importance of the Temple for Ancient Jews

Lawrence H. Schiffman

The topic of this chapter is the theological question: What did the Temple mean to the Jews in ancient times? It will present a synthesis drawn from various sources. In fact, with certain exceptions, the ideas are fairly uniform in most of our sources from late antiquity. We will not deal here with New Testament sources since they exhibit specific early Christian attitudes to the Temple and so would require a separate study of their own.[1]

One of the most important passages for understanding the way later Jews understood the Temple is the prayer attributed by 1 Kings to Solomon upon dedicating the Temple, of which this is just one small part:

> But will God really dwell on earth? Even the heavens to their uttermost reaches cannot contain You, how much less this House which I have built! Yet turn, O Lord my God, to the prayer and supplication of Your servant. . . . May Your eyes be open day and night toward this House, toward the place of which You have said, "My name shall abide there." (1 Kgs. 8:27-29)[2]

---

1. See the survey in J.J.M. Roberts, "Temple, Jerusalem," *New International Dictionary of the Bible* 5.507–8; C. Rowland, "The Temple in the New Testament," in *Temple and Worship in Biblical Israel: Proceedings of the Oxford Old Testament Seminar*, ed. J. Day (London: T.&T. Clark, 2007), 469–83; Y.Z. Eliav, *God's Mountain: The Temple Mount in Time, Place, and Memory* (Baltimore: Johns Hopkins University Press, 2005), 46–82. Cf. also, L.H. Schiffman, "Temple, Sacrifice and Priesthood in the Epistles of the Hebrews and the Dead Sea Scrolls," in *Echoes from the Caves: Qumran and the New Testament*, ed. F. García Martínez (Leiden: Brill, 2009),165–76.

2. Translations from the Hebrew Bible follow the New Jewish Publication Society translation.

Solomon meditates on the propriety of God's possessing a house. Will God really dwell on earth? Can God, who fills the entire universe and rules it, be located in any one place? This tension between the immanence of God and His transcendence is actually a fundamental part of the Jewish prayer service in which the Isaianic verse, "Holy, holy, holy is the Lord of hosts; the whole earth is full of His glory" (Isa. 6:3) is recited along with Ezekiel's doxology, "Blessed be the presence of the Lord from His place" (Ezek. 3:12). The former verse underscores God's immanence and the latter His transcendence.

Scholars in the field of biblical studies have debated the extent to which monotheism as we know it was already normative in the First Temple period. There are indeed remnants of earlier pre-monotheistic points of view in biblical literature, and there is no question that this very tension was understood in the Deuteronomistic layer of Kings. That is the question that Solomon asks outright in 1 Kings 8, and basically the message of that prayer is very typical of what Jews believed throughout the ages: Even though God is transcendent, there is a place where God is deemed even more available—the Jerusalem Temple.

All Jewish groups maintained this point of view about the Jerusalem Temple, even if they opposed the way in which the rituals were being performed. Therefore, already in the Hebrew Bible and in later Jewish ritual, there is the idea of the significance of coming to Jerusalem on the pilgrimage festivals, and the concept of this national gathering unifying the Jewish people.[3] The Psalmist put it clearly:

> I rejoiced when they said to me,
> "We are going to the House of the Lord."
> Our feet stood inside your gates, O Jerusalem:
> Jerusalem built up, a city knit together,
> To which tribes would make pilgrimage,
> The tribes of the Lord,
> —As was enjoined upon Israel—
> To praise the name of the Lord. (Ps 122:1-4)

The Temple was also seen as a unifier of the Jewish people. Ideally built into its architecture according to the *Temple Scroll* was a replication of the residence areas of the twelve tribes in the desert camp.[4]

---

3. See M. Goodman, *Judaism in the Roman World: Collected Studies* (Leiden: Brill, 2007), 59–68.

4. L.H. Schiffman, *The Courtyards of the House of the Lord: Studies on the Temple Scroll*, ed. F. García Martínez, Studies on the Texts of the Desert of Judah 75 (Leiden: Brill, 2008), 215–32.

Jerusalem was known in Deuteronomy as "the place which the Lord will choose to cause His name to dwell,"[5] although in Deuteronomy it had not yet been revealed what city would be that holy place. Nevertheless, by the Second Temple period, everyone knew what the place was that God had chosen, because it was the site of the First Temple. God, in the view of the Jewish people, had already chosen Jerusalem in First Temple times. The idea that Jerusalem had been chosen "from eternity" is reflected in the non-canonical Psalms from Qumran:

> [Jeru]salem [the city which the Lo]rd [chose] from eternity,
> [as a place of residence for] the holy ones.
> [For the na]me of the Lord has been invoked upon it,
> [and His glory] has appeared over Jerusalem [and] Zion.
> (*Non-Canonical Psalms A Scroll* 1 1 1–8)[6]

Among the Dead Sea Scrolls, there are those that are sectarian and those that are nonsectarian.[7] "Sectarian" pertains to the specific group of Qumran sectarians with their particular ideology, language, and separateness. "Nonsectarian" designates the general literature of the Jewish people found along with the sectarian corpus at Qumran. The document above, *Non-Canonical Psalms A*, does not represent sectarian ideology. It expresses the commonplace Jewish idea that God's name is invoked over this particular place. The Deuteronomic theology of the divine name now becomes divine presence theology, so that the name is equal to the *kavod* (the glory) and the *shekhinah* (the divine presence, in rabbinic terms).[8] This is a notion quite prominent in all the Qumran scrolls. God's presence is not really located in the Temple, as we saw in the passage from Kings. Rather, this is the place where God is available to the human being.

The Temple, in certain Dead Sea Scrolls, is equivalent to the Tabernacle in the desert camp. This desert sanctuary was remembered by all Second Temple Jews as concretized in the First Temple and then in the Second. When the Qumran sectarians contemplated the ideal Temple, as we see in the Halakhic

5. Deut. 12:5, 11, 21, 26; 14:24, 25; 16:6; 17:8; 18:6; 26:2.

6. Trans. L.H. Schiffman, *Reclaiming the Dead Sea Scrolls: The History of Judaism, the Background of Christianity, the Lost Library of Qumran* (Philadelphia: Jewish Publication Society, 1994), 388.

7. D. Dimant, "The Qumran Manuscripts: Contents and Significance," in *Time to Prepare the Way in the Wilderness: Papers on the Qumran Scrolls by Fellows of the Institute for Advanced Studies of the Hebrew University, Jerusalem, 1989–90*, ed. D. Dimant and L.H. Schiffman, STDJ 16 (Leiden: Brill, 1995), 23–58.

8. Cf. E.E. Urbach, *The Sages: Their Concepts and Beliefs*, trans. I. Abrahams (Jerusalem: Magnes, 1987), 2:37–65.

Epistle (4QMMT, also known by its first line, *Some Works of the Torah*), a foundational document of the Qumran sect, they determined that the Temple was equivalent to the Tabernacle that stood in biblical times:

> But we hold the view that the Temple is [the (equivalent of the) Tabernacle of the Tent of Meeting, and Je]rusalem is the camp, and outside the camp [is (equivalent to) outside Jerusalem]; it is the camp of their cities. (4QMMT B29-31)[9]

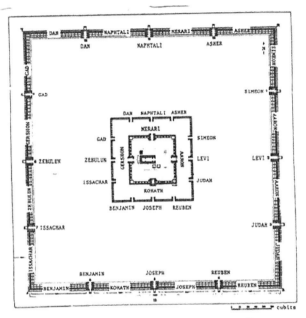

The Temple Plan according to the Temple Scroll

Fig. 3.1. The Temple Plan according to the Temple Scroll. Adapted by the author from Yigael Yadin, The Temple Scroll, vols. 1–3 (Jerusalem: Israel Exploration Society, 1983).

Furthermore, Jerusalem is the camp, that which the rabbis called the "camp of the Levites," for in the Book of Numbers the Levites encamp around what the rabbis called the "camp of the divine presence," the area where the Tabernacle was erected. The most restricted part was the Tabernacle area where only the priests could go; then the camp of the Levites; beyond was the rest of the residency area.[10] The rest of the residency area in this text is the area outside

9. Trans. Schiffman, *Reclaiming the Dead Sea Scrolls*, 389.

10. Schiffman, *Courtyards*, 381–401.

the city of Jerusalem where the rest of the people lived. This point of view also underlies the *Temple Scroll*'s plan for how the Temple should be set up. The *Temple Scroll* depicts the Temple building surrounded by three concentric courts (see Fig. 3.1). It adds a third court so that the camp of the divine presence of the Temple building is in the center, the camp of the Levites is the middle court, and the outer court is the camp of Israel. It symbolizes the dwelling places of all Israel and hence there are gates in the outer walls and then again in the middle court for each one of the tribes. These gates symbolize the access of the entire nation to the Temple because God's presence is there. There is a similar illustration in the mural at Dura Europos of twelve streams of water coming from a well in the middle (see Fig. 3.2). This symbolizes the idea that the divine presence goes out to all the tribes of Israel. To this day, there is a custom that a synagogue should have twelve windows.[11]

Another aspect of this entire picture is that often the Temple is seen in some Second Temple sources as being connected with the primeval Garden of Eden, for example, in the *Book of Jubilees*, found in the library at Qumran, and dated to c. 170 BCE:[12]

> [Noah] knew that the Garden of Eden is the holy of holies, and the dwelling of the Lord, and Mount Sinai the center of the desert, and Mount Zion—the center of the Navel of the universe: these three were created as holy places facing each other. (*Jub.* 8:19)[13]

In this text, the Garden of Eden, Mount Sinai, and Mount Zion (the Temple Mount) are basically lined up as the navel of the universe, the *omphalos*. The Temple is the place from which the divine powers emanate to the world.

Another interesting connection of the Garden of Eden and the Temple comes up in the *Book of Jubilees* (3:10-14) and a Dead Sea Scrolls text entitled *Miscellaneous Laws* (4Q265 7 11-17).[14] These texts extrapolate from the laws of purification in Lev. 12:1-8 concerning purification of the mother after childbirth and impose this need for purification on Adam and Eve. They are

---

11. Ibid., 227–32.

12. J.C. VanderKam, "Jubilees, Book of," *Encyclopedia of the Dead Sea Scrolls* 1.434–35.

13. Trans. C.T.R. Hayward, *The Jewish Temple: A Non-biblical Sourcebook* (London: Routledge, 1996), 89.

14. Cf. J.M. Baumgarten, *Qumran Cave 4.XIII: The Damascus Document (4Q266-273)*, Discoveries in the Judaean Desert 18 (Oxford: Clarendon, 1996), 60–61, 70–72.

Fig. 3.2. Moses strikes a rock and water issues forth to the twelve tribes; fresco from Dura-Europos, third century. National Museum of Syria.

required to be purified, as if they were their own mother, for the number of days that a woman is considered impure after the birth of a male or female child. For this reason they may not enter the Garden, which is equivalent to the Temple, until they are suitably purified.

Rabbinic sources concretize the centrality of the Temple by stating that a Jew is called upon to pray the Eighteen Benedictions facing in the direction of Jerusalem, and if in Jerusalem, to pray towards the Temple. If he is in the Temple, he must pray towards the Holy of Holies.

[If] one was riding on a donkey, he should dismount [to pray]. But if he is not able to dismount, he should turn his face [and pray]. And if he is unable to turn his face, he should concentrate his thoughts toward the Chamber of the Holy of Holies [while praying]. If he was sitting in a boat or wagon, or on a raft, he should concentrate his thoughts toward the Chamber of the Holy of Holies [while praying]. (*Berakhot* 4:5-6)

This prescription indicates the geographic nature of the symbolism of the availability of the divine presence. This is also basically the message of the parts of Solomon's prayer in 1 Kings that we did not quote above: If you are in trouble somewhere, you should turn to this House, meaning that you should pray towards this House (1 Kgs. 8:33-40). This has become the basis for the fact that synagogues are required to face Jerusalem, and when a Jew prays as an individual, he or she is supposed to face Jerusalem.[15]

This basic notion links up with another Mishnaic notion of the levels of holiness:

There are ten levels of holiness:
1. The Land of Israel is holier than all other lands.
2. Walled cities [in the Land] are holier than it....
3. Within the walls [Jerusalem] is holier than they....
4. The Temple Mount is holier than it....
5. (Within) the barrier around the Temple is holier than it....
6. The Women's Courtyard is holier than it....
7. The Israelites' Courtyard is holier than it....
8. The Courtyard of the Priests is holier than it....
9. Between the antechamber to the Temple building and the altar is holier than it....
10. The Temple building is holier than it....
11. The Holy of Holies is holier than they. (*Kelim* 1:6-9)

The closer one gets to the Temple Mount, the more the sanctity of the Land of Israel increases until finally the most holy is the Temple building, and within it the Holy of Holies. Again, we see a connection to that same quotation from Solomon's prayer: Is God really in one place or is He everywhere? Both these ways of looking at the same thing here operate together. There is no debate in Second Temple sources—or for that matter in other Jewish sources—between the concept of God's transcendence and God's immanence. The biblical

---

15. On the orientation of ancient synagogues, see L.I. Levine, *The Ancient Synagogue: the First Thousand Years* (New Haven, CT: Yale University Press, 2000), 302–6.

message as understood by Jews is that God is both. How can one talk in both forms at the same time?

Philo and Josephus attack this problem from a different point of view.[16] To them, the Temple is basically a microcosm of the universe, and the messages projected by entry into the Temple project this idea in a physical sense.

Josephus has the idea that there is a publicly used area in the Temple that symbolizes the earth and the sea.

> . . . By apportioning the tabernacle . . . into three sections giving over two portions to the priests as if it were a public place and permitted for human use, he signifies the earth and the sea, for indeed these are accessible to all. But he marks out the third portion for God alone. . . . By placing on the table the 12 loaves, he indicates [the] months . . . the candlestick composed of 70 portions . . . alluded to the decans [10-degree portions of the Zodiac occupied by each planet] . . . . and by seven lamps . . . he hinted at the orbit of the planets. (*Ant* 3:180-182)[17]

> The seven lamps represented the seven planets . . . and the twelve loaves on the table the circle of the Zodiac and the year; and the altar of incense, because of the thirteen fragrant ingredients with which it is compounded from sea and land both inhabited and uninhabited, signified that all things are of God and for God. (*War* 5:217-218)[18]

The private part of the Temple that no human being enters constitutes God's private house. Here was located the table with the Twelve Loaves of the Bread of the Presence (showbread) (cf. Exod. 25:23-30, 37:10-16). Since Second Temple Hellenistic Jews did not believe that God was eating those loaves,[19] they saw them as symbolic of the twelve months. The candlestick, the Menorah, seventy portions—often symbolic of the seventy nations—and the ten-degree portions of the zodiac, all symbolized the heavenly bodies and their orbits. Finally, the seven lamps that burn on the Menorah hint at the orbits of the seven planets known to the ancients.[20]

---

16. Cf. Hayward, *Jewish Temple*, 108–53.

17. Ibid., 148.

18. Ibid., 146.

19. See L.J.M. Claassens, "Bread of Presence," *New International Dictionary of the Bible* 1:499–500.

20. Cf. R.R. Stieglitz, "The Hebrew Names of the Seven Planets," *Journal of Near Eastern Studies* 40 (1981): 135–37. The seven planets are Sun, Moon, Venus, Mercury, Mars, Jupiter, and Saturn.

What is the point of the Temple's symbolizing the universe? The notion is to teach that God is the ruler over the entire universe and not just a local god here on earth. By Second Temple times there is no question that the notion of God's ruling over what we call the universe, as opposed to some particular part of it, was definitely normative in Judaism. Again, the seven lamps, seven planets, twelve loaves, the thirteen fragrant ingredients in the incense coming from sea and land, all things are of God and for God. Everything is created by Him or to serve Him.

> Now in front of these was a veil . . . of Babylonian woven cloth embroidered in blue and linen as well as scarlet and purple, worked in marvelous fashion. The combination of material it possessed did not lack theoretical significance, but was like an image of the universe. For it appeared that fire was hinted at in the scarlet, the earth in the fine linen, the air in the blue, and the sea in the purple. (*War* 5:212-214).[21]

Within the same general framework is the veil (*parokhet*). This is the curtain that hangs over the Temple entrance (Exod. 36:21-31-37; 36:35). Josephus provides us with a beautiful description of how the veil was "worked in marvelous fashion," but the materials in it were understood to symbolize the entire universe. The Temple structure teaches that God rules over that universe.

A similar notion is found in Philo:

> He placed the candlestick in the south, through which he hints figuratively at the movement of the light-bearing stars, for the sun and moon . . . make their courses in the south. From there, then, six branches, three from either side, issue forth from the central lampstand to make up the number seven [symbol of the planets]. For the sun, just like the candlestick, is ordered in fourth place as the middle of the six, and gives light equally to the three above and to those below it. . . . (*De Vit Mos* 2:102-3)[22]

According to Philo, the menorah symbolized the movement of the light-bearing stars, the sun, and the moon; six branches on each side of the main lamp, the planets with the sun at the center, a heliocentric universe. Note that the text has only accounted for six of the planets.

---

21. Trans. Hayward, *Jewish Temple*, 144–45.
22. Ibid., 125.

Additionally, Josephus declares that the Temple, very much in the sense of the Isaianic vision (Isa. 2:1-4), is for all the nations of the world.

> We slaughter the sacrifices not to get ourselves into a drunken state, for this is disagreeable to God, but to produce a state of moderation in ourselves. And at the sacrifices it is first necessary to pray for the common safety, not for our own selves. For we were born for life in common, and he who honours this above his own personal concerns is especially favoured by God. (*Against Apion* 2:195-97)[23]

In *Against Apion*, from which this quotation comes, Josephus argues against Apion (20s BCE–c. 45–48 CE), who dredged up all kinds of anti-Semitic slurs to present to Greek-speaking readers, many of whom had possibly never met a Jew. Josephus had to show that Jews were not xenophobic, despite the fact that they were expected to marry only their fellow Jews in order to build a religious Jewish home. He answers that the fact that anyone who is truly committed may convert, shows that Jews are not xenophobic (*Against Apion* 2.261; cf. 2.209-10).

In this passage, he continues this trend of thought. He says, "We slaughter the sacrifice not to get ourselves into a drunken state" that is "disagreeable to God," an anti-pagan polemic. It is necessary to pray for the common safety, not just for ourselves: Jews pray for everyone. Indeed, the Jewish prayers until today, with almost no exceptions, are in the plural; there is virtually no prayer in the singular. There are many prayers for the welfare of the Jewish people; there many other prayers which include others as well, the whole world. Josephus is arguing that the Temple, which symbolized the universe, is assumed, following Isaiah's vision, to be a Temple for all of humanity.

Philo also regards the universe symbolically as the Temple of God:

> The whole universe must be regarded it as the highest and, in truth, the holy Temple of God. As sanctuary it has the heaven, the most holy part of the substance of existing things; . . . As for the Temple made by hands—it was necessary that there be no driving back of the eagerness of men who pay the religious dues to piety, and who wish by sacrifices even to give thanks for the good things which happened, what to ask forgiveness and pardon for matters in which they have sinned.[24] (Philo, *Special Laws* 1.66-77)

---

23. Ibid., 152.
24. Ibid., 109.

While the universe is the Temple of God to Philo, the Dead Sea sectarians saw their sectarian way of life as replacing the Temple. They believed that it was forbidden to participate in worship at the Temple because they thought that the Temple was being conducted in an impure manner.

This is the theme of the Halakhic Epistle (4QMMT, also called *Some Works of the Torah*) of which four copies were found at Qumran. The text lists matters about which the sectarians did not agree with the manner in which the Temple worship was being conducted and because of which they had left the Temple service. They write to someone in charge in the hope that he will change the way the Temple is run and conduct the rituals according to the sectarian rulings. This text dates from about 150 BCE and represents a formation document of the sect in the aftermath of the Maccabean revolt when Pharisaic rulings, as opposed to Sadducean views, became the norm in the Temple for some time. These nascent sectarians were protesting and leaving the Temple as a result of their disagreements.[25] Once they stopped participating in the Temple service, they began to explain their own life as a substitute Temple. This is very important to us for historical reasons since eventually rabbinic Judaism as a whole, after the destruction of the Second Temple, would see Torah study and prayer and the Jewish home as a symbolic replacement for the Temple. This symbolism is represented in so many rituals: lighting the Sabbath candles is like lighting the Menorah, and putting the challah bread on the table beforehand is like setting the bread on the showbread table. This kind of symbolism already goes back to these early ideas.

> When the time comes that men such as these are in Israel, then the council of the Yahad will be truly established, an eternal planting, a temple for Israel, and a council of the Holy of Holies for Aaron; true witnesses to justice, chosen by [God's] will to atone for the land and to recompense the wicked their due. . . . a dwelling of the Holy of Holies for Aaron, all of them knowing the covenant of justice and thereby offering a sweet savour. They shall be a blameless and true house in Israel, upholding the covenant of eternal statutes. They shall be an acceptable [sacrifice], to atone for the land and to decide the verdict against evil. When these men have been grounded in the foundation[s] of the Yahad for two years—provided they be perfect in their conduct with no iniquity—they shall be set apart as holy in the midst of the council of the men of the Yahad. (1QS 8.4-11)[26]

25. Schiffman, *Reclaiming the Dead Sea Scrolls*, 83–95.
26. My translation.

Notice that in this passage, there is some garden imagery: the notion of the sect as an eternal planting. The Garden of Eden is somehow symbolic of the Temple, and together with it comes the concept of the sect as a replacement Temple. The sons of Aaron are considered to be the leaders, and because the sect is under their control, their ministry in sectarian life is similar to their ministry in the Jerusalem Temple. Therefore, as it says in the latter part of the passage, "They shall be an acceptable sacrifice atoning for the land and ringing in the verdict against evil so that perversity ceases to exist" (line 10). The sect, having withdrawn from the Temple, has effectively replaced the Temple and its life with their own life and their own religious activities. This becomes a norm later on for the entire Jewish community when the Temple is destroyed. Effectively, the sectarians already faced the challenge of not having a Temple before the Temple was physically destroyed.[27]

The previous passage from *Rule of the Community* (1QS) could be misunderstood to indicate that the withdrawal of the Qumran sect from the Temple was a result of their rejection of sacrifice as a form of worship, or that they withdrew because they were more spiritual. On the contrary, the true reason they withdrew was because the Temple was not conducted according to what they deemed the proper way.

There is a passage in the Scrolls that envisions the conditions that will prevail in the messianic era:

["And no] enemy [will oppress him an]ymore, [and no] son of deceit [shall afflict] him [agai]n, as formerly, from the day that [I appointed judges] over my people Israel" (2 Sam 7:10-11). This is the house which [he will build] for [him] in the latter days, as it is written in the book of [Moses, "The sanctuary,] O Lord, which your hands have fashioned. The Lord will reign for ever and ever." (Exod 15:17-18) This (is) the house which these will not enter] [for]ever, nor an Ammonite, a Moabite, a bastard, a foreigner, or a proselyte forever, for his holy ones (are) there. [His glory shall] be revealed for[ev]er; it shall appear over it perpetually. And strangers shall lay it waste no more, as they formerly laid waste the sanctua[ry of I]srael because of their sin. And he has commanded that a sanctuary of human(s) be built for him, so that they may offer incense in it to him, before him, works of Torah (4QFlor 1–2 i 21).[28]

27. Cf. B. Gärtner, *The Temple and the Community in Qumran and the New Testament* (Cambridge: Cambridge University Press, 1965), 16–46.

A very important debate in Qumran studies concerns this passage. In line 6 there is a reference to the *miqdash 'adam*, "sanctuary of human(s)." Scholars have debated as to whether it refers to a Temple built by humans or a Temple to be built for humans.[29] This text shows that in the end of days the Qumran sectarians assumed that there would be a Temple. The importance of the Temple for the Qumran sectarians is also expressed in the belief that there would be two messiahs: a priestly messiah (the Messiah of Aaron) and a Messiah of Israel. The Messiah of Aaron is the highest messiah who is going to be the priest at the end of days. The expectation of a priestly messiah, expressed in a number of Qumran texts, assumes a sanctuary created in the end of days as part of the messianic vision.

> And I will consecrate my [te]mple by my glory, (the temple) on which I will settle my glory, until the day of blessing[30] on which I will create my temple and establish it for myself for all times, according to the covenant which I have made with Jacob at Bethel (11QT[a] 29:8-10).[31]

This *Temple Scroll* passage maintains that eventually there will be a Temple created by God. This idea is based on a passage at the end of the Song of the Sea, "The Temple, O Lord, which Your hands have founded" (Exod. 15:17). The notion is that in the end of days, there will be a Temple formed by God. "And I will consecrate my [te]mple by my glory" refers to the divine presence that will manifest itself there. This Temple, even in the *Temple Scroll*, is the Temple that exists in their own day, that is, in pre-messianic times "until the day of blessing [and some prefer a different reading, "day of creation"] on which I will create my Temple and establish it for myself." In the end of days, even if the eschatological war were successful and the sectarians conquered the Jerusalem Temple themselves, according to the *War Scroll,* and rebuilt it according to the rules of the *Temple Scroll,* the real Temple would be the "platonic form" of the Temple established by God Himself that is up in heaven, aligned with the lower

28. Trans. J. Milgrom in *The Dead Sea Scrolls Electronic Library*, ed. E. Tov, rev. ed. (Leiden: Brill, 2006).

29. G.J. Brooke, "Florilegium," *EDSS* 1:297–8.

30. Following the reading of Y. Yadin, *The Temple Scroll.* 3 vols. (Jerusalem: Israel Exploration Society and the Shrine of the Book, 1983), 2.129. E. Qimron translates as "blessing" in *The Temple Scroll: A Critical Edition with Extensive Reconstructions* (Beersheva and Jerusalem: Ben-Gurion University of the Negev and Israel Exploration Society, 1996), 44.

31. Trans. Yadin, *Temple Scroll,* 2:128–29.

Temple. That Temple is going to be "for all times according to the covenant which I have made with Jacob at Bethel." The covenant referred to is that of Jacob's dream, when he sees the ladder with the ascending and descending angels and promises that, if God will protect him, he will offer tithes to God of all that he has (Gen. 28:20-22). This covenant is taken as paradigmatic for the relationship of God and the people of Israel (whose name Jacob also bears). The place to present those offerings is the Jerusalem Temple. It is fair to say that virtually all Second Temple Jews would have agreed with this passage about the nature of the acceptance of sacrifices and the divine presence being located in the Temple.

Another aspect of the Temple in Judaism is mourning for its destruction. Already in the Bible we hear that those who were exiled to Babylonia after the destruction of the First Temple in 586 BCE were in mourning.

> By the rivers of Babylon, there we sat, sat and wept, as we thought of Zion.
> There on the poplars we hung up our lyres, for our captors asked us there for songs, our tormentors for amusement, "Sing us one of the songs of Zion."
> How could we sing a song of the Lord on alien soil?
> If I forget you, O Jerusalem,
> let my right hand wither;
> let my tongue stick to my palate
> if I cease to think of you,
> if I do not keep Jerusalem in memory
> even at my happiest hour. (Ps. 137:1-6)[32]

How was the Ninth of Av, which symbolizes the destruction of the Temple, commemorated in Second Temple times? Apparently, the average Jew in Second Temple times continued to mourn the destruction of the First Temple, to read from texts like the biblical book of Lamentations, and to mourn that destruction.

> The Lord has rejected His altar,
> Disdained His Sanctuary.
> He has handed over to the foe
> The walls of its citadels;
> And laid a curse upon His Sanctuary.

---

32. Trans. NJPS.

> They raised a shout in the House of the Lord
> As on a festival day.
> The Lord resolved to destroy
> The wall of Fair Zion. . . . (Lam. 2:7-8)[33]

Surely that mourning was intensified later on when the Second Temple was also razed, but even before that, Jews continued to mourn the destruction of the First Temple.

It is in this spirit that 4Q *Apocryphal Lamentation* mourns the destruction of the Temple and the cessation of its rituals:[34]

> 1. our sins and we have no strength because [we] did not listen
> 2. Judah that all these things befell us. Through the evil [
> 3. of our deeds and we annulled] His covenant. *vacat* Woe for us [
> 4. because] has become burnt by fire, and has turned [
> 5. into] our [magnific]ent glory, and there is no sweet aroma in [our] hou[se of
> 6.] our holy courtyards have become
> 7.] orphan. Jerusalem, city of
> 8. pastu]re for wild beasts and there is no one to f[righten (them)]. And her streets
> 9. are] all her fortresses have become Desolate are
> 10.] and there are no festival visitors in them. All the cities of
> 11.] our heritage has become like a desert, a land not
> 12. sown E]very j[o]y is unheard in it and [there is none who] seeks
> 13. after her] / sore are our injuries [...] all our sins
> 14.] our [re]bellions will [...] our transgressions.
> (4QapocrLam A 1i:1—14)[35]

Accordingly, we have to see this beautiful lament as not just a sectarian text but also as a general Jewish text. It reflects the feeling of loss produced by the destruction of the First Temple in 586 BCE.

This perspective makes it easier to understand how the Qumran sectarians who withdrew from the Temple behaved. For the Dead Sea Scrolls sect, the Second Temple was illegitimate, and they were still in exile. The Temple for them was still destroyed, and there are passages in the Dead Sea Scrolls

---

33. Trans. NJPS.

34. We reproduced the lineation of the MS, since the left of the column is damaged.

35. Trans. M. Bernstein in *Dead Sea Scrolls Electronic Library*.

that lament its destruction. Even though there was a Temple in their day, the Quman sectarians mourned the destruction of the First Temple. Nothing had changed; they were still in the same exile even though they were living in the Land of Israel and the Temple was standing in their times. For them there was effectively no Second Temple.

In the beginning of the *Temple Scroll* there is a very complex calendar of holiday offerings. The same holidays are prescribed in the Bible (New Year, Day of Atonement, Passover, Sukkot, Shabbat, etc.), but the author also presents some additional holidays. After listing all these holidays, the whole section on sacrifice comes to an end with this beautiful message.

> These [you shall offer to the Lord at your appointed feasts] for your burnt offerings (?) and for your drink offerings (?) [...] in the house upon which I shall [settle] my name [...] burnt offerings, [each] on its [proper] day, according to the law of this ordinance, continually from the children of Israel, besides their freewill offerings for all their offerings, for all their drink offerings and all their gifts which they will bring to me that th[ey] may be accepted. And I will accept them (?), and they shall be (?) my people, and I will be theirs forever, [and] I will dwell with them for ever and ever. (11QTª 29:2-8)[36]

"These you shall offer to the Lord," meaning the holiday sacrifices that have to be offered, the daily offering, each on its proper day "according to law," "continually," and these must be prepared—besides the free will offerings and drink offerings and others that people choose to donate. These are the required offerings that are specified. Then it continues in line 6, "that they may be accepted [the sacrifices] and I will accept them, and they shall be my people, and I will be theirs forever, [and] I will dwell with them for ever and ever."

While this statement is the ideal, nevertheless the *Temple Scroll* contains a polemic arguing that the Jerusalem Temple was not being run correctly. From the way the building was built to the way the rituals were performed, down to the minor details of how to sprinkle the blood, this scroll criticized the Temple. The *Temple Scroll* looks very much like the document of a group that did not worship at the Temple because they objected to the way it was conducted. In the *Damascus Document*, also known as the *Zadokite Fragments*, a text very important to the sectarians at Qumran, it is forbidden to worship in the existing Second Temple.

---

36. Trans. Yadin, *Temple Scroll*, 2:127–28.

> None who have been brought into the covenant shall enter into the sanctuary "to light up His altar in vain"; they shall "close the door," for God said, "Who of them shall close My door?" "And they shall not light up My altar in vain." (CD 6.11-13; quoting Mal. 1:10)

In the view of this text, those who have joined the sect may not participate in the lighting of the altar. It is lit "in vain" because the high priests of the Hasmonean period did not perform the purity rites in the correct manner but committed all kinds of transgressions. Then follows a quotation from the prophet Malachi who asks, "Who will close My door?" "To close the door" means to withdraw from illegitimate Temple worship. He replies, "They shall not light up My altar in vain," meaning that for the sectarians it is forbidden to offer sacrifice in the Jerusalem Temple.

This quotation answers the following question: according to the sacrificial codes of the Torah, a person is obligated to offer certain sacrifices, but, if the Temple is not being run properly, what is the right thing to do? Should one stay away or should one go to the Temple and participate in the sacrifices anyhow? According to the Qumran sect, it was best to stay away.

Josephus tells us that the Essenes worshiped in the Temple but that they had a private room where they prepared their sacrifices according to their own standards of ritual purity (*Ant* 18.19). Apparently, the Essenes concurred with the basic rituals, but they thought that the purity laws were not being correctly observed. Therefore, they would take their animal for sacrifice, probably supervise its slaughter themselves, allow the priests to throw the blood on the altar, then take the parts of the animal that were to be eaten, and go to their private room where stricter purity rites, similar to those in the Dead Sea Scrolls, were observed. This is one of the small contradictions between Josephus's description of the Essenes and the Qumran texts. According to the *Damascus Document*, it is forbidden to go into the Temple and to worship at its altar, whereas according to Josephus, members of the Essene sect performed rituals in the Jerusalem Temple.

For Second Temple Jews, and for that matter also for modern Jews, Jerusalem was tied with the idea of the eventual messianic redemption.

> Comfort, oh comfort my people, Says your God
> Speak tenderly to Jerusalem and declare to her
> That her term of service is over, that her iniquity is expiated. (Isa. 40:1-2)

> Awake, awake, O Zion!
> Clothe yourself in splendor;
> Put on your robes of majesty, Jerusalem, holy city!
> Arise, shake off the dust,
> Sit on your throne, Jerusalem! . . . (Isa. 52:1)

The text of this vision of Isaiah had just come into the hands of Professor Eleazar L. Sukenik as part of the great Isaiah scroll on November 29, 1947, on the very night that the Israelis-to-be were dancing in the streets after the United Nations voted for the Partition Plan, dividing Palestine into Arab and Jewish sectors, thereby creating an independent Jewish state. He actually published a special booklet of Isaiah 40 before he published any other Scrolls texts,[37] for this chapter was symbolic of the concept of the messianic redemption that we find in the Scrolls.[38]

We have two competing approaches in the Hebrew Bible regarding whether or not the messianic vision is universalistic or, we might say, only for Israel. The Qumran sectarians went one step further: to them, the messianic redemption was limited only to the sectarians, as opposed to the Isaianic vision that the House of the Lord is for all humanity. The *Scroll of the War of the Sons of Light against the Sons of Darkness* (1QM) describes the messianic battle at the End of Days that ends with the rebuilding of and return to the Temple. It includes a military manual with plans for the battles against all the nations that surround the Land of Israel. According to this text, every single nation is supposed to be defeated and killed, even all the Jews who do not agree with the sectarians.

However, the *War Scroll* is a bit confusing about this issue. The author of the *War Scroll* wanted to pepper his text with some pre-existing poems, and those poems that he inserted speak about the restoration of the nations and how they will all come up, as Isaiah says, to worship in the house of the Lord. So the book is itself self-contradictory: the people that died in one chapter are coming up to the house of the Lord in another chapter. Even in the *War Scroll*, therefore, the ultimate vision of the Temple in the End of Days is the vision of all the nations coming to the Temple. And so I conclude with this vision that was the main view in Second Temple and later Judaism, that is to say, the universalistic messianic idea.

> In the days to come the Mount of the Lord's House shall stand firm
> above the mountains, and tower above the hills. All the nations shall

---

37. E.L. Sukenik, *Naḥamu, Naḥamu ʿAmi* (Jerusalem: Mosad Bialik, 1948).

38. On messianism in the scrolls, see Schiffman, *Reclaiming the Dead Sea Scrolls*, 317–39.

gaze on it with joy, and the many peoples shall go and shall say: "Come, let us go up to the Mount of the Lord, to the House of the God of Jacob, that He may instruct us in His ways, and that we may walk in His paths." For instruction shall come forth from Zion, the word of the Lord from Jerusalem. Thus He will judge among the nations, and arbitrate for the many peoples. And they shall beat their swords into plowshares and their spears into pruning hooks. Nation shall not take up sword against nation; they shall never again know war. (Isa. 2:2-4)

The narrow view was gradually suppressed, even though it certainly existed in the Dead Sea Scrolls. The sectarian Dead Sea Scrolls and some other documents preserve this exclusivist concept of the Temple in the End of Days, but the dominant trend in Judaism is the assumption that all nations would worship the real God in the End of Days. This does not mean that they must all become Jewish, but it means they will no longer be worshiping multiple gods and practicing idolatry, and that they would all come up to join in the worship in Jerusalem at the End of Days.

The Temple provided a religious focus for Second Temple Jews, both in the real world and in the symbolic world. Those who worshipped there experienced the Temple and its many layers of meaning. But even for those who did not, it provided a symbolic framework for understanding God's relationship to the world and to the Jewish people. For some, the Temple even made sense of the larger universe that they inhabited. Yet for all Jews, the Temple stood at the place where God had caused His presence to dwell, the place to which all prayers were turned, the place where a God who could not be contained in the universe He had created could somehow be found waiting for His people.

4

The Psalms as Hymns in the Temple of Jerusalem

Gary A. Rendsburg

From as far back as our sources allow, hymns were part of Near Eastern temple ritual, with their performers an essential component of the temple functionaries.[1] These sources include Sumerian, Akkadian, and Egyptian texts from as early as the third millennium BCE.[2] From the second millennium BCE, we gain further examples of hymns from the Hittite realm, even if most (if not all) of the poems are based on Mesopotamian precursors.[3] Ugarit, our main source of information on ancient Canaan, has not yielded songs of this sort in

1. For the performers, see Richard Henshaw, *Female and Male: The Cultic Personnel: The Bible and Rest of the Ancient Near East* (Allison Park, PA: Pickwick, 1994) esp. ch. 2, "Singers, Musicians, and Dancers," 84–134. Note, however, that this volume does not treat the Egyptian cultic personnel.

2. As the reader can imagine, the literature is extensive, and hence I offer here but a sampling of bibliographic items. For Sumerian hymns, which include compositions directed both to specific deities and to the temples themselves, see Thorkild Jacobsen, *The Harps that Once...: Sumerian Poetry in Translation* (New Haven: Yale University Press, 1987), esp. 99–142, 375–444. Notwithstanding the much larger corpus of Akkadian literature, hymns are less well represented; see the discussion in Alan Lenzi, ed., *Reading Akkadian Prayers and Hymns: An Introduction*, Ancient Near East Monographs (Atlanta: Society of Biblical Literature, 2011), 56–60, with the most important texts included in said volume. For Egyptian hymns, see Jan Assmann, *Ägyptische Hymnen und Gebete*, Orbis Biblicus et Orientalis (Göttingen: Vandenhoeck & Ruprecht, 1999); André Barucq and François Daumas, *Hymnes et prières de l'Égypte ancienne*, Littératures anciennes du Proche-Orient (Paris: Cerf, 1980); and John L. Foster, *Hymns, Prayers, and Songs: An Anthology of Egyptian Lyric Poetry*, Writings from the Ancient World 8 (Atlanta: Society of Biblical Literature, 1995). A sampling of Sumerian, Akkadian, and Egyptian hymns also may be found in William W. Hallo, ed., *The Context of Scripture*, vol. 1: *Canonical Compositions* (Leiden: Brill, 1997).

3. See the discussion in Itamar Singer, *Hittite Prayers*, Writings from the Ancient World 11 (Atlanta: Scholars, 2002), 3. Note, however, that some original Hittite hymns are incorporated into prayer texts, as illustrated by texts no. 8 and 9 in said collection.

the native language, Ugaritic,[4] but strikingly, the documentary evidence from this important site includes the world's oldest hymn containing both the libretto and the musical notation. I refer to the hymn to Nikkal, composed in Hurrian, and whose musical system was deciphered by Anne Kilmer and colleagues, then made available to the public at large with the felicitous title *Sounds from Silence*.[5]

In view of this widespread religious tradition, spanning time and place, it is striking that hymnic recitation is completely absent from the ritual texts in the priestly source of the Torah. Indeed, speech is barely mentioned! The occasional mentions of speech in the Yom Kippur ritual (Lev. 16, though even there by inference only) and in the ordeal of the woman accused of adultery (Num. 5:21-22) do not, in this case, disprove the rule. The great synthesizer of Israelite religion, Yehezkel Kaufmann, whose monumental eight-volume work *Toledot ha-'Emuna ha-Yisra'elit* (*The History of Israelite Religion*) remains a tour-de-force three generations later,[6] opined that the lack of speech and recitation, hymn and psalm, in the priestly conception of the cult resulted from a conscious effort to distance the ritual worship of Yahweh from the ritual worship systems of the polytheistic deities—an estimation with which I concur. In Kaufmann's words, "The priestly temple is the kingdom of silence."[7] This is to say, as one reads through the large chunks of priestly literature—spanning the latter part of Exodus, all of Leviticus, and large portions of Numbers—the lack of spoken word, chanted libretto, and musical instrumentation stands in sharp contrast to

---

4. Note that the term "hymn(s)" appears but once in the index to the massive reference work, *Handbook of Ugaritic Studies*, ed. Wilfred G. E. Watson and Nicolas Wyatt, Handbuch der Orientalisk (Leiden: Brill, 1999), 832 (with reference to pp. 272–73). I am not convinced by the argument of Yitzhak Avishur, *Studies in Hebrew and Ugaritic Psalms* (Jerusalem: Magnes, 1994), 277–307, that CAT 1.108 = RS 24.252 constitutes "A Ugaritic Hymn in Honor of El" (thus the name of his chapter). For alternative understandings of this text, see Gregorio del Olmo Lete, *Canaanite Religion According to the Liturgical Texts of Ugarit*, trans. Wilfred G. E. Watson (Winona Lake, IN: Eisenbrauns, 2004), 184–92; and Dennis Pardee, *Ritual and Cult at Ugarit*, Writings from the Ancient World 10 (Atlanta: Society of Biblical Literature, 2002), 192–95. Both of these scholars link this composition to the royal cult, with specific attention to the deification of the deceased king.

5. Anne D. Kilmer, Richard L. Crocker, and Robert R. Brown, *Sounds from Silence: Recent Discoveries in Ancient Near Eastern Music* (record with booklet), 1976. Now available in CD-format at http://www.amaranthpublishing.com/hurrian.htm or http://www.bellaromamusic.com.

6. Yehezkel Kaufmann, *Toledot ha-'Emuna ha-Yisra'elit*, 8 vols. (Tel-Aviv: Bialik/Devir, 1937–1956). Much more accessible is the abridged English version: Yehezkel Kaufmann, *The Religion of Israel: From its Beginnings to the Babylonian Exile*, trans. Moshe Greenberg (Chicago: University of Chicago Press, 1960), from which I cite herein.

7. Kaufmann, *The Religion of Israel*, 303. For the treatment of this subject in the Hebrew original, see Kaufmann, *Toldelot ha-'Emuna ha-Yisra'elit*, 2:476–78.

the ancient Near Eastern temple traditions outlined above. The effect is clear: in the vision of the priests responsible for these Torah texts, the Tabernacle (and in its wake the Temple) was indeed a "sanctuary of silence."[8] And just as the texts of Lev. 16 and Num. 5:21-22 do not invalidate this statement for the spoken or chanted word, the same is true for Num. 10:10, a passage that might imply that the silver trumpets were used in the cult of Yahweh as envisioned by the priests, though which more likely (with Kaufmann) reflects popular religious practice, as an extension of the trumpets' original role in a military context.[9]

The priestly conception, however, is only one view of the way things are, were, or should be.[10] The Book of Deuteronomy, as is well known, presents a different picture of the ancient Israelite cult,[11] and this book in turn serves as the ideological and theological basis for much of Israelite historical writing, including the Book of Kings. Thus, for example, and perhaps most famously, during the dedication of the Temple as described in 1 Kings 8, the author places into the mouth of Solomon a speech that refers repeatedly to the Temple as a place of prayer—not sacrifice.[12] To gain a flavor of these words, we may consider 1 Kgs. 8:28-30:[13]

> Turn to the *prayer* of your servant and to his *supplication*, O Yhwh my God, to hear the *cry* and the *prayer* which your servant *prays* before you this day. May your eyes be open toward this House night and day, toward the place of which you have said, "my name shall be there," to hear the *prayer* which your servant *prays* toward this place. And when you hear the *supplication* of your servant and of your people Israel, which they will *pray* toward this place, give heed in your abode in the heavens—give heed and pardon.

8. This term serves as the title of a more recent work on the subject by Israel Knohl, *The Sanctuary of Silence* (Minneapolis: Fortress Press, 1995), esp. 148–52.

9. Kaufmann, *The Religion of Israel*, 306. For more on the trumpets, see Jacob Milgrom, *Numbers: The JPS Torah Commentary* (Philadelphia: Jewish Publication Society, 1990), 72–75, 372–73.

10. This point raises an entirely different topic, to which I hope to return on another occasion: the dialectic within ancient Israel and early Judaism. Indeed, the stage is set in the first two chapters of Genesis, with two different creation accounts exhibiting many differences. The way of the Bible (by which I mean its editors/compilers/redactors/et al.) is not to present a single unified voice on any subject but to allow for different voices to be heard.

11. See Moshe Weinfeld, *Deuteronomy* 1–11, Anchor Bible 5 (New York: Doubleday, 1991), 25–44.

12. To be sure, the sacrifices are offered when the ceremony is concluded (see 1 Kgs. 8:62-63), but they are not mentioned in Solomon's speech.

13. I have placed the three Hebrew nouns *rinna* "cry," *tәpilla* "prayer," and *tәḥinna* "supplication" in italics, along with the verb *p-l-l* (T-stem) "pray," to highlight these repeated usages.

And then additional excerpts as Solomon's speech continues:

> *1 Kgs. 8:38*—Every *prayer*, every *supplication*, which will be to every person among all your people Israel.

> *1 Kgs. 8:45*—And you shall hear in the heavens their *prayer* and their *supplication*.

> *1 Kgs. 8:49*—And you shall hear in the heavens, the habitation of your abode, their *prayer* and their *supplication*.

Now, to be sure, there is a difference between prayer, which may contain words alone, and hymns, which include both words and music (with the words sung and with instrumental accompaniment). So it is possible that even the author of 1 Kings 8 did not envision music in the Temple. Regardless, it did not take long for musical traditions to invade the Temple rituals—or perhaps, in light of our first passage to be considered, I should say, temple rituals (with lower/case "t").

Amos 5:21-23 is set in the city of Bethel, and hence in the kingdom of Israel, with its own ritual practices, no doubt at times consonant with the rituals of the Jerusalem Temple, while at other times different. It is here that we gain our first certain reference to hymns and music as part of religious worship. The passage reads as follows:

> [21] I loathe, I spurn your festivals, I do not (delight in the) smell of your solemn-assemblies. [22] If you offer me burnt-offerings, or your meal offerings, I will not accept them; and to the gift of your fatlings, I will pay no heed. [23] Remove from me the loud-sound of your hymns (*šīrīm*), and the music (*zimra*) of your lyres let me not hear.

This passage constitutes one of the most famous of the prophetic critiques of the sacrificial worship system: v. 21 begins with mention of the festivals; v. 22 refers to the different specific sacrifices; and then v. 23 concludes with mention of both vocal and instrumental music. These verses from Amos clearly attest to a well-developed musical tradition in the temple at Bethel by the mid-eighth century.[14] Did such activity also take place in Dan, where a second temple to Yahweh stood in the northern kingdom (1 Kgs. 12:29)?

---

14. Because the verse is so famous, it is worth quoting the following passage here, with Amos's recipe for a better approach to a religious lifestyle: "But let justice well up like water, righteousness like an unfailing stream" (5:24).

Did such activity also take place in the temple to Baal that Ahab built in Samaria (1 Kgs. 16:32)—at least until it was destroyed by Jehu (2 Kgs. 10)? Did such musical traditions penetrate southward to Jerusalem already in Amos's time? We have no way of answering the first two questions concerning Dan and Samaria, though given the evidence of Bethel, I believe that we may posit answers to these questions in the affirmative. We are on firmer ground, however, when we turn our gaze southward, thanks to a single reference which allows us a glimpse into the Jerusalem Temple. I refer to the words of King Hezekiah, spoken c. 710 BCE, as part of his psalm of thanksgiving upon recovery from illness (a poem found in the historical appendix to First Isaiah, but not found in the Book of Kings).[15] The key passage is Isa. 38:20, the last line of the poem:

> Yhwh, to save me, And my musical instruments we will play, All the days of our lives, At the house of Yhwh.

Such is my very literal translation, according to my usual system of rendering biblical Hebrew passages into English. In this case, I admit, a more standard translation such as that of the RSV may capture the sense better:

> The Lord will save me, and we will sing to stringed instruments all the days of our life, at the house of the Lord.

Regardless, the point is clear: musical instruments (and presumably song) are assumed to be a regular part of the Jerusalem Temple ritual during the reign of King Hezekiah, in the late eighth century BCE.[16]

If only we had more explicit evidence to pursue this inquiry into the First Temple period. Unfortunately, though, the next biblical passage that we can cite comes from more than a century after Hezekiah, at the very end of the First Temple period. I refer to Jer. 33:11, a most illuminating text:

---

15. The basic study of this poem is Michael L. Barré, *The Lord Has Saved Me: A Study of the Psalm of Hezekiah (Isaiah 38:9-20)*, Catholic Biblical Quarterly Monograph Series 39 (Washington, DC: Catholic Biblical Association of America, 2005). Contra many scholars, my standpoint here is that the poem dates to the pre-exilic period, c. 700 BCE. As Barré has shown (pp. 216–27), the linguistic evidence certainly points in that direction—and let us recall that such testimony remains the most objective manner for the dating of biblical texts (even if many biblical scholars continue on their merry way and ignore such data).

16. For a detailed discussion on the crucial centuries separating Amos in the mid-eighth century and Hezekiah in the late eighth century, see the Excursus.

> The voice of joy, the voice of gladness, the voice of bridegroom and
> the voice of bride, the voice of those who say, "Give thanks to Yhwh
> of Hosts, for Yhwh is good, for his kindness is forever!" as they bring
> the thanksgiving-offering to the House of Yhwh. For I will restore
> the captivity to the land, as of old—says Yhwh.

The prophet Jeremiah not only witnesses the destruction of the First Temple in
586 BCE, but he also anticipates a time when it will be rebuilt, when worshippers
will once again bring their offerings to the locus of Jewish ritual worship.
The "voices" at the beginning of the verse refer not to spoken words, most
obviously, but rather to joyous vocal music.[17] No doubt Jeremiah observed
people singing the words "Give thanks to Yhwh of Hosts, for Yhwh is good,
for his kindness is forever!" as they brought their thanksgiving-offering (tōdā) to
the Temple, a scene which he assumes will be recreated in the rebuilt Temple.

Now, what is truly remarkable about this passage is its connection to
Psalm 100, whose superscription (v. 1) reads "a psalm of thanksgiving" (mizmōr
lə-tōdā), whose penultimate line (v. 3) bids the offerers "enter his gates with
thanksgiving (tōdā)," and whose concluding line (v. 5) reads:

> For Yhwh is good, his kindness is forever, and until every generation
> is his faithfulness.

with the a-line of this couplet echoing the words that Jer. 33:11 reproduces!
And while the word "thanksgiving" (tōdā) appears elsewhere in the Book of
Psalms, only Psalm 100 bears the superscription "a psalm of thanksgiving"
(mizmōr lə-tōdā) with its concomitant description of individuals arriving at the
Temple with offering in hand.[18] Let us recall that the interconnection between
these two texts cannot be a "set-up," as if the final editor of Jeremiah and
the final editor of Psalms were in conversation with one another. Quite the
contrary, these two books have very different editorial histories, a point that
makes the nexus between Jer. 33:11 and Psalms 100 all the more noteworthy.

With our nod to Psalm 100, this essay arrives at its logical destination,
adumbrated in the title, the Book of Psalms. Linguistic analysis reveals that most
of the psalms were composed in the First Temple period[19] though the crucial
question still remains: how many of the individual poems were used in the

---

17. For additional passages, where Hebrew qōl "voice" clearly refers to singing, see 2 Sam. 19:36, Isa.
24:14, 52:8, Ezek. 33:32. See David J.A. Clines, The Dictionary of Classical Hebrew, 8 vols. (Sheffield:
Sheffield Phoenix, 1993–2011), 7:215.

18. Though see also Psalm 50.

Temple rituals, say, by individuals arriving with offerings, as we saw in the case just described?[20] A further insight in this direction may be forthcoming from the following converging lines of evidence.

Of the 150 canonical psalms, eleven bear the superscription assigning them to the "sons of Korah" (Pss. 42, 44–49, 84–85, 87–88), while twelve bear the superscription attributing them to the "sons of Asaph" (Pss. 50, 73–83)—*bǝnē qōraḥ* and *bǝnē 'asap*, respectively. As we shall see below, these two groups are associated with the Temple rites in the Book of Chronicles, written during the post-exilic, or Persian, period. The question arises: since there are no unequivocal pre-exilic texts which indicate Korahites and Asaphites serving as Temple singers, can we nonetheless push this tradition back to the era of the First Temple? A hint, but no more than that, is forthcoming from a Hebrew inscription found at Arad in southern Judah. The epigraph, known as Arad ostracon 49, contains a list of officials, some as groups ("sons of X"), some as individuals, and among the former are the BNY QRḤ, that is, *bǝnē qōraḥ* "sons of Korah" (more properly "Qorah").[21] The location of this inscription, moreover, is most revealing: the ostracon was found in a room adjacent to the Arad temple, a structure that existed and operated as a local or regional cultic center for about a century or two, until it was destroyed c. 700 BCE.[22] It is most enticing to connect the mention of the "sons of Korah" at Arad in a late eighth-century

19. This is one of the conclusions forthcoming from the work of Avi Hurvitz, *Ben Lashon le-Lashon* (English title: "The Transition Period in Biblical Hebrew: A Study in Post-Exilic Hebrew and its Implications for the Dating of Psalms") (Jerusalem: Bialik, 1972). Also of note are the many points of contact between the language of Psalms and Ugaritic poetry, which suggests an earlier rather than a later date for most of the compositions. This point was grossly overstated and pushed to the extreme by Mitchell Dahood, *Psalms*, 3 vols., Anchor Bible (Garden City, NY: Doubleday, 1966–1970), but the general conclusion still can be sustained, for which see Jonas C. Greenfield, "The Hebrew Bible and Canaanite Literature," in *The Literary Guide to the Bible*, ed. Robert Alter and Frank Kermode (Cambridge, MA: Harvard University Press, 1987), 545–60; and James L. Kugel, *How to Read the Bible: A Guide to Scripture Then and Now* (New York: Free Press, 2007), 467–70. To be sure, the conclusions of some early twentieth century scholars, that many of the Psalms date to the Hellenistic, even Maccabean, period, is simply untenable.

20. For an imaginative recreation of how the psalms may have operated in such a setting, see Kugel, *How to Read the Bible*, 463–65.

21. For photograph, line drawing, transcription, and translation, see Shmuel Aḥituv, *Echoes from the Past: Hebrew and Cognate Inscriptions from the Biblical Period*, ed. Anson F. Rainey (Jerusalem: Carta, 2008), 145–48.

22. The destruction of the Arad temple either was caused by the Assyrian invaders (see 2 Kgs. 18:13; and with greater detail the three prism inscriptions of Sennacherib [London, Chicago, Jerusalem] with the Assyrian perspective) or was due to the centralization of worship program initiated by King Hezekiah (see 2 Kgs. 18:4-6).

context, during the heyday of the monarchy, with the contemporaneous poems ascribed to them and the (albeit later) biblical tradition that Korahites were Temple singers (2 Chron. 20:19).

Regardless of what we make of the mention of "sons of Korah" in Arad ostracon 49, one point remains clear. The testimony of Amos's critique in Amos 5:21-23, Hezekiah's prayer in Isa. 38:20, and Jeremiah's description of the Temple ritual in Jer. 33:11 converge to demonstrate that hymns and music found a home in ancient Israel's ritual spaces, most famously the Jerusalem Temple. The priestly conception in the Torah may be a fine ideal—but the populace at large could not countenance the "sanctuary of silence" forever. The basic human need to communicate with its deity, especially with song,[23] could not be quieted, and thus psalmody entered the Jerusalem Temple rituals by at least the end of the eighth century BCE.

One still may wish to ask, why is it that the biblical sources from the monarchic period, especially the Book of Kings (note that our three passages above derive from prophetic works), tend to ignore this point? Especially in light of the contrast with the Book of Chronicles, which, as we shall see, places such importance on this feature of ritual worship. The question is hardly ever asked, but we may venture a hypothesis. First, if Amos 5:21-23 and Arad ostracon 49 are an indication, it is possible that psalmody arose outside the Jerusalem Temple, developed by guilds of singers, which only later made their way to the main locus of worship in the capital city of Judah.[24] Secondly, this new mode of devotion to Yahweh must have remained secondary in the Jerusalem Temple, with the focus clearly on the sacrifices themselves. It was only in the Second Temple period, as we shall see, that hymns took their pride of place in the official cult.

And with that comment, we may segue nicely to the Book of Chronicles, mentioned several times thus far. Both Kings and Chronicles relate the history of the Judahite monarchy (and in the case of the former, the history of the northern kingdom of Israel as well), but there is a major difference between these two sources. Kings is based on authentic archival material, composed during the reigns of the individual kings, whether they be rulers of Israel (c. 930–721 BCE) or Judah (c. 930–586 BCE),[25] with its final editing during the Babylonian Exile. For the period that precedes c. 930 BCE, the epoch of

---

23. And dance, I should add!—a point that Michal did not understand (see 2 Sam. 6:14-16).

24. See the classic study by Nahum M. Sarna, "The Psalms Superscriptions and the Guilds," in *Studies in Jewish Religious and Intellectual History: Presented to Alexander Altmann on the Occasion of his Seventieth Birthday*, ed. Siegfried Stein and Raphael Loewe (Tuscaloosa, AL: University of Alabama Press, 1979), 281–300. We will explore this point further in the Excursus.

the united monarchy under David and Solomon, we also have more or less contemporaneous sources incorporated into the canonical Book of 2 Samuel (re: David) and the first eleven chapters of 1 Kings (re: Solomon).[26] Chronicles, by contrast, was written/compiled in the fifth (if not fourth) century BCE, during the Persian period, with the goal to glorify the former kings of Judah (from David onward). Much of Chronicles parallels (verbatim or nearly so) the books of Samuel and Kings; when new information, not encountered in the earlier books, is provided, scholars typically debate how historical the portrayal may or may not be. Throughout, however—as is true of all authors—the compiler/ redactor of Chronicles betrays his own epoch, the Second Temple period.[27] This is especially the case when the Temple rituals are described, and it is here that one reads repeatedly of the use of vocal and instrumental music mentioned. Also relevant to this discussion is the Book of Ezra-Nehemiah (a single work in the Jewish tradition, two separate books in the Christian tradition), which relates the history of the fifth century BCE, and thus serves as a valuable source of information for the Persian period.

To demonstrate a crucial distinction between Samuel-Kings, on the one hand, and Chronicles-Ezra-Nehemiah, on the other, we need only look at the use of a single lexeme in these different compositions. The verb *h-l-l* "praise" occurs only twice in all of Samuel-Kings, neither with reference to God,[28] whereas this verb occurs twenty-five times in Chronicles-Ezra-Nehemiah, almost always with reference to God.[29] Similarly, the derived noun form *təhilla*

25. See such statements as 1 Kgs. 14:19 (re: Israel) and 1 Kgs. 14:29 (re: Judah), which repeat throughout the Book of Kings. For the relevant linguistic data, see Gary A. Rendsburg, *Israelian Hebrew in the Book of Kings*, Occasional Publications of the Department of Near Eastern Studies and the Program of Jewish Studies, Cornell University 5 (Bethesda, MD: CDL Press, 2002).

26. Most of the material concerning David is characterized by epic treatment (hence we have superb narrative prose in tales such as the adultery with Bathsheba in 2 Sam. 11–12), while most of the material concerning Solomon betrays its origins in the archival record (as may be indicated, for example, by 1 Kgs. 11:41)—though both types of writing "smack of an intimate familiarity with the events narrated." For the transition from the epic style to the annalistic style, see Cyrus H. Gordon and Gary A. Rendsburg, *The Bible and the Ancient Near East* (New York: Norton, 1997), 207–08; for the quote just given, see p. 215.

27. This is certainly true from the linguistic standpoint, since Chronicles is written in Late Biblical Hebrew, as opposed to the Book of Kings, written in Standard Biblical Hebrew (at least for the parts emanating from Judah; see previous note).

28. In 2 Sam. 14:25, the object of the admiration is Absalom; while in 1 Kgs. 20:11, the context is self-praise or boasting by a military man. I do not include here 2 Sam. 22:4, which occurs within a poem, indeed one paralleled in Ps. 18.

29. The only exceptions are 2 Chron. 23:12-13.

"praise" never occurs in Samuel-Kings, whereas it occurs four times in Chronicles-Ezra-Nehemiah, each time with reference to God.

Now, to be sure, the Chronicles frequently uses the term anachronistically, as for example in the following passages:

> *1 Chron. 16:4*—"And he [David] placed before the Ark of Yhwh from among the Levites ministers, to invoke and to give thanks and to praise Yhwh the God of Israel."

> *1 Chron. 23:5*—"And four thousand praises of Yhwh with instruments that I [David] have made for praising."

As noted earlier, there is no indication of such activity by David in the Book of Samuel (nor any reflex thereof in the Book of Kings), so clearly these "data points" constitute imaginations by the Chronicler reflecting his contemporary Second Temple period, during which time song and music had been upgraded to a central role within the cult. The authors of our Persian-period books even provide the names of singers, both individual ones and groups thereof. The name that emerges most of all is Asaph (see especially 1 Chron. 16:5, where said individual is appointed as "head (singer)" [Hebrew: *rōš*], but also Ezra 2:41 // Neh. 7:44); while among the other names we also find Korah (2 Chron. 20:19)—hence our attention above to the various poems ascribed to Asaph and Korah in the Book of Psalms.

Of the many texts within Chronicles on which one could focus, a very crucial one is 1 Chronicles 16 (an excerpt of which appears just above), which constitutes the Chronicler's understanding of how the Ark of God was transferred to Jerusalem during the reign of king David. The text first speaks of the sacrifices that were performed (vv. 1-2), we then read (as per the above) of the appointment of the Levites with musical responsibilities (vv. 4-7), after which follows an actual hymn, comprised of excerpts from three psalms that eventually found their way into the canonical Book of Psalms. Without presenting the actual words here, we may chart this material as follows:

1 Chron. 16:8-22	=	Ps. 105:1-15
1 Chron. 16:23-33	=	Ps. 96:1-13
1 Chron. 16:34	=	(see below)
1 Chron. 16:35-36	=	Ps. 106:47-48

Of the various verses from these poems, one may be cited, since it is so characteristic of ancient Israelite hymnic psalmody (indeed, let us transcribe the Hebrew here: *hōdū la-yhwh kī ṭōb / kī lǝ-ʿōlam ḥasdō*), to wit, 1 Chron. 16:34:

> Give thanks to Yhwh for he is good, For his kindness is forever.

Indeed, a variation of this couplet was quoted above in Jer. 33:11 ~ Ps 100:5. The exact words, with both stichs, appear in Ps. 106:1, 107:1, 118:1, 118:29, 136:1; variations appear in Ezra 3:11, 2 Chron. 5:13, 7:3, 20:21; and the second stich alone appears three additional times in Psalm 118 (vv. 2-4) and a whopping twenty-five times more, as the refrain, in Psalm 136 (vv. 2-26).[30] Finally, at the end of this pericope, we read in 1 Chron. 16:48:

> "Blessed is Yhwh God of Israel from eternity until eternity"; and all the people said "Amen," and they praised Yhwh.

A narrative that began with the sacrifices, a ritual limited to the priests, transitions to the Levites' singing psalms of praise, and ends with the population at large engaged by proclaiming "amen," along with (apparently) their own words of praise to God. In this snapshot, we see the movement in ancient Judaism from a cult limited to the priesthood to one in which everyone may participate in devotional worship.

As one other indication of this transition, we may note the difference between Solomon's dedication of the Temple in 1 Kings 8 (which we discussed earlier) and the same event as handled by the Persian-period writer in 2 Chronicles 6. 2 Chron. 6:1-40 parallels closely 1 Kgs. 8:12-52; the main difference is what follows. In the Kings version, Solomon adds a single line of prose (1 Kgs. 8:53) to complete his long speech. In the Chronicles version, he pronounces two poetic lines (2 Chron. 6:41-42):

> And now, arise O Yhwh God, to your resting place, you and your mighty Ark; Your priests, O Yhwh God, are clothed in triumph, And your loyal-ones rejoice in goodness. O Yhwh God, do not turn away from the face of your anointed-one; Remember the loyalties of David your servant.

---

30. Note that this makes for twenty-six repetitions of the refrain "for his kindness is forever," thus equaling the numerical equivalent of Yhwh, whose name is invoked in the opening verse of Psalm 136. I do not believe that this is a coincidence, but rather speaks to the (albeit sporadic) use of *gematria* in biblical times already.

If this poetic coda to Solomon's prose prayer in the Chronicles version was not enough to demonstrate the trend at hand, the picture comes into greater focus when we realize that these verses appear (with minor variants) in Ps. 132:8-10. Which is to say, taking into consideration both 1 Chron. 16 and 2 Chron. 6, by sometime c. 425 BCE and c. 350 BCE, when the Book of Chronicles was written/compiled/edited/redacted, hymns of praise and thanksgiving that eventually would be canonized in the biblical Book of Psalms, already were well ensconced in the Temple ritual.

As we move beyond the biblical period, we have additional evidence for the use of psalms in the Temple liturgy, from three sources. The first is Ben Sira (also called Sirach or Ecclesiasticus), the Jewish sage who wrote his book of wisdom c. 180 BCE. In his paean to the heroes of old, towards the end of his long opus, Ben Sira has this to say about King David (Ben Sira 47:9-10):

> [David] established harp-singers before the altar, also to make sweet melodies with their ringing sounds. He gave dignity at the feasts, and he arranged seasons until completion, When they were praising his holy name, and from early morning the holy precinct was resounding.

Ben Sira was written in Hebrew and then translated into Greek by his grandson in the year 132 BCE. The above passage is taken from the Greek version,[31] because (and how often does this happen in scholarship!) the Hebrew manuscript (MS B) that contains this portion of the text (Bodleian MS.Heb.e.62 folio XVI verso) is damaged. Nevertheless, we can make out the following Hebrew words: NGYNWT "tunes," ŠYR "song," and Q[W]L "sound," as well as QWL MZMWR HN'YM "sound of sweet music" in a marginal note. The reader will realize the same anachronistic thinking in Ben Sira's portrayal of David as appears in Chronicles, but that is irrelevant for our present purposes.

A more accurate reflection of Temple practice, contemporary with the author's own time period, occurs several chapters later, when Ben Sira describes with great detail the wonder and splendor of the high priest Shim'on ben Yoḥanan (Simeon son of John) (Ben Sira 50:1, with this pericope continuing through v. 21). After the poetic depiction of the sacrificial service, Ben Sira states (again using the Greek as the basis[32]):

---

31. I have used here the translation of Benjamin G. Wright, "Sirach," in *A New English Translation of the Septuagint*, ed. Albert Pietersma and Benjamin G. Wright (New York: Oxford University Press, 2007), 758.

And the harp-singers sang praises with their voices, a melody was made sweet with a full tone. (Ben Sira 50:18)

Which is to say, by Ben Sira's time, the use of hymns in the Temple was, as we would expect, a fundamental part of the ritual.

The glory exhibited in Ben Sira's description of the high priest and the Temple ritual came to an end (from the perspective of the "Yahweh only" party, at least) within a decade or so of this ancient composition. I refer, of course, to the persecutions introduced by Antiochus IV Epiphanes, the Seleucid ruler of the land of Israel, in 168–167 BCE, which included the transformation of the Temple into a temple to Zeus. This transformation was short-lived, though, for in 164 BCE, the Maccabees successfully rebelled and restored the Temple to the worship of the God of Israel. The relevant texts from that period again provide testimony to the use of hymns in the Temple rituals.

> *1 Macc. 4:54*—At the very season and on the very day that the gentiles had profaned it, it [the Temple] was dedicated with songs and harps and lutes and cymbals.

> *2 Macc. 10:7-8*—They offered hymns of thanksgiving to him who had given success to the purifying of his own holy place. They decreed by public ordinance and vote that the whole nation of the Jews should observe these days every year.

Notwithstanding the fact that the events described here are connected to a specific festival occasion (a second Sukkot, according to 2 Macc. 10:5-8, which eventually morphed into Hanukkah), once more we observe the use of hymns in the Temple ceremony.

The third of our relevant sources from this general period is Josephus (fl. 70–90 CE). His great work, *Antiquities of the Jews*, echoes the material in Chronicles and Ben Sira, by attributing to David the institution of hymns sung by the Levites (*Ant* 7.12.3):

> [David] taught the Levites to sing hymns to God, both on the sabbath day and on other festivals.

---

32. Though not because the Hebrew is not extant or is damaged, but rather because the Greek is more expressive than the very terse Hebrew original, which also requires emendation to gain sense. See Moshe Zvi Segal, *Sefer Ben Sira ha-Shalem* (Jerusalem: Bialik, 1971–72), 346. Once more the English presented here is that of Wright, "Sirach," 760.

If only for its quaintness, based on Josephus's need to explain Judaism to his Greco-Roman audience, I also quote here his identification of the Levites as Temple singers (*Ant* 20.9.6):

> The Levites, which is a tribe of ours, were singers of hymns . . . and a part of this tribe ministered in the temple.

Until this point, we have spoken only in the most general of terms, concerning the recitation of Psalms in the Temple. True, Chronicles allows us an occasional glimpse into a specific text used in the Temple service (see above), but by and large we have no contemporary material that provides further information on this subject. Fortunately, a later rabbinic text may offer additional insight. The Mishnah was compiled c. 200 CE by Rabbi Judah ha-Nasi, in Sepphoris in the Galilee, approximately 130 years after the destruction of the Temple. Yet at least one-third of this compendium of Jewish religious practices (as observed by the rabbinic class at least)—and whose importance cannot be overstated—includes information relevant to Temple practices (sacrifices, purity laws, etc.).[33] The question debated by scholars is the following: to what extent does the Mishnah's descriptions of Temple rituals reflect the historical reality of the pre-70 CE period? This is clearly not the place to delve into this question in depth, but we can state the following. One of the major findings emanating from Dead Sea Scrolls research is that the very issues discussed in the Mishnah, including specific stances taken by the rabbis, underlie the polemics of the Qumran sect (as seen most of all in 4QMMT, the Halakhic Letter).[34] To my mind, accordingly, the default position in response to the question posed above should be this: unless there is evidence to the contrary, one may assume that the Mishnah reflects earlier practice.

With this as background, we turn to the Mishnah's mention of specific Psalms used in the Temple ceremony, starting with the list provided in Mishnah

---

33. For general orientation, see David Kraemer, "The Mishnah," in *The Cambridge History of Judaism*, vol. 4: *The Late Roman—Rabbinic Period*, ed. Steven T. Katz (Cambridge: Cambridge University Press, 2006), 299–315.

34. See the brief statement by Lawrence H. Schiffman, *Reclaiming the Dead Sea Scrolls* (Philadelphia: Jewish Publication Society, 1994), 87. Additional literature includes Lawrence H. Schiffman, "Qumran and Rabbinic Halakhah," in *Jewish Civilization in the Hellenistic-Roman Period*, ed. Shemaryahu Talmon (Philadelphia: Trinity Press International, 1991), 138–46; Elisha Qimron, "The Halakha," in *Qumran Cave 4: V: Miqṣat Maʿaśe ha-Torah*, eds. Elisha Qimron and John Strugnell, Discoveries in the Judaean Desert 10 (Oxford: Clarendon, 1994), 123–77, especially the succinct conclusion on p. 177; and Yaʿakov Sussmann, "The History of the Halakha and the Dead Sea Scrolls," in *Qumran Cave 4: V: Miqṣat Maʿaśe ha-Torah*, 179–200.

Tamid 7:5 for the psalms recited on a daily basis.[35] In this particular case, we also may add that many specialists in rabbinic literature aver that Tamid is one of the oldest tractates (if not *the* oldest tractate) in the Mishnah (which is to say, it incorporates *written* material from several generations before Judah ha-Nasi),[36] and hence regardless of one's position on the question addressed in the preceding paragraph, one may utilize Tamid as a reliable source on older practices. The relevant passage reads as follows:

> The song that the Levites would recite in the Temple: on the first day, they would recite, "to Yhwh is the earth and its fullness, the world and its inhabitants"; on the second [day], they would recite, "Yhwh is great and much praised, in the city of our God, his holy mountain"; etc.

In typical Jewish tradition, this text provides only the incipit for each psalm. To translate this into our system of numbering the Psalms—including not only the two cited above, but the entire roster of seven poems (note the 'etc.' at the end of the excerpt)—we gain the following list:[37]

Day 1	Psalm 24
Day 2	Psalm 48
Day 3	Psalm 82
Day 4	Psalm 94
Day 5	Psalm 81
Day 6	Psalm 93
Sabbath	Psalm 92

In the Masoretic codices, only one of these psalms bears a superscription that connects it to a specific day; not surprisingly that psalm is the last on this list, whose introductory verse reads as follows:

Ps 92:1 'A psalm, a song, for the Sabbath day'

---

35. The term Tamid means literally "continual"; in this context it refers to the daily sacrifices offered each morning and afternoon in the Temple.

36. See especially Louis Ginzberg, "Tamid: The Oldest Treatise of the Mishnah," *Journal of Jewish Lore and Philosophy* 1 (1919): 33–44, 197–209, 265–95; and Jacob N. Epstein, *Mevo'ot le-Sifrut ha-Tanna'im*, ed. E.Z. Melamed (Tel-Aviv: Devir 1957), 27–31. For a dissenting voice, see Jacob Neusner, "Dating a Mishnah-Tractate: The Case of Tamid," in *History, Religion, and Spiritual Democracy: Essays in Honor of Joseph L. Blau*, ed. Maurice Wohlgelernter (New York: Columbia University Press, 1980), 97–113.

37. In both this chart and the one following, I opt to use the Jewish system of "counting" the days of the week, which lack individual names, except for the Sabbath day.

Quite remarkable, however, is the additional testimony of the Septuagint (LXX), which assigns specific days to five of the seven psalms, namely:[38]

Day 1	Psalm 24 (LXX Psalm 23)
Day 2	Psalm 48 (LXX Psalm 47)
Day 4	Psalm 94 (LXX Psalm 93)
Day 6	Psalm 93 (LXX Psalm 92)
Sabbath	Psalm 92 (LXX Psalm 91)

Moreover, there is agreement between this list and the rabbinic list (notwithstanding the omission of the psalms for Day 3 and Day 5 in the Septuagint). These lines of evidence (which are very much independent of each other) converge to allow us to reconstruct the ritual recitation of these psalms in the Temple during its last century of existence.

An inspection of these individual psalms reveals (in most cases) why these particular compositions would have found their way into the Temple ritual.[39] Pertinent passages, which disclose the Temple setting, include the following:[40]

Psalm 24 [3] Who may ascend the mountain of Yhwh? And who may stand in his holy place? [4] He who has clean hands and a pure heart. ... [7] Lift up your heads, O gates, And be raised, you everlasting doors, So that the King of Glory may enter. [8] Who is the King of Glory? Yhwh, mighty and valiant, Yhwh, valiant in battle. [9] Lift up your heads, O gates, And lift up, you everlasting doors, So the King of Glory may enter. [10] Who is he, the King of Glory? Yhwh of Hosts – He is the King of Glory!

38. Yes, the system is complicated because the numbering of the individual psalms in the Septuagint typically does not correlate to the numbering system commonly used for the Hebrew text of Psalms. The vast majority of English translations adhere to the latter scheme.

39. I would not, however, go so far as Peter L. Trudinger, *The Psalms of the Tamid Service: A Liturgical Text from the Second Temple*, Supplements to Vestum Testamentum 98 (Leiden: Brill, 2004), who claims, as per the title, a) that these seven psalms may be read as a coherent whole, with a continuous them running through them, and b) that the group was in place "perhaps in the mid-second century, if not earlier" (p. 54). See the review by Eileen Schuller, *RBL* (August 2006), available at http://www.bookreviews.org/pdf/4373_4384.pdf.

40. Note the intriguing suggestion by Moshe Weinfeld, "Instructions for Temple Visitors in the Bible and in Ancient Egypt," in *Egyptological Studies*, ed. Sarah Israelit-Groll, Scripta Hierosolymitana 28 (Jerusalem: Magnes, 1982), 224–50, that texts such as Ps. 24:3-6 (along with Ps. 15, Isa. 33:14-16), with the listing of "moral qualities required for admission to the Temple" (p. 224), were posted at the entrance to the Temple (see esp. 237–38).

Psalm 48 [2] Yhwh is great and much praised, In the city of our God, his holy mountain. [3] Beautiful view, joy of all the earth, Mount Zion, summit of Zaphon, City of the Great King. . . . [10] We envision, O God, your kindness, In the midst of your temple, [11] As is your name, O God, so is your praise, Unto the ends of the earth. . . . [15] For this is God, our God forever, He will lead us evermore.

Psalm 93 [5] Your decrees are indeed enduring, In your house, befitting holiness, Yhwh, for length of days.

Psalm 92 [13] The righteous shall flourish like the palm, Like a cedar in Lebanon he shall grow strong. [14] Like seedlings in the house of Yhwh, In the courts of our God they shall blossom.

The Mishnah furnishes additional information concerning other psalms recited on other occasions.[41] Mishnah Middot[42] 2:5 reads,

> And there were fifteen steps that went up from its midst to the court of Israel, corresponding to the fifteen Songs of Ascent that are in [the Book of] Psalms, on which the Levites would stand in song.

The reference is to Psalms 120–134, each of which bears the superscription *šīr ham-maʿalōt* "a song of ascents."[43] The attentive reader will note that this Mishnah passage (which occurs in a tractate devoted to the Temple layout and measurements [see n. 42], not to Temple ritual practice) does not inform us *when* such a recitation of these fifteen psalms would have occurred. That information is forthcoming from another tractate, Sukkah 5:4, which describes a ceremony held during the days of Sukkot (Feast of Booths):

> Pious and distinguished men would dance before them with torches, and they would recite hymns and words of exaltation before them.

41. For a general survey, see Mark S. Smith, "The Psalms as a Book for Pilgrims," *Interpretation* 46 (1992):156–66.

42. The term means literally "measurements," in this context with reference to the Temple layout and measurements.

43. Ps. 121:1 contains the slightly variant Hebrew wording *šīr lam-maʿalōt*, though with the same meaning, "a song of ascents." This is typical of Hebrew literary style, to break the monotony of verbatim repetition, even if the remaining thirteen superscriptions return to the wording of the first one.

> And the Levites accompanied them with harps, lyres, cymbals, and musical instruments without number—on the fifteen steps that go down from the court of Israel to the court of the women, corresponding to the fifteen Songs of Ascent in [the Book of] Psalms, on which the Levites would stand and would recite in song.

Even at a distance of two thousand years, one can envision the scene and well nigh hear the vocal and instrumental music produced by the Temple professionals, that is, the Levites.

And why might this collection of psalms be appropriate for recitation on the festival of Sukkot? During this holiday (and also on Pesaḥ [Passover], though most likely to a lesser extent on Shavuʿot [Weeks]), large numbers of Jews made the pilgrimage to Jerusalem. Two passages from the beginning and the end of Psalms 120–134 are especially suitable for such a setting. Ps 120:5 reads,

> Woe is me, that I reside in Meshech, That I dwell amongst the tents of Kedar.

Meshech is a region in Anatolia, to the far north of Jerusalem, while Kedar is a region in Arabia, to the far south of Jerusalem.[44] These places represent the extremes of Israel's geographical horizons,[45] the farthest extent from which pilgrims would come to Jerusalem (even if but once in their lifetimes, certainly not annually).

Ps. 134:1-3 provides a fitting farewell:

> [1] A song of ascents: Behold, bless Yhwh, all servants of Yhwh; Who stand in the house of Yhwh at night; [2] Raise your hands to the holy-place, and bless Yhwh. [3] May Yhwh bless you from Zion, the maker of heaven and earth.

Here one can imagine the visitors to Jerusalem taking their leave, with v. 3 suggesting the words spoken by those (the priests, for example) who were remaining in the city. In addition, we cite a passage that we have seen earlier,

---

44. Meshech is to be identified with the Mushki known from Assyrian sources and the Moschoi known from Greek sources. Kedar (more properly Qedar) occurs in Assyrian and Arabian sources as a people connected to the desert; see Israel Eph'al, *The Ancient Arabs* (Jerusalem: Magnes, 1984), 223–27.

45. At least for this poet, since technically speaking Cush (= Nubia, Sudan, etc.; see Amos 9:7) is still more distant.

namely, Ps. 132:8-10, which occurs towards the end of the "Song of Ascents" collection:

> [8] Arise O Yhwh God, to your resting place, you and your mighty Ark. [9] Your priests are clothed in righteousness, And your loyal-ones exult. [10] On account of David your servant, do not turn away from the face of your anointed-one.

The reader will recall that the Chronicler placed these words (with slight textual variants) in the mouth of Solomon upon the conclusion of his prayer (2 Chron. 6:41-42). This case represents, accordingly, a correlation between a Psalms passage known from the liturgy as preserved in rabbinic tradition and a much earlier reference in the narrative of the Book of Chronicles.

The third key Mishnah text is Pesaḥim[46] 5:7, which informs us very succinctly that while individual Israelites appeared before the priests with their personal sacrifice in hand, "they read the Hallel." The term means literally "praise" (see above, for our earlier discussion), with specific reference to Psalms 113–118, due to the ten-fold presence of the verb h-l-l "praise" in these poems. While not stated explicitly (note the generic "they"), one assumes that the Mishnah intends that the Levites recited the Hallel psalms while this ritual took place.

To return to Sukkot, we also know from Mishnah Sukkah 3:9 that specifically Psalm 118 was chanted during that festival ceremony, and so we may extrapolate that the Hallel psalms as a whole were part of the ritual for both holidays, Pesaḥ and Sukkot.[47] In fact, a particular passage in Psalm 118 seems to refer to Sukkot explicitly:

> [26] Blessed is he who comes in the name of Yhwh; we bless you from the house of Yhwh. [27] Yhwh is God, and he has given us light, bind the festival-offering with branches, unto the horns of the altar. (vv. 26-27)

The Hebrew word for "branches" here is 'abōtīm, the very word used for "branch" (in the singular: 'abōt) in Lev. 23:40 with reference to Sukkot.

---

46. The Hebrew term for "Passover," though actually in the plural form here, as per typical Mishnaic Hebrew usage.

47. And by extension Shavuʿot as well, as per later rabbinic practice, and still part of Jewish liturgy to the present day.

Finally, we learn from Mishnah Taʿanit[48] 4:5 that a fast could not be proclaimed on the first day of the month of Tevet, because the community recites Hallel on said day. This date falls within the eight days of Hanukkah, and hence we learn from this rabbinic text that Psalms 113–118 were recited on this festival as well—a point which makes sense, given our statement above that Hanukkah originated as a second Sukkot, with explicit mention in 2 Macc. 10:7-8 to the singing of hymns during the holiday.[49]

In sum, as these Mishnah texts make clear, a variety of psalms were used in the Temple ritual on different occasions, with the seven Tamid psalms recited on a daily basis, one for each day of the week, with Psalms 120–134 playing a special role on Sukkot (and perhaps, if not presumably, at other times), and with the Hallel psalms (113–118) filling a significant role on the major festivals. While individual psalms may not have been written with the cult in mind, by the time that the canonical Book of Psalms received its final editing, clearly these stirring poems had found a home in the liturgy.[50] For how else, one may ask, can one explain the placement of Psalm 150 as a coda to the compilation,[51] with its central verses presenting the complete orchestra, as it were, of the ancient Temple:[52]

Praise him with the blast of the shofar, Praise him with lute and lyre.
Praise him with timbrel and dance, Praise him with strings and pipe.

48. This term means "fast," with the tractate devoted to public and private fasts on different dates during the year.

49. Once more this remains Jewish practice to the present day.

50. On the subject of the final shape of the Book of Psalms, see Gerald H. Wilson, *The Editing of the Hebrew Psalter* Society of Biblical Literature Dissertation Series 76 (Chico, CA: Scholars, 1985); Susan Gillingham, "The Zion Tradition and the Editing of the Hebrew Psalter," in *Temple and Worship: Proceedings of the Oxford Old Testament Seminar*, ed. John Day (London: T&T Clark, 2005), 308–41; and Susan Gillingham, "The Levitical Singers and the Editing of the Hebrew Psalter," in *The Composition of the Book of Psalms*, ed. Erich Zenger, BETL 238 (Leuven: Peeters, 2010), 91–123 (along with many other contributions to this volume).

51. As intimated below, a different arrangement of the individual psalms obtains in 11QPs[a], so that Ps. 150 does not serve there as the coda to the compilation. Nonetheless, it appears very near the end of the scroll, with the succeeding material as codas to the coda, one might say.

52. One also should note the Late Biblical Hebrew usage in vv. 3-4, with the three-fold non-repetition of the preposition in the collocations "with lute and lyre," "with timbrel and dance," and "with strings and pipe." In Standard Biblical Hebrew, the preposition would be repeated before each noun. This is a little-known point in the historical development of the Hebrew language, for which see Abba Bendavid, *Leshon Miqra u-Leshon ḥakhamim*, 2 vols. (English title: "Biblical Hebrew and Mishnaic Hebrew"; Tel-Aviv, Devir, 1967–1971), 2:455–56. This linguistic usage reveals Ps. 150 to be a Persian-period poem, further demonstrating that it was composed specifically for placement as the finale to the Book of Psalms.

> Praise him with cymbals of sound, Praise him with cymbals of clashing. (vv. 3-5)

No survey of our topic would be complete without a look at Qumran. Amongst the biblical manuscripts found at Qumran, the best-represented book is Psalms, with thirty-nine different manuscripts (all fragmentary, with the largest extant scroll, 11QPs[a], containing about a third of the canonical book, albeit with the psalms in a different order).[53] This point alone speaks to the importance of these compositions within the religious life of the Yaḥad members.[54]

As for use of the Psalms, the most telling evidence from the Dead Sea Scrolls is the prose addendum to the aforementioned 11QPs[a], which reads as follows (11QPs[a] col. 27, lines 4-10):[55]

4. and he wrote: psalms,
5. 3,600; songs to sing before the altar accompanying the
6. daily-perpetual burnt-offering, for all the days of the year, 364;
7. for the Sabbath offerings, 52 songs; and for the New Moon offerings,
8. all the festival days and the Day of Atonement, 30 songs.
9. The total of all the songs that he composed was 446, and songs
10. to play on the seasonal-encounter days, 4. And the sum total was 4,050.

Indeed, David was one busy man! But apart from the obvious hyperbole inherent in this text, our attention is drawn to the statement that David composed a special song for each day of the year (numbering 364, according to the Qumran calendar). The Hebrew word used here, in line 6, is the very word *tamīd*, which we have explored earlier, rendered here as "daily-perpetual," describing the daily sacrifice offered in the Temple. In addition, special hymns

53. By comparison, we note thirty-one manuscripts of Deuteronomy (again all fragmentary) and twenty-two manuscripts of Isaiah (including one complete copy, 1QIsa[a]).

54. On the Psalms at Qumran, see Peter W. Flint, *The Dead Sea Psalms Scrolls and the Book of Psalms*, Studies on the Texts of the Desert of Judah 17 (Leiden: Brill, 1997). For the theory that 11QPs[a] represents a liturgical reordering of the Masoretic Book of Psalms, with Flint's assessment thereof, see p. 209. For a more recent and more succinct treatment, see Peter W. Flint, "Psalms and Psalters in the Dead Sea Scrolls," in *The Bible and the Dead Sea Scrolls*, vol. 1: *Scripture and the Scrolls*, ed. James H. Charlesworth (Waco, TX: Baylor University Press, 2006), 233–72.

55. See James A. Sanders, *The Psalms Scroll of Qumrân Cave 11 (11QPs[a])*, Discoveries in the Judaean Desert 4; Oxford: Clarendon, 1965); and James A. Sanders, *The Dead Sea Psalms Scroll* (Ithaca, NY: Cornell University Press, 1967), esp. 86–87, with discussion on pp. 134–35.

accompany each of the Sabbath, New Moon, and festival offerings, according to this text. And while the Qumran sect distanced itself from the Temple (given their much stricter purity concerns, with their concomitant belief that the Temple was impure and polluted), nevertheless, in their minds (and in some reality?) they continued to perceive themselves as observing a Temple-centered cult. It was important, accordingly, to continue to declaim the daily Tamid psalms, as well as the special festival hymns, as a ceremonial complement to the sacrificial cult. We therefore gain a modicum of support for the hypothesis advanced above, that the performance of psalms in the Temple, as mentioned in the Mishnah (Tamid 7:5, Middot 2:5, Sukkah 5:4, Pesaḥim 5:7, Taʿanit 4:5) reflects an actual practice dating back to the late Second Temple period.

The Dead Sea Scrolls provide additional evidence for the use of hymns (though not necessarily the canonical Psalms) in the liturgy. The most prominent texts are:

a. the *Hodayot* scroll, or *Thanksgiving Hymns* (1QH), comprised of about twenty-five individual hymns (many commencing with the expression *ʾōdeka ʾadōnay* 'I give thanks to you, O Lord'), though their exact use still is open to debate;[56]
b. the *Works of the Luminaries* (4Q504-506), admittedly more like prayers than hymns, but noteworthy is the ascription of particular texts to be recited on particular days, with one section of the text introduced as a hymn for the Sabbath day (4Q504 20:5 *hwdwt bywm hšbt*) and with its style and vocabulary evoking the biblical Psalms;[57]
c. two very fragmentary manuscripts (4Q380-381) containing non-canonical psalms, with superscriptions such as "psalm of Obadiah" and "psalm of the man of God";[58] and
d. the *Songs of the Sabbath Sacrifice* (4Q400-407, 11Q17, plus one Masada manuscript), poems chanted by the angels in heaven on each of the first thirteen Sabbaths of the year, to accompany the sacrifices

56. For an interesting suggestion, connecting the Hodayot poems to the use of hymns among the Therapeutae, as described by Philo, see Geza Vermes, *The Complete Dead Sea Scrolls in English* (Harmondsworth: Penguin, 1997), 244.

57. Esther Chazon wrote her Hebrew University doctoral dissertation (1991) on this composition and is preparing the text for its official publication in the Discoveries in the Judaean Desert series. For the nonce, see Vermes, *The Complete Dead Sea Scrolls in English*, 364–67.

58. Eileen Schuller, *Non-Canonical Psalms from Qumran: A Pseudepigraphic Collection*, Harvard Semitic Studies 28 (Atlanta: Scholars, 1986).

offered in the Temple,[59] thereby implying, in Geza Vermes's felicitous words, "the simultaneity of heavenly and earthly worship"[60] (and is not that a lovely thought). So while none of these texts constitutes evidence for the use of psalms specifically in the religious worship at Qumran, taken collectively they indicate that a hymnic tradition was very much alive and well among the Dead Sea sectarians.[61]

Finally, we arrive at that one other crucial source for Jewish religious life at the end of the Second Temple period, to wit, the New Testament. In light of all that has been said until this point, it will come as no surprise to learn that Psalms is the most commonly quoted book in the Christian scriptures, with sixty-nine citations.[62] Jews (and Luke too!) simply knew their Psalms during the time of the florescence of the Jerusalem Temple—and indeed after its demise as well.

59. Carol Newsom, *Songs of the Sabbath Sacrifice: A Critical Edition*, Harvard Semitic Series 27 (Atlanta: Scholars, 1985).

60. Vermes, *The Complete Dead Sea Scrolls in English*, 321.

61. For general discussion, see Bilhah Nitzan, *Qumran Prayer and Religious Poetry*, trans. Jonathan Chipman, Studies on the Text of the Desert of Judah 12 (Leiden: Brill, 1994),190–200; and Esther G. Chazon, "Hymns and Prayers in the Dead Sea Scrolls," in *The Dead Sea Scrolls after Fifty Years: A Comprehensive Assessment*, 2 vols., ed. Peter W. Flint and James C. Vanderkam (Leiden: Brill, 1998), 1:244–70, esp. 264–67 concerning hymns. For hymns in the larger context of early Judaism, see James C. Charlesworth, "A Prolegomenon to a New Study of the Jewish Background of the Hymns and Prayers in the New Testament," *Journal of Jewish Studies* 33 (1982): 265–85 [= *Essays in Honour of Yigael Yadin* (ed. Geza Vermes and Jacob Neusner)], with the very useful catalogue on pp. 274–75; and George J. Brooke, "The Psalms in Early Jewish Literature in the Light of the Dead Sea Scrolls," in *The Psalms in the New Testament*, ed. Steve Moyise and Maarten J. J. Menken (London: T&T Clark, 2004), 5–24. Finally, for a recent treatment of the subject of liturgy in general, see the programmatic essay by Esther G. Chazon, "Shifting Perspectives on Liturgy at Qumran and in Second Temple Judaism," in *The Dead Sea Scrolls in Context: Integrating the Dead Sea Scrolls in the Study of Ancient Texts, Languages, and Cultures*, 2 vols., ed. Armin Lange, Emanuel Tov, and Matthias Weigold, Supplements to Vestus Testamentum 140 (Leiden: Brill, 2011), 2:513–31.

62. By comparison, the next most cited books are Isaiah (fifty-one times) and Deuteronomy (thirty-two times). Psalms holds pride of place across genres, be it the Gospels, Acts, Romans, or Hebrews. The reader will recall (see above) that Psalms was also the most widely read book at Qumran, at least judging from the number of manuscripts found amongst the Dead Sea Scrolls. On the other hand, judging by the lists compiled by Armin Lange and Matthias Weigold, *Biblical Quotations and Allusions in Second Temple Jewish Literature* (Göttingen: Vandenhoeck & Ruprecht, 2011), overall it appears that Deuteronomy outranks Psalms, when all of the relevant Jewish texts of the age are taken into consideration. While this important reference tool does not produce actual counts, I have reached this conclusion, based on the number of pages devoted to each biblical book in the catalogue (Deuteronomy, 18 pages; Psalms, 16 pages; Isaiah, 16 pages; and so on).

Obviously, the use of Psalms in the New Testament is a topic deserving of its own treatment, and space considerations do not allow a thorough discussion here.[63]

I elect, accordingly, to focus on one particular verse, Ps 118:26—the only Psalms passage to be quoted by all four gospels:

Mark 11:9 = Matthew 21:9 = John 12:13
Blessed is he who comes in the name of the Lord.
Εὐλογημένος ὁ ἐρχόμενος ἐν ὀνόματι κυρίου

Luke 19:38
Blessed is the king who comes in the name of the Lord.
Εὐλογημένος ὁ ἐρχόμενος,
ὁ βασιλεύς ἐν ὀνόματι κυρίου

Mark, Matthew, and John quote the verse verbatim (indeed, this is the reading of the LXX) – although John adds "the king of Israel" afterwards (not indicated above), while Luke takes the liberty of tweaking the verse by inserting the word "king" (βασιλεύς) as the explicit subject. The setting, of course, is Jesus' arrival in Jerusalem, as he is greeted by his followers with this Psalm passage. Moreover, the next event narrated, at least in the synoptic gospels, is Jesus' entrance into the Temple (Mark 11:11, Matt. 21:12, Luke 19:45). In light of this venue, the verse proclaimed by Jesus' followers is a most fitting one, indeed, perhaps *the* most fitting one that people would invoke at this point. The reader will recall our discussion of this verse above, in the context of Sukkot and the explicit mention of Psalm 118 in Mishna Sukkah 3:9. When one notices that Jesus' followers also greet him with palm branches (John 12:13), which are a central feature of the festival of Sukkot (see Lev. 23:40), then our picture is complete. One can hardly imagine a better window into the use of the Psalms by Jewish worshippers in the last century of the Temple's existence.

EXCURSUS: THE KORAH AND ASAPH PSALMS

The picture presented in the main body of this article, regarding the origin of the liturgical use of Psalms in temple sites outside Jerusalem, with a focus on Bethel and Arad (since our evidence stems from these two locales), speaks in general terms only. This excursus attempts to refine that picture, even if, by necessity, it must do so with a modicum of speculation.

---

63. The reader will find a series of essays in *The Psalms in the New Testament*, ed. Steve Moyise and Maarten J.J. Menken (London: T&T Clark, 2004).

Our attention is turned to the Psalms of Korah and Asaph, especially since these two names appear as Levitical singers (or groups of singers) in the post-exilic books of Chronicles and Ezra-Nehemiah (Asaph in particular [1 Chron. 16:5, etc.], though see 2 Chron. 20:19 for Korah). Several scholars, the present writer included, have opined that the Psalms of Korah included in the canonical Book of Psalms originated in the northern kingdom of Israel.[64] In the words of Michael Goulder, "The Korah series contains several references which read as though the water available were plentiful."[65] Thus, for example: "Therefore I recall you from the land of the Jordan" (Ps. 42:7); "The deep calls to the deep at the sound of your cataracts, all your breakers and waves pass by me" (Ps. 42:8); "The river, its streams gladden the city of God" (Ps. 46:5); and "All my springs are in you" (Ps. 87:7). In addition, one finds reference to northern toponyms, such as *ḥermōnīm* and *har miṣʿar* (both in Ps. 42:7)—the former is an unusual plural form, referring to the multiple peaks of the Hermon range; while the latter is to be identified with *zaʿōra*, a place three miles south of Banias.[66] A striking passage is Ps. 46:3-4:

> Therefore we will not fear should the earth shift,
> And should the mountains tumble into the heart of the sea;
> Should its waters rage and foam,
> Should the mountains quake in its swell.

These verses describe the meeting of mountains and the roaring and foaming sea. The only places where such occurs in Israel is in the north, with mountains such as Carmel and Rosh ha-Niqra cascading down into the sea (especially the latter, which is my personal choice for the setting of this passage).

Ps 48:3 famously refers to *yarkōtē ṣapōn*, "the far north," even if it is used as a synonym for Mt. Zion[67]—a point to which we will return below (see n. 75).

Finally, there is the toponym *ʿmeq hab-baka* "the valley of Baka" in Ps. 84:7, a term that has engendered much debate in biblical studies.[68] The best solution

---

64. See most importantly, John J. Peters, *The Psalms as Liturgies* (New York: Macmillan, 1922), esp. 62–64; and Michael D. Goulder, *The Psalms of the Sons of Korah*, Journal for the Study of Old Testament Supplement Series 20 (Sheffield: JSOT, 1982); along with my linguistic analysis: Gary A. Rendsburg, *Linguistic Evidence for the Northern Origin of Selected Psalms*, Society of Biblical Literature Monograph Series 43 (Atlanta: Scholars, 1990), 51–60.

65. Goulder, *The Psalms of the Sons of Korah*, 13–14.

66. The original identification was made by Gustaf Dalman, "Zu Psalm 42, 7.8," *Palästinajahrbuch* 5 (1909): 101–103, and has been adopted by several Psalms commentators such as Morris Buttenweiser, *The Psalms* (Chicago: University of Chicago Press, 1938), 231; and Hans-Joachim Kraus, *Psalmen*, 2 vols. (Neukirchen: Neukirchener Verlag, 1960), 1:320.

is Goulder's, which identified the Baka of Ps. 84:7 with the Baka (Baka) in Upper Galilee mentioned by Josephus in *Jewish War* 3.3.1.[69] It is also tempting, moreover, to associate the *b3k3*-tree mentioned in Papyrus Anastasi I, col. 23, line 7, referenced in connection with the tribe of Asher.[70]

All of this, in short, associates the Psalms of the sons of Korah (nos. 42, 44–49, 84–85, 87–88) with northern Israel (notwithstanding the threefold reference to "Zion" in Psalm 48 [one of which we alluded to above], along with an additional mention in Ps. 84:8; again see further below).

As with the Psalms of Korah, so too with the Psalms of Asaph. Here too, scholars have detected a northern provenience, based once more on items mentioned in these poems, along with the linguistic evidence.[71] The former include the following:

1. northern tribes such as Joseph (77:16, 78:67, 80:2, 81:6) and Ephraim (78:9, 78:67, 80:3), with single mentions of Benjamin (80:13) and Manasseh (80:13);
2. northern cities, to wit, En-dor and Adamah (both in 83:11);
3. enemies from northern Israel's historical past, such as Sisera and Jabin (83:10) and Oreb, Zeeb, Zebah, and Zalmunna (83:11); and
4. northern topography, e.g., *hararē 'ēl* "mountains of God" (50:10), *naharōt 'ētan* "rivers of might" (74:15), and *'arzē 'ēl* "cedars of God" (80:11), all of which evoke the Galilee region.

67. See Frank M. Cross, *Canaanite Myth and Hebrew Epic* (Cambridge, MA: Harvard University Press, 1973), 38 (where the reference to Ps. 43:8 is a misprint for Ps. 48:3); and A. Robinson, "Zion and *Saphon* in Psalm XLVIII 3," *Vetus Testamentum* 24 (1974): 118–23.

68. See A. Robinson, "Three Suggested Interpretations in Ps. lxxxiv," *Vetus Testamentum* 24 (1974): 378–79.

69. Goulder, *The Psalms of the Sons of Korah*, 40.

70. For the Egyptian text, see Alan H. Gardiner, *Egyptian Hieratic Texts* (Leipzig: Hinrichs, 1911), 25*. 70. I first made this suggestion in Rendsburg, *Linguistic Evidence for the Northern Origins of Selected Psalms*, 53. This is not to say that this particular tree (whatever its official botanical identification) is limited to northern Israel, for it also is mentioned in 2 Sam. 5:23-24 (// 1 Chron. 14:14-15) in a southern geographical setting.

71. For earlier discussions, see Martin J. Buss, "The Psalms of Asaph and Korah," *Journal of Biblical Literature* 82 (1963): 382–392; Harry P. Nasuti, *Tradition History and the Psalms of Asaph*, Society of Biblical Literature Dissertation Series 88 (Atlanta: Scholars, 1988); and H.L. Ginsberg, *The Israelian Heritage of Judaism* (New York: Jewish Theological Seminary, 1982), 31–34 (on Psalms 77, 80–81, not the entire Asaph collection); along with the linguistic evidence in Rendsburg, *Linguistic Evidence for the Northern Origin of Selected Psalms*, 69–81.

At this point, the reader may wish to know: Why is all this information about the northern provenience of the Korah and Asaph Psalms relevant to our study? As we saw in the main essay, the post-exilic Judean tradition placed a great emphasis on these two groups (the Asaph one, in particular) as levitical singers in the Jerusalem Temple, anachronistically retrojecting them in this role back to the time of David—even though our pre-exilic sources are silent on this matter. I would like to suggest that the priestly source of the Torah represents the manner in which the Jerusalem Temple indeed operated, in whole or in part, for its first several centuries of existence. In other parts of the country, however, a different approach was in place. I find it rather striking that our first reference to music in a temple context comes from Amos, with reference to Bethel c. 750 BCE, and only later do we find evidence from southern Judah, in the more or less contemporary documentation from Hezekiah (embedded in Isaiah) and the Sons of Korah at Arad (by inference, to be sure). What transpired in between the former (Amos) and the latter (Hezekiah / Arad)? The answer: The destruction of the northern kingdom of Israel by the hands of the Assyrians in 721 BCE.

As we know both from the Bible and from archaeological sources, a significant portion of the population of the northern kingdom of Israel, especially from its southern borderland area, emigrated to Judah to escape the Assyrian devastation.[72] Among these sources is the description in 2 Chronicles 30 of Hezekiah's invitation of northern Israelians to participate in the observance of Passover in the Jerusalem Temple along with their southern Judahite compatriots.[73] And while the author of Chronicles introduces hymns and music into the Temple at various times in his narrative, the following verse (2 Chron. 20:31) is rather intriguing:

> And the Israelians who were present in Jerusalem observed the holiday of matzot seven days, with great joy—with the Levites and the priests praising Yhwh every day with musical instruments, unto Yhwh.

---

72. For a recent discussion, with much bibliography, see William M. Schniedewind and Gary A. Rendsburg, "The Siloam Tunnel Inscription: Historical and Linguistic Perspectives," *Israel Exploration Journal* 60 (2010): 188–203.

73. The historicity of this episode is greatly debated by scholars. For discussion, see Hugh Williamson, *1 and 2 Chronicles*, New Century Bible Commentary (Grand Rapids, MI: Eerdmans, 1982), 361–64; and Sara Japhet, *I & II Chronicles*, Old Testament Library (Louisville: Westminster John Knox, 1993), 934–36.

Equally curious is the author's use of the phrase kɔlc ʿōz for "musical instruments," a term used only here in the Bible.[74] This suggests that the term is not one of the Chronicler's "pet phrases," but rather, just perhaps, an expression found in his historical source.

In light of the above evidence, I would propose, with all due caution, that the musical traditions attached to the ancient Israelite cult began in the northern kingdom, where apparently there was less attention paid to the major break with polytheism attempted by the Judahite priesthood, as described by Kaufmann. The northerners, after all, were the ones who permitted physical representations of Yahweh, the god of Israel (1 Kgs. 12:28-30), and hence one can imagine their continuation of the ancient Near Eastern musical traditions associated with temple rituals. It may not be coincidental, therefore, that Amos 5:21-23 constitutes the earliest biblical text to mention music and song alongside altar and sacrifice. In such fashion, moreover, we can understand the origin of the Asaph and Korah Psalms in northern Israel, especially if they represent two early collections of religious poetry.[75]

All of this, of course, came to an end in 721 BCE—in the north, that is. For as intimated above, the Israelians brought these traditions with them to Judah, not only to Jerusalem, where they would remain in place until 70 CE.

To repeat, none of this can be proved to the extent that would satisfy a historian with more evidence at his or her disposal. But based on the clues presented in the biblical sources, I am content to speculate, with all due caution, on the matter. In the very least, should the reader of these pages find the hypothesis too speculative, he or she will have gained some insights into, and hopefully also some appreciation for, two of the poetic collections incorporated into the Book of Psalms.

---

74. Or, if one follows the reading of the Septuagint, then in 2 Sam. 6:14 as well. Note that the two Hebrew nouns collocated in Exod. 15:2 (quoted in Isa. 12:2, Ps. 118:14), namely, ʿōz and zimrat both bear double meaning, with one set of connotations relating to music and the other set to strength. The phrase thus can be read as both "Yah is my music and my song" and "Yah is my strength and my might." Such literary brilliance is typical of the ancient Hebrew literati who provided us with so much wonder to behold. Though most scholars do not recognize the point made here and thus typically opt for one set of meanings only; for discussion of the individual terms, see William H.C. Propp, Exodus 1–18, Anchor Bible 2 (New York: Doubleday, 1998), 511–13.

75. To be sure, the term "Zion" appears in these psalms (for example, three times in Psalm 48), which may indicate that these poems were doctored (ever so slightly, though, given their northern linguistic profile) when they were incorporated into the Jerusalem cult.

5

Reverence for Jerusalem and the Temple in Galilean Society

Mordechai Aviam

Galilee is about 200 km from Jerusalem if one measures by the as the bird flies. It is almost 300 km on the road. The shortest route is to travel through the Samaritan territory that was so hostile to Galileans and Judeans.[1] A longer route follows the Jordan Rift Valley, but the journey is hot, dry, and climbs from 900 feet below sea level to 3000 feet above sea level. During the days of Hillel and Jesus, there were aggressive wolves, leopards, bears, and even lions that threatened pilgrims on the way.[2] Galileans took about six days to travel by foot from Galilee to Jerusalem.

Jerusalem was the metropolis and the Holy City. Taxes were paid by the Galileans to the Temple and to the Jerusalem authorities. Numerous questions appear before us historians and archaeologists. The following seem the most important:

- Did these obstacles and differences create an emotional gap between Galileans and Jerusalem?
- Did historians "invent" a chasm between Galilee and Judea, misinterpreting Jesus' "rejection" of the Temple and the Holy City?
- What can we learn from new archaeological discoveries regarding the emotional and physical attitude of Galileans towards Jerusalem? Or, in other words, was Jerusalem in the hearts of the Galileans?

---

1. *War* 2.232

2. b*Baba Kama* 17:1. Bones of leopard and bear were discovered in our excavations at Yodefat, a first-century Galilean town.

RELIGIOUS PRACTICES

RITUAL BATHING

The discovery of *mikvaot* (Jewish baths for ritual immersion) throughout Judea and Galilee, from Hasmonean times to at least 70 CE, has an enormous impact on our new interpretation of Judaism. Most scholars who have studied ritual purity are pointing to its appearance in the Hasmonaean era. In 1980, R. Reich identified the early *mikvaot* at Tel Gezer. The earliest identified, dated *mikveh* is probably the one excavated at the "buried" Hasmonaean palace in Jericho, under the "fortified" palace, dated by the excavator to 125–115 BCE. There are other Hasmonaean *mikvaot* in Jerusalem, Qumran, Sepphoris, Gamla and the fortress at Qeren Naftali. The *mikveh* at Qeren Naftali (Fig. 5.1) has a special importance as it is not in a private home or a rich palace but in a military structure that was used only by soldiers.[3]

Fig. 5.1. The mikveh at Qeren Naftali; photo by the author.

When did *mikvaot* first appear? Recently, a major study was focused on the origin and use of *mikvaot*.[4] In his detailed survey of the studies, Y. Adler surveys three main suggestions about the origin of the *mikveh* as an installation. The first argument is that it derives from the First Temple period bath installations. Adler supports Reich's strong objection to such a suggestion. The second and third arguments follow Reich's suggestion to identify the origin of the *mikveh* with the arrival of the Greeks. On the one hand, Greek baths in the Land of Israel in the Hellenistic period[5] influenced the origin of *mikvaot*. On the other hand, the Greek "Spring house," especially in the rituals of Asclepius, included immersion

---

3. .M Aviam, *Jews, Pagans, and Christians in Galilee* (Rochester, NY: University of Rochester Press, 2004), 59–88.

4. .YAdler, "The Archaeology of Purity" (PhD diss., Bar Ilan University, 2011).

into stepped pools helped with the evolution of *mikvaot*.[6] Adler concludes that the arrival of the Greek bath implicated the creation of the *mikveh* but suggests that the entirely new system of bathing caused changes in the Jewish ritual bathing and these necessitated the creation of Jewish *mikveh*.

I now suggest another conclusion. The Greek bathing system and the Greek baths arrived in the Land of Israel by the end of the fourth century BCE, but the appearance of Jewish *mikvaot* do not appear until 115–100 BCE. This is too long a period for us to suppose Greek baths to have been the origin of *mikvaot*. I am convinced that although there were religious, social, and cultural components in the creation of *mikvaot*, the most important factor was the establishment of a powerful, aggressive, and expanding Jewish kingdom, creating an enlarged territory that should be populated in a short period of time with new Jewish villages and towns. The success of the Maccabean-Hasmonaean revolt, the freeing of Jerusalem, and the purification of the Temple increased the inner religious feelings towards the Holy City and its Temple. Recently, both Joseph Baumgarten and Steve Cohn have suggested that many religious traditions and customs were first established during the Hasmonean reign.[7]

In my view, the appearance of the *mikveh* installation is one of these innovations. The vast and speedy expansion of territory, including the conversion to Judaism of pagans such as the Edomites and Ituraeans (by the sword or persuasion), as well as new settlements of immigrating Jews from Judea and "colonies" of veterans from the Jewish armies, all together were a boon for the new installation—a "portable" purification installation, one that could be built anywhere, not requiring any connection to a cave filled by rain water in the winter or in close proximity to a spring or a river. Every converted Jew, or any new resident of the Galilee, could immerse in the *mikveh* and be in as pure a state as everyone in the courtyard of the Temple. The new innovation made a direct and fast connection to the holiness of the Temple and the Holy City in the young kingdom, a kingdom of religion, a kingdom in which one of its motives was to "purify" the "sacred land" from any idolatry and paganism.

---

5. R. Reich, "Archaeological Evidence of the Jewish Population at Hasmonean Gezer," *Israel Exploration Journal* 31 (1981): 48–52.

6. Ibid., 140–141.

7. J.M. Baumgarten, "Invented Traditions of the Maccabean," in *Geschichte–Tradition–Reflexion: Festschrift für Martin Hengel zum 70 Geburtstag*, vol. 1, ed. P. Schäfer (Tübingen: Mohr-Siebeck, 1996), and S.J.D. Cohn, *The Beginning of Jewishness: Boundaries, Varieties, Uncertainties* (Berkeley: University of California Press, 1999).

The *mikveh* was a tool of religious power.[8] If the Galilee was annexed to Judea at the very end of the second century BCE, already after the campaign against Scythopolis,[9] or even a little later during the reign of Alexander Janneus, then the fortress of Keren Naftali was taken during these days and the *mikveh* was then built there as a second phase in one of the rooms of the Tyrian-Seleucid fort.[10] This is, so far as excavations up until now have revealed, the earliest *mikveh* in the Galilee. From that point onwards, *mikvaot* appear in almost every excavation of first-century BCE to first-century CE farm,[11] village,[12] town,[13] and city in Galilee, Judea, and Peraea.[14]

The existence and use of a *mikveh* originate within the holy connection of territories with Jerusalem. It solidified a bond between Jews in the periphery and in the core of holiness in Jerusalem. After the destruction of Jerusalem and the Temple in 70 CE, we observe a major decline in the number of *mikvaot* in Jewish sites. This fact helps prove the connection between the *mikvaot* and the holiness of the Temple, Zion, God's House.

STONE VESSELS

The earliest stone vessels in Judea are usually dated to the second half of the first century BCE and they were produced in the hills around Jerusalem. However, it is not yet clear that the stone vessel industry first appeared in the late Hasmonaean era. Maybe, similarly to the *mikvaot*, the origin of these vessels is to be derived from the luxurious, hard-stone Hellenistic period vessels; but in Jewish life, they quickly became a crucial part of purity as well as other religious practices, as reflected in the well-known story of the wedding at Cana (John 2). Recently a better understanding of these vessels has been enriched by the discovery in Jerusalem of a stone cup with magic inscriptions.[15]

8. This suggestion was first made by my colleague and friend W.S. Green who excavated Yodefat with me and he brought it up when we discussed the *miqvaot* of Yodefat.

9. Aviam, *Jews, Pagans, and Christians*, 44–45.

10. Ibid., 69–70.

11. .YHirschfeld, *Ramat Hanadiv Excavations* (Jerusalem: Israel Exploration Society, 2000), 16–26.

12. At Karem e-Ras, near Kefar Kana some miqvaot were discovered in the houses of the Early Roman period Jewish village. See http://www.hadashot-esi.org.il/report_detail.asp?id=602&ag_id=114

13. For Yodefat, see M. Aviam, *The New Encyclopedia of Archaeological Excavations in the Holy Land* (Jerusalem: Israel Exploration Society & Carta, 2008). For Gamla, see D. Syon and Z. Yavor, *Gamla II. The Architecture* (Jerusalem: Israel Antiquities Authority, 2010).

14. For an updated map of miqvaot see Adler, "The Archaeology of Purity."

15. An unusual and important stone vessel with an inscription on it was discovered in Jerusalem. It is in some cryptic script, and according to the excavator it "does seem as if the inscription must have had some mystical or liturgical significance." See S. Gibson, "New Excavations on Mount Zion in Jerusalem and an

While scholars have not yet discerned the precise extent and function of stone vessels in the religious life of Palestinian Jews, it is obvious that this custom expanded rapidly, during the Herodian period, from Jerusalem to other Jewish regions, especially Galilee and Peraea. Although the exact use of these stone vessels is not yet resolved, it is clear that they were not intended for ordinary daily use. These types of stone vessels are not of large number and they include mainly hemispheric bowls, flat dishes, cups, pitchers, large craters, and square deep bowls.[16] The most common types are mugs (small and large) and pitchers (mugs with spouts).

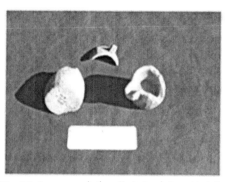

Fig. 5.2. Stone vessels (small pitchers) from Yodefat.

There are no parallels for these types of vessels in clay, and according to the design of the outer face of the mugs, they do not imitate metal vessels.[17] The stone vessels were certainly made for a very specific purpose. It is possible that the mugs with their large handles were created for ritual hand washing.[18] I suggest that the pitchers were used to fill oil lamps with oil. The small ones contain the right quantity to fill up a regular oil lamp and the large ones can fill large or multi-nozzled oil lamps, not necessarily those that were lighted for Shabbat (Fig. 5.2).

I contend that the distribution of stone vessels from Jerusalem, similarly to the *mikvaot*, is an attempt to "export" the purity and holiness of Jerusalemand of the Temple to the periphery. Jewish people, especially in the Land of Israel,

Inscribed Stone Cup/Mug from the Second Temple Period," in *New Studies in the Archaeology of Jerusalem and its Region Collected Papers*, ed. D. Amit, O. Peleg-Barkat and G.D. Stiebel (Jerusalem: Israel Antiquities Authority, 2010), 32–43.

16. For the entire repertoire see Y. Magen, *The Stone Vessel Industry in the Second Temple Period* (Jerusalem: Israel Exploration Society, 2002), 174–180.

17. Magen suggested that the mugs imitate wooden carved mugs. Ibid., 99.

18. Ibid.,138–147, 163–164. See also Gibson, "New Excavations," 41.

adopted quickly these customs. They became part of the daily life of Jews and solidified the spiritual connection of Galileans to the Temple. Archaeological excavations in Judea and Galilee prove that the stone vessel industry in Jerusalem collapsed after its destruction in 70 CE. In both Judea and Galilee, it disappeared during the second century CE.

CLAY OIL LAMPS

In the 1980s, Y. Gounevag examined the petrography of the "Herodian" or "knife-pared" oil lamps (Fig. 5.3) from different locales in Israel and concluded that all were manufactured in Jerusalem.[19] During the final phases of the excavations at Yodefat, we checked the petrography of the same type of oil lamps from Yodefat and Gamla and arrived at the same conclusion as Gounevag. More recently, D. Adan-Bayewitz published the results of his chemical and physical analysis of different groups of oil lamps from various sites and concluded that all "knife-pared" oil lamps from Jewish sites, whether Galilee or Judea, were produced in Jerusalem from Motza's clay. The Jewish nature of these lamps is highlighted by the fact that "knife-pared" oil lamps not produced in Jerusalem but from local clay have been recovered, but they were found only in the Gentile locations.[20]

When we studied the oil lamps from the Yodefat excavations, we realized that although Yodefat had its own pottery production, and although there is a local type of oil lamp (the "boot-shape" type) that could have been produced at Yodefat, about 60% of all the lamps at the site were imported from Jerusalem.

This fact sharply contrasts oil lamps from other clay vessels. All Yodefat cooking pots, storage jars, jugs, juglets, and other vessels are of local production. Only the oil lamps (and most of them) were brought to Galilee from Jerusalem. Not surprisingly, it is the same situation at Gamla and probably in all Galilee. No technical reason helps to explain this phenomenon. The size and capacity of the two types is similar, their strength is similar, so there is only one explanation to the large import of the oil lamps to the Galilee and it is the holiness of the place in which they were manufactured, the holiness of the city, Jerusalem.

With those who study the history of symbolism, and with most theologians of world religions, I think that there is a strong mystical and emotional

19. J. Gunewag and I. Perlman, "The Origin of the Herodian Lamps," *Bulletin of the Anglo-Israel Archaeological Society 1984-5* (1984): 79–83.

20. D. Adam Bayewitz, et. al., "Preferential Distribution of Lamps from the Jerusalem Area in the Late Second Temple Period (Late First Century BCE–70 CE)," *Bulletin of the American Schools of Oriental Research* 350 (2008).

Fig. 5.3. Gray knife-pared oil lamp from Yodefat. Photo by the author.

connection between light and holiness. The flame from the spout of the Jerusalem lamp, in the darkness of the room, brought with it a direct connection to the Temple in Jerusalem, to the flames of the sacred seven branched candelabrum, the Menorah, which was a focal symbol of the Temple for the Jewish people as reflected from its appearance in many places, notably on the coins of Mattathias Antigonus, in the artworks found in the Upper City of Jerusalem, and the Arch of Titus in the Roman Forum. Many Galilean Jews who made the mandatory pilgrimage to the Temple would remember in the flames that brought light to a dark Galilean home the symbolic power of the Menorah in the Temple.

SYNAGOGUES

The existence of first-century synagogues was, for many years, heavily debated among scholars. Yet, in the last twenty years the debate slowly lost its intensity as more and more buildings from this period were identified as synagogues. The first buildings to be identified as first-century synagogues in the 1950s were Masada and Herodium, but they were treated as "synagogues of refuge" built by the Zealots, as they were far from the Temple.

It was only after the discovery of Gamla's synagogue (Fig. 5.4) that the attitude was changed and scholars realized that there is a clear architectural group of first-century synagogues.

Fig. 5.4. The synagogue at Gamla (courtesy of D. Syon)

Although the debates did not subside, the archeological discovery of other synagogues during these years, and especially the synagogue at Khibet Badd Issa (Kiryat Sefer),[21] finally convinced most scholars of the existence of buildings that were purposely built to be used as synagogues. However, because only one synagogue has been found in the north (at Gamla, and not in Galilee but in the Golan), some scholars raised questions as to whether the building at Gamla is a unique phenomenon and, as such, perhaps is not a synagogue. Some experts, therefore, claimed that there were no first-century buildings that were synagogues in the Galilee and that the connections between episodes from Flavius Josephus and the NT should be explained differently. If so, how can we trust Josephus and the Evangelists who reported synagogues in the Galilee?

If we take Masada and Qiryat Sefer as models of the Second Temple period's synagogues, then there is no doubt that the building at Gamla is a synagogue (Fig. 5.4). It is a large, public building; and the gathering people sat on stone benches around the walls facing the center. Moreover, there is a niche in the wall, presumably to house a wooden chest to preserve Torah scrolls.

21. Y. Magen, et. al. *The Land of Benjamin* (Jerusalem: Israel Antiquities Authority, 2004), 179–242.

If we are right, where are the other Galilean synagogues? For years I have been claiming that finding a synagogue in the Galilee is only a question of "archaeological luck," which is connected with the number of excavations being carried out in the region, as well as their size.

In 2009, an important discovery was made at the ancient site of Migdal. In a salvage excavation by the Israel Antiquities Authority (IAA), a first-century synagogue was unearthed. Finally, archaeologists have unearthed a building that was certainly a synagogue in first-century Galilee.

Migdal is a well-known site of historical significance in Galilee. It is mentioned in both Josephus and the New Testament. This square building with benches around the walls has a footpath, part of which is paved with a mosaic floor, and walls and pillars that were covered with frescoes.[22] The central floor is made of pebbles. If this was the original floor, it was probably covered with rugs or mats. To the west, there is another room with benches that could be used as a smaller study room, similar to the one at Gamla.

The earliest synagogues dated so far are the first phase of the synagogue at Modiin,[23] which is dated to the Hasmonaean period, and the synagogue at the Royal Hasmonaean palace in Jericho.[24]

Although there are not yet any remains of Hasmonaean-period synagogues in Jerusalem, I do believe that the phenomenon of building synagogues as public spaces for "reading and studying the Torah" started in Jerusalem and maybe even near the Temple, as hinted from the Theodotos inscription and the Toseftah, which probably mentions a synagogue within the Temple courtyards.[25] The concept of a building for communal gathering for reading the Torah spread fast with the Hasmonaean expansion and arrived in the Galilee and Golan. The earliest dating that we have up until now is probably the end of the first century BCE. The strong connection between the Temple and the synagogue was proved with the discovery of the decorated stone from the synagogue at Migdal.

22. The description of the building and its design, as well as the discussion of the decorated stone is from the web site of the IAA, lectures given by the excavator D. Avshalom-Gorni as well as many websites such as:http://bibleillustration.blogspot.com ; http://www.youtube.com/watch?v=VX83jUdeKE; http://www.lomdim.org.il/photos?album=Migdal; http://www.bib-arch.org/bar/article.asp?PubID=BSBA&Volume=37&Issue=4&ArticleID=7

23. A. On and S. Weksler-Bdolah, "Khirbet Um el-Umdan: A Jewish Village with a Synagogue from the Second Temple Period at Modiin," *Qadmoniot* 130 (2005).

24. E. Nezer, et. al. "A Hasmonaean Synagogue at Jericho," *Qadmoniot* 117 (1999).

25. Toseftah Sukkah 4:5.

THE DECORATED STONE FROM MIGDAL

The strong connection of the Galileans to the Temple, and the Menorah as its central symbol, is proven now by the symbolic decorated stone discovered on the floor of the first-century synagogue at Migdal.

The proof that the Menorah was a central symbol for the Temple, already in the first century BCE, came from the coin of Mattathias Antigonus, which was minted probably in 63–64 BCE during Pompey's campaign. The reverse of the coin carries a depiction of the Showbread Table that was located near the Menorah. These two objects also appear on Titus's Arch as they were carried by Roman soldiers in the triumphal march of Vespasian and Titus, and on chunk of wall plaster from the Jewish Quarter in Jerusalem.[26]

The appearance of the Menorah in a synagogue dated to the Second Temple period, although it is one of its kind, proves, in my opinion, that the synagogue is a "representative" of the Temple, especially for the Jewish settlements in the distant periphery of the Land of Israel. This phenomenon was strengthened after the destruction of the Temple when the synagogues were "temporary replacements" for the Temple until the third one should be built.

There is almost no doubt that the Menorah symbolized the Temple for Jews in the Land of Israel as well as in the Diaspora. Therefore, I suggest that all other "decorative" objects that appear on the stone (and will be discussed below) are symbolic as well, and I'll try to show the meaning of each one of them and the entire holistic outlook.

As a first step I will give the description of the stone accompanied by line drawing of each side, and their interpretation as suggested by the excavator (Figs. 5.5, 5.6, 5.7, 5.8).[27]

Here is a rectangular limestone block, 0.6 m. long, 0.5 m. wide and 0.4 m. high, which stands on four short, massive legs.

The façade of the stone, if it was discovered in its original place, is facing to the south, towards Jerusalem. The depiction here includes the seven-branched candelabrum (Menorah), standing on a square stage, flanked by two amphorae, all placed between two pillars with bases and capitals, and under an arch.

26. L. Habas, "An Incised Depiction of the Temple Menorah and Other Cult Objects of the Second Temple Period," in *Jewish Quarter Excavations in the Old City of Jerusalem*, ed. H. Geva, vol. 2 (Jerusalem: Israel Exploration Society, 2003).

27. The photos of all sides of the stone appeared in many websites on the Internet. A copy of the stone was displayed in the Notre-Dame in Jerusalem and it was discussed by the excavator D. Avshalom Gorni public lectures.

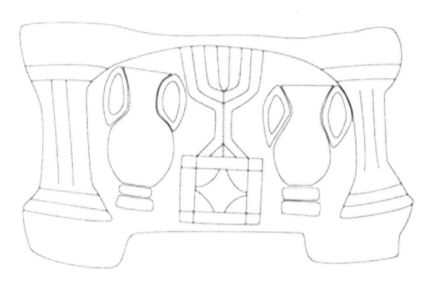

Fig. 5.5. The façade with the Menorah. Drawing courtesy of D. Shalem.

The two long sides are identical to each other: An arcade of four arches and within three of them a depiction of what looks like a sheaf of corn, as suggested by the excavator. In the forth one, at the beginning of each row is a hanging object, perhaps, as suggested by the excavator, an oil lamp.

The back side is also designed as architectural frame, but not with two pillars like the front and slightly different arcade from the sides. There are three pillars of which the central capital is slightly different. At the top of the two arches, there are two objects that were identified by the excavator as rosettes. Below each of these are six triangles arranged in half of a circle.

Above the arcade, on both corners, there are two geometric designs in frame.

The entire rectangular upper face of the stone is covered with low relief objects, decorative according to the excavator. Almost in the center there is a large rosette, made of six petals and surrounded by six other identical petals. On both sides of the rosette are long objects; they are suggested by the excavator as palm trees. The rest of the space is taken by twelve other motifs, both floral and geometric.

A New Holistic Interpretation of the Symbols

The front side gives a view into the inner hall of the Temple in Jerusalem, the sanctuary (*Heichal*), where the Menorah, the Gold Altar, and the Showbread

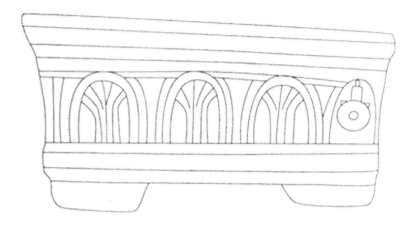

Fig. 5.6. The long sides. Drawing courtesy of D. Shalem.

Fig. 5.7. The back side. Drawing courtesy of D. Shalem.

Table stood. I believe that the square object that looks like a podium for the
Menorah represents, as a matter of fact, the altar itself and is standing in front
of the Menorah. A similar description and arrangement of the objects was
found engraved on a plaster chunk of a large mansion in the Jewish Quarter
of Jerusalem, dated to the first half of the first century CE.[28] The two amphorae

---

28. Habas, "An Incised Depiction."

Fig. 5.8. The face of the stone. Drawing courtesy of D. Shalem.

on both sides of the Menorah represent the symbolic and mystic olive trees or branches (Bnei HaYizhar, בני היצהר in Hebrew) which are mentioned in Zechariah 4:10-14. Amphorae on both sides of the menorah also appear on ancient Jewish glass from Rome, dated to the Late Roman period.[29] All these elements appear under an arch and between the pillars, which symbolize the architectonic façade of the Temple, as seen while looking into the sanctuary.

Inside each of the arches of the stone's side arcades, there is not a sheaf of corn but rather another arch. There is a complete similarity between the design of the arcade's pilasters and the depiction inside the arch, which I understand

29. See http://www.lootedart.com/news.php?r=N4L90B393991

as an arcade behind an arcade or, in other words, building within a building, a symbolic representation of the Holy of Holies inside the temple building.

The hanging object inside the first arch is not an oil lamp as was suggested. Although it has some similarities to an oil lamp, I do not think it is. First of all, it does not have the complete shape of an oil lamp as it misses the "mouth," the hole at the end of the nozzle. Second, it has a small handle on each side. Third, it is hanging from its long side. As all other elements on this stone are symbolic, I think this one is also. I suggest it is an incense vessel—a censer. Those were in use in the Temple: "And the dish was in it, full and heaped up with incense." Also, there was a kind of covering on it (in the Hebrew מטטלת, which could mean hanging cover). [30] Two of these were in use on the Showbread Table [31], and two are depicted on the stone.

On, the back side, the two circular objects in the upper part of the arches are wheels, not rosettes. First of all, rosettes are usually designed as leafs and not as lines. Second, there is a difference between the centers of each of the objects. On the left one, it is a protruding knob and on the right one it is a sunken one. I speculate that the artist depicted two chariot wheels: one is viewed from its inside and one from its outside. The set of small triangles at the bottom represent flames of fire. This is a well-known representation of the divine chariot: "I beheld till the thrones were cast down, and the Ancient of days did sit, whose garment was white as snow, and the hair of his head like the pure wool: his throne was like the fiery flame, and his wheels as burning fire" (Daniel 7:9 KJV). The vision of the divine chariot appears in few mystical books of the Bible and apocrypha such as Ezekiel, Zechariah, and Enoch.

Above the wheels and the pilasters, there are three objects. Two, on each side, are of unusual geometric design, like four-point stars, and the third, in between what looks like a long rectangular table. It looks as if the upper part of the stone is eroded or worn and this table is missing its upper part. The only explanation I could find is to try and connect it to the imaginary structure of the frame of the chariot above the wheels.

If my interpretation is correct, then what we see depicted on the back side of the Migdal stone is a mystical, allegorical view directly into the Holy of Holies, through its architectural frame into the place of the divine spirit, represented by its chariot. It is important to note that in early Jewish art there is a somewhat similar depiction of God seated on a winged, wheeled throne on a YHD coin from the fifth century BCE.[32]

---

30. *Tamid.* 5:4.

31. See also the discussion about the Showbread Table depicted on the mosaic floor of the synagogue at Sepphoris; Z.Weiss, *The Sepphoris Synagogue* (Jerusalem: Israel Exploration Society, 2005), 95.

On, the face of the stone, the central and largest object is the rosette. The design of it is unusual among the hundreds of rosettes we know from the Second Temple period.[33] The outer circle, which is made of six petals, is completely rounded, while in many other examples from the architecture and funerary world, these petals are creating straight lines between the tips of the rosette's petals. Modern scholars such as Rahmani,[34] followed recently by Hachlili,[35] rejected the idea that the rosette is a symbol, and Hachlili even suggested that there is no symbolism yet in the world of Second Temple period Jewish art.[36] As I am trying to prove that all objects on this stone are symbolic, I am supportive of the opposite conclusion. I believe that the rosette, especially this one with its twelve petals, and probably most of the rest, are symbolic as well. The location of this rosette (almost in the middle of the face of the stone), its size, and its design show that it has a focal meaning. I believe that it has a celestial symbolism. The complete circle of twelve petals can symbolize the heavens—the sky including the time frame of twelve months (an element that will later be replaced by the zodiac). The number twelve is connected directly to the number of loaves on the Showbread Table and the cosmos is certainly clear in the only place where we have an explanation about the number of loaves. Note the description provided by Flavius Josephus: ". . . the loaves on the table, *twelve* in number, the circle of the zodiac and the year . . ." (*War* 5.217).

The two objects on the sides of the rosette are not palm trees. They are not designed as palm trees and a simple comparison to other known examples of palm trees from the same period will prove this point.[37] I think that what we have here are two holy tools that were used during the sacred work of sacrifice. They are the *rakes*—the Magrefot (מגרפה in Hebrew). These tools (there is also another musical tool with the same name used in the Temple) were used to rake the ash and burnt bones from the main altar.[38] A deeper look at the stone and the drawings will show that the "trunk" of the "palm tree" is designed as a handle.

32. Y. Meshorer, *Ancient Jewish Coinage*, vol. 1 (Dix Hills, NY: Amphora Books, 1982), 1:21–25.

33. See, for example, L.Y. Rahmani, *A Catalogue of Jewish Ossuaries* (Jerusalem: Israel Antiquities Authority, 1994), 39–41.

34. Ibid.

35. R. Hachlili, *Ancient Mosaic Pavements: Themes, Issues, and Trends* (Leiden: Brill, 2009).

36. Ibid., 13–14.

37. For example the trees on the lintel from Gamla: O. Peleg-Barkat, "Architectural Decoration," in *Gamla II, The Architecture*, ed. D. Syon and Z. Yavor, Israel Antiquities Authority Reports 44 (Jerusalem: Israel Antiquities Authority, 2010), 168–9.

38. *Tamid.* 2:1.

which is wrapped with a string to hold together a bunch of limbs which creates the shape of a rake at the end of the tool.

There are also twelve objects on the surface of the stone that are designed as floral and geometric patterns and are arranged in couples. Each couple is designed differently and with no other parallels whatsoever to first-century Jewish artistic objects (ossuaries, for example). There are small, medium, and large couples of ivy leafs, a couple of rhombuses within a square frame, a couple of rhombuses within a square frame and a cross in the center, and a couple of unfamiliar objects that look like something folded. In all the artistic work of the first century, including the rich material from the funerary world of ossuaries, we have no parallels to such a concentration and unusual group of artistic elements. My suggestion is that this group represents, in a very symbolic way, the twelve loaves that were placed on the Showbread Table.

The information on the shape of the loaves is varied and probably contains many different traditions, and so is the case about the way they were arranged on the Table. The most common approach is two piles of six loaves in each.

On the reverse of the coin of Mattathias Antigonus is a depiction of the Table with two piles of six concave objects.[39] The Talmudic sources speak about two types of loaves. One is an "open, broken box" (תיבה פרוצה), which probably had some kind of a square design. The second is a "rocking boat" (ספינה רוקדת), which probably had more of a triangular shape. There is no consensus today regarding the shape and the way the loaves were folded. On the mosaic floor of the Samaritan synagogue at el-Khirbe, there is a depiction of the Showbread Table; it is a round one and only four of the twelve loaves are now preserved. Three of them are round, but each one is carrying a different pattern of what could be a stamp or remains of folding. The fourth is elliptical and looks like it is folded.[40]

According to Josephus, the loaves were baked in groups of two and then they were placed on the Table in two groups of six (*Ant* 3:255). In the Kabala are remains of traditions that the loaves were divided into six groups of two. In summation, my suggestion is that the collection of the twelve objects on the face of the stone represents, symbolically, the Showbread Table in the Temple.

A careful look at the corners of the stone's face shows that there are remains of four broken, round elements. I believe that these are the remains of four stone

---

39. For the large and detailed discussion on the depictions on these coins, see Z. Amar, "The Showbread Table on the Coins of Mattathias Antigonus: A Reconsideration," *Israel Numismatic Journal* 17 (2010).

40. See Weiss, *Sepphoris Synagogue*, 97–98.

legs or four stone bases for wooden legs, on which a table (stone or wood) was placed. It is the table on which the Torah was read (Fig. 5.9).

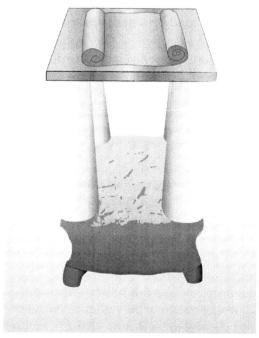

Fig. 5.9. A reconstruction of the Torah Reading Table from Migdal

If this reconstruction is correct, not only do we have the first evidence for a "Torah reading table," but we also have a strong and informative connection between the synagogue, the Torah, and the Jerusalem Temple. Here at the Migdal synagogue, the base for the Torah reading table is the Showbread Table in the Temple and the Temple itself described in pure symbolism and allegory. When the Torah was read, it was in a direct connection to the holiness of the Temple.

It is extremely important to perceive that this Migdal stone, with its decorations, is the first and only collection of symbols of the Temple to show the importance of the Temple to the people who frequented the synagogue. Moreover, it also heralds the massive use of the Temple's symbols in third to sixth century CE synagogue decorations, whether on stone or mosaic floors. The most prevalent Temple symbol is the Menorah, as it appears on the stone from Migdal. The second is the façade of a building, which represents the architecture of the Temple in the shape of the Torah Shrine which stood in the synagogue.

There is more. On the stone from Migdal, is a representation of the *magrefot* (rakes), which are sacred objects from the sacrifice work in the Temple .This symbol was later replaced by shovels that were used to carry the embers as well as the ash from the altar. Both of these symbols were connected to the holy work on the altar. Another symbol is the Showbread Table, which appears in some of the synagogues' decoration as are the cases in Dura Europus and Sepphoris.[41] I think that the best example to show the continuity of the symbols from the Migdal stone is the decorated stone fragment from the synagogue at Capernaum. On this stone, there is a building shown on three-fourths view, surrounded by pillars or pilasters; it has wooden doors on the façade, and a gabled roof with roof tiles (Fig. 5.10).

The entire building is carried on four wheels and it was usually explained during the 1960s and 1970s as the "portable Torah Shrine" representation, in a time when no structures of Torah shrines were identified in what were called then "Early Galilean Synagogues." When the new discoveries came during the 1980s and 1990s (and it was clear that there are permanent "bemas" for the Torah Shrines in almost every excavated Late Roman and Byzantine synagogue), it was suggested that this representation from Capernaum is, as a matter of fact, the representation of the Ark of Covenant making its way back from captivity with the Philistines (1 Sam. 6:10-17), similar to the description in Dura Europos. I always wondered why, in front of the "building on wheels," there is no evidence for cows or any yoke. I think now that this stone also represents the combination of the Temple and the divine chariot, similar although different, from the back side of Migdal's stone.

Although my attempt to explain the complex of art on the Migdal stone as ancient Jewish mysticism and symbolism is new, the antiquity of Jewish mysticism in literature is well known. There are at least three biblical compositions in which the heavenly mysticism is deeply involved: Ezekiel, Zachariah, and Daniel. I think that the closest imagery to the description on the Migdal stone is either the Book of Daniel or the exegetical expansion of Daniel found in the *Parables of Enoch*.

In the Book of Daniel, the author mentions three times that a prayer is said in the direction of Jerusalem. It is a strong belief among scholars that the synagogue in the first century was not a place for communal pray, but if private

---

41. Ibid., 95–101.

Fig. 5.10. The decorated stone from Capernaum's synagogue

prayers were said towards Jerusalem and the stone was faced towards Jerusalem, we have here an archaeological evidence for the importance of the holy city and its Temple in the hearts of ancient Galilean Jews.

It is also very important to emphasize the importance of another book from the pseudepigrapha, the *Book of Enoch*. The final editing of the book, especially the final editing of the *Parables of Enoch*, is dated to the time of the Herodian Dynasty, the time for the erection of the synagogue at Migdal. The *Book of Enoch* also contains heavenly, celestial, and mystical scenes. It is very important to note that the earliest place in which we find a group of angels by the name of "Ofanim" is in the *Book of Enoch* (61:10). It later appears in the Talmud. The Hebrew translation of the word "Ofanim" is wheels, which undoubtedly derives from the divine chariot.

The "merkava" also appears in Second Temple period non-religious works such as Philo from Alexandria. He compares the Menorah to the movement of the planets.[42] Also in Josephus's writings, there are hints for a serious discussion on empirical issues; for example, when he describes the Menorah he writes: ".

42. Y. Liebes, "The Work of the Chariot and the Work of Creation as Esoterical Teachings in *Philo of Alexandria*," in *Scriptural Exegesis: The Shapes of Culture and the Religious Imagination,*ed. D. Green and L. Lieber (Oxford: Oxford University Press, 2009), 90–105.

. . from its single base right up to the top, having been made to consist of as many portions as are assigned to the planets with the sun. It terminated in seven branches . . . recalling the number of the planets . . ." (*Ant* 3:146).

Non-Religious Behavior

The Gamla Coin

In the excavations at the Second Temple period, a unique type of coin was discovered in Golan town of Gamla, which was one of Josephus's fortified towns that was besieged, conquered, and destroyed by the Romans at the beginning of the First Jewish Revolt.[43] The Jerusalem Revolt probably influenced the design of this bronze coin, as coins were minted from the beginning of the revolt, probably under the order and administration of the Revolt Government. The similarity can be seen in the two elements that appear on the coin: the metal cup as on the Jerusalem Sheqel, and the paleo-Hebrew script that is used in Jerusalem coins. Both cup and inscription are crudely made in an attempt to imitate the Jerusalem coin. It is important to emphasis that not even one Jerusalem coin (Sheqel, half a sheqel, or perutah) was discovered in the scientific excavations at both sites of the early Revolt (Yodefat and Gamla). It seems that only a few specimens, if at all, arrived at the Galilee before the war started. Whether the Galileans or people of Gamla had the Jerusalem coin in hand or only saw it, there was something behind their decision to mint a coin that imitated the coins from Jerusalem (Fig. 5.11).

I believe there was the spiritual and emotional connection to Jerusalem and the Temple. It can clearly be seen in the legends on both sides of the coin. According to the common reading it says: "to the redemption of holy Jerusalem" ([לג]אולת [ירושלים הק[דושה]).[44] What redemption? Jerusalem was in Jewish hands, the Temple was functioning, the revolt just started (although the Galilee already fell in front of the massive attack of the Roman legions led by Vespasian). In the hearts of the freedom fighters of Gamla and its leaders, the battle in Galilean towns and cities were a crucial part in the political and national freedom that should be led by Jerusalem, the Temple, and its High Priest, who is already at the head of the leadership of the revolt. This coin reflects the wish of the Gamla and Golan people, as well as Galileans, to be the

---

43. D. Syon, "Tyre and Gamla" (PhD diss., Hebrew University, 2004), 54–57.

44. On the discussion of the inscription, see D. Syon, "Yet Again on the Bronze Coins Minted at Gamla,"*INR* 2 (2007): 117–122.

Fig. 5.11. The Gamla coin

first defending line for Jerusalem, the holy city and Capital with the Temple in its center, maybe similar to the Mattathias Antigonus's coin.[45]

SUMMARY

Displayed here is a change in the study of Judaism of the Second Temple period, especially in the origins of Christianity. In previous scholarship, scholars succeeded in creating an emotional gap between the Galilean Jews and Jerusalem because, in the traditional approach, the mutual relationship between Jesus and the Temple were declared as "hostile" and was studied through Jesus' words on the Temple and his acts in its courtyards, as well as through pieces of Josephus's writings on the connection between Galileans and Jerusalem and the "triple taxation."

For the first time, there is a large collection, a bulk of material, cultural evidence to prove the opposite. I am not sure that the Galileans were happy to pay taxes, first to the King (Herod the Great in Jerusalem or Herod Antipas in Tiberias), second to the Roman authorities, and third to the Temple, but I

45. Meshorer, *Ancient Jewish Coinage*, 1:116–119.

deeply believe that of the three they felt strong ties to the Temple taxation. They were attached to the Temple in their hearts and in their souls, as was Jesus himself.

6

Jesus and the Temple

James H. Charlesworth

I first went to Jerusalem in September 1968, passing near the walls of the Old City late at night. A little more than one year after the Six-Day War, when Jews again ruled Jerusalem after almost two thousand years, I witnessed contagious excitement as archaeologists excavated around the Temple Mount. I recall vividly an animated conversation between Benjamin Mazar and Nelson Glueck. Around us were two thousand-year-old stones and debris. Time zoomed backwards; stones and structures not seen since Jesus' time lay eloquently before our feet. Stones pushed by Roman soldiers from the top of the Sanctuary (the precinct around the Temple; Heb. *ha-miqdash*) in late summer 70 CE were uncovered before 1970. Amazement was shared as we saw unearthed the destruction of "the House of the Lord" some two thousand years earlier.

In the spring of 1969, beneath Robinson's massive arch that is attached to the southwestern wall of the Temple, I bent over, noticing something riveting. I soon placed in a glass jar ashes and burned timbers from the conflagration of 70. Subsequently, archaeologists exposed streets, first-century shops, numerous *mikva'ot* (Jewish ritual baths) and sewers in which terrified women with their children had hidden moments before Roman soldiers slaughtered them.[1] The outlines of the gates in the Temple Mount known to Hillel and Jesus were studied and appreciated in a more perceptive manner than we could have imagined before the excavations.

After decades of excavations around the Temple Mount, we can appreciate that the Temple built by Herod the Great (40 to 37–4 BCE) was as magnificent as Josephus reported (and as the archaeologists writing in the present book reveal).[2] Josephus (37–100 CE), the valuable first-century Jewish historian and

---

1. Decades later, the southern sewer was discovered and unearthed. In a place where the women and children had hid, I picked up the remains of cooking pots.

priest, reported that the walls of the Temple were the greatest in human history (*Ant* 15.396). Josephus also judged the southern portico or "Royal Portico" to be "a construction more worthy of reporting than any other under the sun" (*Ant* 15.412).[3] Leading archaeologist Eilat Mazar evaluated the Temple known to Jesus as "truly one of the wonders of the world."[4]

The Temple was truly one of the unparalleled wonders of antiquity. We can imagine the loss felt by the future emperor, Titus, when he saw the Temple explode into flames and received only the spoils of war. What can be seen today gives us an indication of its magnificence. The massive, two-thousand-year-old retaining walls stand majestically before us, especially, in the Kotel, the Western Wall. Here, today, Jews come from all over the world to lament the destruction of "the House of God" and the "Holy City" by Roman soldiers in September of 70 CE.

Traditionally, the Temple's destruction is commemorated on the ninth of Av. That is also the designated day on which the Babylonians destroyed Solomon's Temple, approximately 650 years earlier. The ninth of Av remains a day of mourning for the Jews throughout the world; on it they remember the destruction of the First and Second Temples.

Beneath the Temple Mount one may today examine Corinthian columns; these sentinels may be imagined to bespeak exceptional porticoes, including the Royal Portico, which once existed in the Sanctuary far above the first-century streets. The walls of the Temple mount are finely chiseled stones with incised borders; these elegant stones are called Herodian ashlars.

Gates can now be seen on the west of the Temple Mount (others are to the north, now under the homes of Arab Israelis). On the south, the Huldah Gates remain visible (that name derives from memories of the First Temple). The ancient architects made exits larger than entrances; they knew that worshippers trickle in but pour out.

The stairways and entrances under the El Aksa mosque (not open to the public) indicate the grandeur that Jews like Jesus would have witnessed as they ascended to the Hill of the Lord. Like no temple in Rome and few temples in antiquity, the Jerusalem Temple dominated and defined Jerusalem, one of the most amazing cities of the ancient world. The *Temple Scroll* indicates the widespread veneration of the Temple by Jews already in about 100 BCE, when

---

2. See the description of the Temple by Josephus in *Ant* 15.11. Josephus hailed Herod's Temple as "the most glorious of his actions."

3. ἔργον δ' ἦν ἀξιαφηγητότατον τῶν ὑφ' ἡλίῳ.

4. Eilat Mazar, *The Walls of the Temple Mount* (Jerusalem: Shoham Academic Research and Publication, 2011), 13.

it was written. This scroll defines what was to be allowed, in terms of *halakot* (Jewish laws and customs),[5] in Jerusalem, and elsewhere in the Holy Land. Note for example this passage:

> And you shall make a rampart around the Sanctuary one hundred cubits wide which shall separate between the holy Sanctuary and the city, so they shall not enter confused into the midst of my Sanctuary and they shall not profane it; but they shall sanctify my Sanctuary. And they shall revere my Sanctuary [in] which I shall dwell in their midst. (*Temple Scroll* 46.9-12)[6]

Archaeologists working in the Lower Galilee, the setting of much of Jesus' ministry, have uncovered first-century houses made of stone or basalt. They are usually one story high and made of stones two men could carry. The Temple Mount, on the other hand, boasts some of the most majestic stones ever used by engineers. A person near the Temple Mount today can see stones weighing over thirty-five tons; one is part of Robinson's Arch. Further north in an underground tunnel, one may stop and touch one gigantic stone that weighs approximately 570 tons. It is in the western retaining wall of the Temple. The builders of Herod the Great placed it there shortly before the birth of Jesus of Nazareth.

The stupendous nature of such large stones needs to be contextualized. The largest stones in the Temple Mount dwarf those used in the construction of Egypt's massive pyramids. No stone in the pyramids weighs over seventy tons. And no stone used by builders with massive equipment today weighs over one hundred tons. Yet, the stone put in place by builders just before Jesus' birth weighs about 570 tons. Herod's Temple Mount in Jerusalem was the largest in the ancient world, being more than twice the size of Trajan's later temple in Rome.

---

5. Jews in antiquity, maybe primarily after 70 CE, considered the basic study curriculum to include Torah (Old Testament) and Oral Torah. The latter was a mixture of *halakot* (rules), *tosafot* (supplements to Mishnah and Torah), and *aggadot* (non-legal traditions and semi-narratives). Some rabbinic traditions privilege Oral Torah (p. *Ber* 1.7 3b) others imply the "Two Torahs" are equal (*Sifre Deut. Piska* 351 [ed. Finkelstein, 408]). What had been Oral Tradition in Jesus' day was redacted into Mishnah about 200–220. Social needs, the crises of the two massive revolts against Rome, and the vast geographical diffusion of Jews from Spain to Adiabene helped shape Mishnah and Tosephta (late third century CE). See Steven T. Katz in *The Cambridge History of Judaism*, vol. 4 (Cambridge: Cambridge University Press, 2006), 16–18.

6. J.H. Charlesworth, with L. Schiffman et al., eds. *The Temple Scroll and Related Documents*, Princeton Theological Seminary Dead Sea Scrolls Project 7 (Tübingen: Mohr Siebeck, 2011), 349–51.

Jesus' Galilean followers were used to simple dwellings. Jerusalemites knew some of the most sophisticated architecture anywhere in the ancient world, including not only the Temple but also Herod's palaces, the houses of high priests, and the Antonia Fortress. Note the assessment of Eilat Mazar:

> As seen today, the Temple Mount compound is the fruit of Herod's vision. He rebuilt the Temple on a grand scale, doubling the size of the existing compound and making it inestimably more magnificent than ever before . . . It was Herod's creativity, originality, power, perfectionism, and audacity that made the endeavor a reality, and one that captured his spirit and persona.[7]

Now, some passages in the New Testament take on new meaning thanks to archaeological research. Recall the amazement of Jesus' disciples: "As Jesus came out of the Temple, one of his disciples said to him, 'Teacher, look, what wonderful stones and what wonderful buildings!'" (Mark 13:1 [my translation]).

WHAT WAS THE TEMPLE?

For many early Jews, the Jerusalem Temple was the *axis mundi*; that is, the Temple was the center of the world, and the specific spot where heaven meets earth was Zion. Jerusalem's Temple is the only official site for worship and sacrifice according to the Pentateuch, which early Jews imagined was written by Moses.

The Temple was the cause of some factionalism within Judaism, as we know from studying the Dead Sea Scrolls, the Samaritan texts, and Josephus. Nevertheless, the Jerusalem Temple was primarily the magnetic force that united Jews throughout the civilized world. At least once, Philo traveled from Alexandria to Jerusalem to observe the required pilgrimages. Following Ezekiel's claim (38:12), the authors of *1 Enoch* 26:1 and *Jubilees* 8:19, pre-100 BCE Jewish compositions, declared that Jerusalem was the center of the earth.

Second, the Temple was the center for the arts and music. The Levites chanted and led worship. The Book of Psalms, believed by early Jews to be composed by David, was the "Hymnbook of the Temple." It was celebrated with drums, trumpets, cymbals, and harps. Dancing was a way of expressing joy for knowing God and revealing God's will.

Third, the Temple was not only the official place for sacrifice and celebration; it was a bank depository for Jews throughout the world. Wealth,

---

7. Mazar, *The Walls of the Temple Mount*, 15.

the "Temple tax," and gifts poured into the Holy City from far to the East and from far to the West; for example, from Adiabene (whose royalty converted to Judaism about the time of Jesus), from Alexandria, Antioch, Rome, and Spain.

Fourth, it was the center for teaching. Jews focused study on Torah and explained the oral interpretation of it. Most likely the form of the Hebrew Scriptures (the Old Testament) that is used by Jews and Christians today was the version preferred by Sadducees and others connected with the Temple cult.

Fifth, those in the Temple defined the time of prayer and festivals. From the Temple, Jewish heralds announced the times of the day, the festivals, and the year. These were signaled by the blowing of the trumpet or shofar. A stone with the inscription "for the blowing of the trumpet" has been found on pavement near the southwest corner of the Sanctuary (to be discussed later in this chapter). It fell there in 70 when Roman soldiers pushed it from the top of the wall.

THE THREE MAJOR TERMS FOR "THE TEMPLE" IN THE NEW TESTAMENT

Besides *Jerusalem* and *Zion*, which, intermittently, are employed as synonyms for "Temple," at least three important terms designated the Temple.

First, the Greek noun *hieron* (ἱερόν) denotes "the holy place," or "Sanctuary"; that is, the whole Temple precinct with its buildings and courts (the Hebrew term is *miqdaš*). The noun *hieron* occurs seventy-one times in the New Testament (nine in Mark, eleven in Matthew, fourteen in Luke, twenty-five in Acts, eleven in John, and once in Paul).

Second, the Greek noun *naos* (ναός) usually specifies the building within the Sanctuary; that is, the Temple building (the Hebrew term is *beth miqdaš*, literally "House of the Sanctuary"). The noun *naos* occurs twenty-one times in the Gospels (three times in Mark, nine in Matthew, four in Luke, two in Acts, and three in John), eight times in the Pauline corpus (four times in 1 Corinthians, twice in 2 Corinthians, and once each in Ephesians and 2 Thessalonians), and sixteen times in Revelation. Twenty of these forty-five times, an author intends to mean the Jerusalem Temple.

Third, New Testament authors employed the Greek noun *oikos* (οἶκος) to signify the Temple; they inherited this term from the Old Testament (the Hebrew term is *beth*, or "house"). As many other early Jews, the New Testament authors refer to the Temple as "the House of God." In the Old Testament, "the House of God" denoted the tabernacle (Deut. 23:18; 1 Kgs. 8:11-20), Solomon's Temple (1 Kgs. 12:27; Jer. 20:1), and even pagan temples (Judg. 9:4; 2 Kgs. 10:21). In the New Testament, the "House of God" continues to denote the Jerusalem Temple (Matt. 12:4; Mark 2:26; 11:17; Luke 6:4; John 2:16, 17). Jesus spoke of "my Father's house" (cf. John 2:16), which was to be an international house for prayer (Mark 11:15-17; cf. Isa. 56:7; 60:7 [lxx]) rather than a "house for trade" (John 2:16; cf. Zech. 14:21).

Early Jews choose "house" to denote the earthly and the heavenly Temple that was above the physical structure in east Jerusalem. New Testament authors chose "house of prayer" (οἶκος προσευχῆς) sometimes to refer to the Temple. Eventually, Jesus' followers innovatively extended the meaning of "God's house" to denote the "church" (e.g. Eph. 2:19-22; Heb. 3:1-6), whose communal character was emphasized in the concepts of the "spiritual house" (1 Pet. 2:5) and God's Temple (1 Cor. 3:16; 6:19).

PRESUPPOSITIONS: JESUS AND THE TEMPLE

One of the main purposes of the symposium at which these papers were first presented was to evaluate the supposition, or claim, that Jesus led a movement that was, in principle, opposed to the Temple or its worship. Here I choose four different scholars to illustrate how, in various ways, the academy and church have been informed that Jesus was against the Temple cult and sought, symbolically at least, to destroy the Temple.

WALTER BAUER

Among early twentieth-century German scholars, the desire to distance Jesus from the life and practice of the Temple was bound up with larger efforts to disassociate Jesus from Judea, while emphasizing his Galilean provenance. Judea is the home of Judeans or Jews; but Galilee, it was thought, was not Jewish.

A clear expression of this false portrayal is found in an important 1927 article entitled "Jesus der Galiläer" by the erudite Walter Bauer, who was then a professor at the University of Göttingen in Germany. Bauer's essay serves to emphasize the influence of Galilean traditions—over against those of Judea—upon Jesus. Concerning Jesus and the Temple, he writes,

> According to tradition, Jesus, when he examined his teaching in connection with Scripture, did so from the perspective of prophetic preaching. He did not work as a herald of the law. Much more can be said to the contrary. Never had he stressed the necessity for sacrifice. The Temple is for him a battleground during his last days, not a place of worship. He adopts the saying of Hosea as his own: "I desire mercy and not sacrifice." He does not believe in Levitical purity and rejects for himself and his own the Fast. [My idiomatic translation][8]

Bauer influenced generations of Europeans to adopt the hypothesis that Jesus was not only against any form of sacrifice but was against the Temple. That institution was not a place of worship; it was a battlefield. In contrast to Bauer, I am persuaded that some traditions imply that Jesus was not against sacrifice and appreciated the necessity for ritual purity. Indeed, he must have entered a *mikveh* to purify himself or he could not have entered the Temple; and he advised a man whom he healed to go and immerse in the Pool of Siloam (John 9:7), which is a very large pool for ritual purification.

JOHN DOMINIC CROSSAN

More recently, one of the most influential effects of the Jesus Seminar has been to drive a wedge between Jesus and the Temple. John Dominic Crossan, in his *The Historical Jesus: The Life of a Mediterranean Jewish Peasant*, explicitly portrays Jesus as setting himself against the Temple. In discussing what he sees as the inevitable tension between the Temple and Jesus, Crossan states,

> Jesus was, as we have seen, atopic, moving from place to place, he coming to the people rather than they to him. This is an even more radical challenge to the localized univocity of Jerusalem's Temple, and its itinerancy mirrored and symbolized the egalitarian challenge of its protagonist. No matter, therefore, what Jesus thought, said, or did about the Temple, *he was its functional opponent, alternative,* and substitute; his relationship with it does not depend, at its deepest level, on this or that saying, this or that action. (355, emphasis added)

For Crossan, Jesus led a movement that challenged the Temple. Later, Crossan further states,

> I am not sure that poor Galilean peasants went up and down regularly to the Temple feasts. I think it quite possible that Jesus went to Jerusalem only once and that the spiritual and economic egalitarianism he preached in Galilee exploded in indignation at the Temple as the seat and symbol of all that was nonegalitarian,

---

8. W. Bauer, "Jesus der Galiläer." The origin: "Die Überlieferung läßt Jesus, soweit er bei seiner Verkündigung überhaupt den Anschluß an die Schrift sucht, an die prophetische Predigt anknüpfen. Als Herold des Gesetzes hat er nicht gewirkt. Weit eher läßt sich das Gegenteil sagen. Niemals betont er die Notwendigkeit der Opfer. Der Tempel ist ihm in seinen letzten Tagen Kampfplatz, nicht Stätte der Anbetung. Und er macht sich den Hoseaspruch zu eigen: "Barmherzigkeit will ich und keine Opfer." Von levitischer Reinheit hält er nichts und lehnt für sich und die Seinen das Fasten ab" (28).

patronal, and even oppressive on both the religious and the political level. His symbolic destruction simply actualized what he had already said in his teachings, effected in his healings, and realized in his mission of open commensality. (360)[9]

This understanding of Jesus and the Temple is also echoed in Crossan's more recent work. Commenting on passage about Jesus' "cleansing" of the Temple, Crossan states,

> Notice, first of all, the balance of deed and word, action and comment. The action is not, of course, a physical destruction of the Temple, but it is a deliberate symbolic attack. It *destroys* the temple by *stopping* its fiscal, sacrificial, and liturgical operations. (148)[10]

According to Crossan, Jesus attempts to destroy the Temple symbolically and stop its work and worship.

E.P. SANDERS

Far different from Bauer's attempt to distance Jesus from Judaism and from Crossan's portrayal of Jesus as a revolutionary who opposed the Temple's oppressive function are some proposals by E.P. Sanders. In his *Jesus and Judaism*,[11] Sanders focuses on Jesus' actions in the Temple. Sometimes, Sanders gives the impression that Jesus directs his words and actions against the Temple as an institution. Note these excerpts:

> Thus far, it appears that Jesus' demonstration was against what all would have seen as necessary to the sacrificial system, rather than against present practice. (66)

> Jesus' action is to be regarded as a symbolic demonstration . . . (69). The discussion of whether or not Jesus succeeded in interrupting the actual functioning of the temple points us in the right direction for seeing what *the action symbolized* but did not accomplish: it symbolized *destruction*. (70, emphasis added)

---

9. John Dominic Crossan, *The Historical Jesus: The Life of a Mediterranean Jewish Peasant* (New York:HarperOne, 1991). I deeply appreciate Crossan's insights and reflections on the historical Jesus, but I must confess that it is misleading to talk about a social construct called "a Mediterranean peasant."

10. John Dominic Crossan, *Jesus: A Revolutionary Biography* (New York: HarperCollins, 1994).

11. E.P. Sanders, *Jesus and Judaism* (Philadelphia: Fortress Press, 1985).

The import to those who saw or heard of it was almost surely, at least in part, that Jesus was attacking the temple service which was commanded by God . . . Thus I take it that the action at the very least symbolized an attack, and note that "attack" is not far from "destruction." But what does this mean? On what conceivable grounds could Jesus have undertaken to attack—and symbolize the destruction of—what was ordained by God? The obvious answer is that destruction, in turn, looks towards restoration. (70–71)

Thus *we conclude that Jesus publicly predicted or threatened the destruction of the temple,* that the statement was shaped by his expectation of the arrival of the eschaton, that he probably also expected a new temple to be given by God from heaven, and that he made a demonstration which prophetically symbolized the coming event. (75, emphasis added)

Our interpretation has the additional advantage of making sense of the acceptance of temple worship by the early apostles (Acts 2:46; 3:1; 21:26). They did not think that Jesus had considered it impure, but only that *the days of the present temple were numbered.* (76, emphasis added)

These influential opinions need to be brought into central focus. They have a common emphasis. All three influential scholars state or imply that Jesus resisted, rejected, or wanted to replace the Temple and its services. Is that historically accurate?

NICHOLAS PERRIN

In the recently published book entitled *Jesus the Temple*, Nicholas Perrin claims that the historical Jesus is to be perceived within a trajectory of counter-Temple movements. Perrin is convinced that Jesus claimed to embody the Temple. Note Perrin's words: "I wish to argue that Jesus of Nazareth saw himself and his movement as nothing less than the decisive embodiment of Yahweh's eschatological temple" (12).[12]

Perrin's conclusion would mean that Jesus himself, before 30 CE, rejected the present Temple and put himself in place of it. While it is clear that, prior

---

12. I am appreciative of J.P. Sweeney's overview and critique of N. Perrin's *Jesus the Temple*. Sweeney presented his paper during the 2011 annual meeting of the Evangelical Theological Society in San Francisco.

to Jesus, there were Jews who rejected and resisted one or another aspect of the Temple cult or the power of those who administered it, it appears artificial and a distortion of history to position all dissident Jews on a single anti-Temple trajectory, or even to describe these as movements in a single direction. The tension between those in power and those who lost power was often shifted rhetorically onto the Temple itself, but as we shall see, the polemic was intended sometimes against the representation of Jerusalem as the only place in which to worship God (the Samaritans), sometimes against all the priests in the Temple (the early Qumran texts), sometimes against some anti-Torah legislation of the priests (some Jesus traditions), and sometimes against only one or another High Priest (the struggles within the Temple and perhaps some of Jesus' followers from 30 to 70).

Although Perrin seeks to set Jesus within the context of early Judaism, the real effect of his work is to remove Jesus from Judaism by attributing to him a Christology that in fact appeared only after Jesus. It is also far from clear that Jesus, or his followers, saw the Jesus Palestinian Movement replacing the Temple; in fact, I will seek to argue in the next chapter that Jesus' followers hallowed the Temple and worshiped in it (which is the picture Luke paints in Acts). For the present, it must suffice to agree with the judgment of David Catchpole: "Some of those who pursue the current quest . . . of the historical Jesus are much inclined to find him somehow undermining, bypassing, or even substituting for, what the Temple represented."[13]

DISCRIMINATION

As we proceed to discern Jesus' attitude to the Temple, we need to be discriminating. Diverse architectural and sociological aspects of the Temple and its functions need to be distinguished. The Holy City, Jerusalem, the Temple, the Temple services, the Temple cult, the administration of a financial and political institution, and the changing of coinage in the Temple when lumped together present a complexity that may becloud the diversities in pre-70 Judaism. For example, Jesus may have loved the Temple but became enraged by the way Sadducees officiated in and controlled the Temple services and its cultic functions.

Another possibility presents itself. We have many Jewish texts in the canon and on its so-called fringes that laud the Temple but despise its operation. Thus, Jesus, as a devout adherent of Torah, could well have loved Jerusalem

---

13. David Catchpole, *Jesus People: The Historical Jesus and the Beginnings of Community* (Grand Rapids, MI: BakerAcademic, 2006), 228.

and Zion, worshiped in the Temple, chanted with the Levites, sacrificed under the tutelage of the High Priest,[14] even admired the Temple cult, but despised the way business was often conducted. Further, this objection to "operational" aspects of the Temple might have taken different forms. Later I will discuss the offensiveness caused by the image of a pagan god, Melkart, on the silver coins that were chosen to pay the Temple tax. It is quite understandable that such coins would have offended Jesus and caused a righteous outrage because they broke the second of the Ten Commandments. He would most likely have hated not only the pagan iconic coins used for exchange in the Temple by the "money changers," but also the unjust measures employed for exchanging coinage. (During Jesus' time, weights did not have a number that specified their heaviness; scales could be unbalanced without any perceptible defect. That unjust weights and measures were used in the Temple is not a creation of "Christian" writings; they are noted in Rabbinic writings as well.) Jesus' action might well have been intended to support the holiness of the Sanctuary against those who were polluting it and making God's House a house for trade. We should also distinguish between the ancient holy area of the Temple and the non-traditional extensions to the Temple Mount south, west, and probably north, made by Herod—who despite his self-presentation was regarded by many Jews as an outsider to Judaism and Torah observance. Herod's expansions were in the southern area of the Sanctuary, where the moneychangers are reputed to have been located. Did some Jews consider that because this area was Herod's addition, the moneychangers were not within the holy precincts of the Temple (and thus not bound to observe Temple-appropriate sanctity there)? Jesus may well have considered that *all* of the Sanctuary was holy ground, *including* Herod's extensions.

The historical context of Jesus' actions against the "moneychangers" brings into focus the possible interaction of a stew of abuses that we know from time to time prompted protests from ordinary Jews: corrupt on the part of high-placed Temple authorities, Roman incursion into the Holy Land, and greed on

---

14. The polemics against Caiaphas, the High Priest, who had a very long tenure (18 to 36–7 CE), increase as New Testament documents are composed. Caiaphas has been presented with too much negative bias; yet, the prophecy attributed to him about Jesus in John 11:47-53 needs ample discussion. It is virtually impossible to reconstruct the historical Caiaphas, although Josephus, who surprisingly seldom mentions Caiaphas during episodes of importance to the High Priest, gives his full name (Joseph Caiaphas [*Ant* 18]) and this name appears on an ossuary (bone box) found south of Jerusalem's first century walls. See James C. VanderKam, *From Joshua to Caiaphas: High Priests After the Exile* (Minneapolis: Fortress Press, 2004) and Adele Reinhartz, *Caiaphas the High Priest* (Minneapolis: Fortress Press, 2013). For a discussion of the Caiaphas ossuary, see Gibson, *The Final Days of Jesus* (New York: HarperCollins, 2009), 82–83.

the part of Jerusalem elites for more power. Jesus would have known about the Hasmoneans (the dynastic descendants of the Maccabees) and Herod the Great's hatred of them. Before Jesus' ministry, many Jews had resented the practice of rolling the office of king and priest into one powerful position, a practice that clearly began with the first Hasmonean king, Aristobulus, about 102 BCE. The Qumran Essenes, those who collected (or wrote) what we call the Dead Sea Scrolls, hated the Hasmonean priests with a vengeance, claiming they were destined for Sheol, or Hell. Many Scrolls indicate that the reason for the Essenes' retreat to the wilderness of Judea was to prepare the Way of YHWH and to decry the loss of the only true priestly lineage, the Zadokites and Aaronites. The desecration of the high priest's office continued under the Herodian dynasty; in my judgment, it is quite possible that illegitimate priests were appointed who were widely perceived as owing allegiance more to Rome than to God. Hence, Jesus' explosive actions in the Temple would have pleased many Jews, including some priests.

DID JESUS AVOID THE TEMPLE?

Too many Christians today assume, without adequate reflection, that Jesus despised the Temple. They might develop such perceptions from a focus on passages that indicate the priests' plot to kill Jesus, such as Mark 14:1-2 (cf. Matt. 26:1-5; Luke 22:1-2; John 11:45-53):

> It was two days before the Passover and the festival of Unleavened Bread. The chief priests and the scribes were seeking a way to arrest Jesus by stealth and kill him; for they said, "Not during the festival, or there may be a riot among the people."

The setting is the Temple and the time is Passover. According to this tradition, opposition to Jesus seems to come from some priests and authorities in the Temple. At the outset of our questioning, let us be open to the possibility that the quoted passage concerns an actual plot against Jesus, but this does not inform us of Jesus' attitude toward the Temple; most likely, however, the passage is not objective history, but reflects traditions that were shaped and reshaped between 30 and 70 CE that reveal strife between Jesus' earliest Jewish followers and other Jews connected with the Temple.

Many pastors, and some New Testament critics, tend to conclude that Jesus had no use for the Temple and only went to Jerusalem to fulfill the prophecies that he, as the Son of Man, was destined to die in (or in the vicinity of) Jerusalem (Mark 3:22; 7:1; 10:32-33; 11:1, 15, 27). They might connect those ostensible prophecies with Gospel depictions of concerted antagonism toward Jesus on the part of Temple personnel, as in Mark 11:27-28 (compare Matt. 21:23-27; Luke 20:1-8): "Again they came to Jerusalem. As he was walking in the Temple, the chief priests, the scribes, and the elders came to him and said, 'By what authority are you doing these things? Who gave you this authority to do them?'" Mark 11 does suggest a tension between the leaders in the Temple and Jesus, but this does not indicate Jesus' attitude toward the Temple. Again, distinctions are fundamental for answering our focused question: What did Jesus think of the Temple?

As we seek a clearer perception of Jesus' attitude to the Temple, we should distinguish among many concepts, notably Jerusalem as the Holy City versus a commercial center, the Temple as the holy House of God versus the religious and administrative institutions devised by Sadducees to control it, the Temple as a place of worship versus the Temple as a political extension of Rome, and the institution versus institutional rules and regulations. We should take into account *halakot* and folksongs that have come down to us that describe the manipulation of rules by corrupt priests, even the High Priest (e.g., Tosefta, *Minḥot* 13.21; Babylonian Talmud, *Pesaḥim* 57.1), and we should distinguish the abuses of the sacrificial cult, for which we have such documentation, from the cult itself.

Too often, the Temple as a holy place is not perceptively distinguished from excesses within the sacrificial cult. In the symposium from which these papers are drawn, we stressed distinctions and sought to improve perceptions through interrogative explorations of scientific, historical, archaeological, architectural, and theological issues related to the Temple.

Distinctions also should be made between Jesus and his disciples and between chronological periods. For perceptual clarity, it is imperative to distinguish between Jesus' time and the Evangelists' time. The first century may be divided into two phases: before 70 CE, when the Temple dominated Jewish culture and lives, and after 70, when the worship in the Temple ceased, since Jerusalem lay devastated and burned by Roman soldiers under the leadership of a future emperor.

ARCHAEOLOGY AND JESUS' PATH

Jesus heard Jews blow trumpets from the mount of the Temple. (The location of the trumpeters on the southwest corner of the Temple Mount is confirmed by the recovery of a stone that fell from above. The broken inscription seems to report the place of the trumpeting to announce the sacred hours or feasts.[15]) Over the past fifty years, archaeologists working south and west of the Temple

Mount have discovered walkways that would have been used by Hillel and Jesus, and *mikva'ot* they would have entered to make themselves pure so they could enter the Temple.

We can imagine the gates Hillel and Jesus entered and exited, and the porticoes they knew and frequented. We can see portions of the balustrades that warned non-Jews not to proceed further within the Sanctuary. Although these railings were supposedly in Greek and Latin, according to Josephus, only two have been found, both in Greek.[16] The warning is clear: Gentiles who proceed further into the Temple will lose their lives.

Archaeology gives substance and detail to what we can learn through biblical exegesis.[17] After all, the Gospels indicate that Jews from Galilee joined Jews from Judea and elsewhere in marveling at the massive and elegant Temple. Jesus perceived that the Temple was the place where God dwelt among his people Israel (Matt. 23:21; John 2:16). He believed that the Temple sanctified things within it (Matt. 23:17-21). We turn next to examine the textual (literary) evidence that may be relevant to Jesus' experience of the Temple.

JESUS' INFANCY AND THE TEMPLE

An early Christian composition not included in the New Testament canon, called *The Birth of Mary* or the *Protoevangelium of James*, highlights Mary's youth from the age of three to her marriage to Joseph. Prominent attention is given to the Temple and its institutions, and will merit further discussion in this volume. (The work mentions the name of Jesus' maternal grandmother, Anna, or Hannah. Another "Anna" is mentioned by Luke, an elderly widow of the tribe of Asher who serves daily in the Temple and was present when Jesus was first taken into the Temple; Luke 2:36-38. Perhaps Luke intends his readers to assume this was the time of Jesus' circumcision. According to this text, like Simeon, Anna, a prophetess, recognized Jesus as the Messiah.)

JESUS' YOUTH: BAR MITZVAH IN THE TEMPLE?

Only Luke describes Jesus' time in the Temple as a youth (Luke 2:41-51). One may dismiss the report as legend and a topos: Jesus is a wise youth, like Daniel, sharing wisdom with the great teachers in the Temple. But there may be a kernel of history in the story. Luke may be describing Jesus' bar mitzvah. As to

---

15. See the images in Leen Ritmeyer, *The Quest: Revealing the Temple Mount in Jerusalem* (Jerusalem: Carta, 2006), 57–58.

16. Ibid., 346.

17. See J.H. Charlesworth, ed., *Jesus and Archaeology* (Grand Rapids, MI: Eerdmans, 2006).

the description of Jesus' "amazing" understanding of the Torah, if Mozart could accomplish before the age of thirteen what another musical genius might not accomplish in adulthood, why could Jesus not have shown keen biblical insight? Genius is not defined by age. But it can be shaped by passion. Jesus was indeed obsessed with God. We shall never be able to discern how much history is in the Jesus story, but it is not wise to jettison too much as legend at the outset. No one can prove that Jesus went to the Temple for his bar mitzvah, but no one can disprove it either. It is conceivable, but certainly does not reveal Jesus' attitude as an adult to the Temple.

JESUS' JUDEAN MINISTRY

The Synoptic Gospels—Matthew, Mark, and Luke—portray Jesus as teaching primarily in Galilee and going to Jerusalem only at the end of his life. Near the end of Mark, the impression is given that after his death and resurrection, Jesus' disciples are to return to Galilee. Recall the last words of the "young man" in the last chapter of Mark (two angels in Matthew): "But go, tell his disciples and Peter that he [Jesus] is going before you to Galilee; there you will see him, as he told you" (16:7). According to this text, Galilee is the center of salvation, the Temple and Jerusalem are left behind; they are no longer the center of God's salvific work.

The author of the Gospel of John, however, describes Jesus going more than once to Jerusalem. For John, Jesus has a public ministry in Judea, and it is centered on the Temple. A careful reading of Mark as well often gives a reader the impression that Jesus has been to Jerusalem before.

Once, it was fashionable to jettison the Gospel of John from Jesus Research;[18] now, it is no longer acceptable to dismiss John in studying the historical Jesus.[19] The Fourth Evangelist knows Jerusalem intimately. He has amazing knowledge of the Temple and its environs, describing quite accurately the pools north and south of the Temple, at Bethzatha and Siloam, respectively.[20] According to John, Jesus hails the Temple as "my Father's house"

18. The use of the capital "Jesus Research" indicates the technical term I suggested should replace the unfortunate concept of "The Quest of the Historical Jesus." Christians may be devoted to Jesus Research, but they are not questing for someone they have lost. See Charlesworth, *Jesus Within Judaism*, Anchor Bible Reference Library 1 (New York: Doubleday, 1988).

19. See Charlesworth, "The Historical Jesus in the Fourth Gospel: A Paradigm Shift?" *Journal for the Historical Jesus* 8 (2010): 3–46.

20. See Charlesworth, "The Tale of Two Pools: Archaeology and the Book of John," *Near East Archaeological Society Bulletin* 56 (2011): 1–14.

(2:16). If these texts are reliable, Jesus evidenced a deep zeal for the Temple and worshipped there (John 2:17).

JESUS SITS IN THE TEMPLE AND WATCHES THOSE NEAR THE TREASURY

According to Mark and Luke, Jesus was known to sit in the Temple and watch proceedings. Recall the well-known account of the widow who put a two tiny copper coins in the Temple Treasury:

> He sat down opposite the treasury, and watched the crowd putting money into the treasury. Many rich people put in large sums. A poor widow came and put in two small copper coins, which are worth a penny. Then he called his disciples and said to them, "Truly I tell you, this poor widow has put in more than all those who are contributing to the treasury. For all of them have contributed out of their abundance; but she out of her poverty has put in everything she had, all she had to live on." (Mark 12:41-44; cf. Luke 21:1-4)

Frequently, scholars focus upon the widow in this passage. Now, let us refocus the lens to see Jesus in the Temple, watching events unfold. He observes something that allows him to share wisdom with his disciples. It is a social setting in which Jesus appears to be comfortable. Others, namely the priests, seem to accept and welcome him.

Other related passages suggest that, in the Temple, Jesus sometimes simply observed others. What do we learn? We comprehend that Jesus and his disciples felt at home in the Temple. It is not inconceivable that they, like many of their Jewish contemporaries, were attracted to the Temple as if it was a massive magnet. Imagining such events brings new connotations to Jesus' affirmation that the Temple is his Father's house.

JESUS' TEACHING IN JERUSALEM: THE TEMPLE

Many passages in the Gospels portray Jesus teaching in the Temple; he seems to teach there habitually. Perhaps the clearest report comes at the end of his teaching career, in words he speaks on the Mount of Olives as he looks at those who crossed the Kidron Valley and up into the Garden of Gethsemane to arrest him:

> Then Jesus said to them, "Have you come out with swords and clubs to arrest me as though I were a bandit? Day after day I was with you

in the Temple teaching, and you did not arrest me." (Mark 14:48-49 NRSV)

This report is supported by many other interludes in Jesus' life, according to the Evangelists. Jesus customarily and daily taught in the Temple, for the last week of his life, according to the Synoptics, and for some months, according to John.

Clearly, Jesus taught frequently in the Temple. Each Evangelist makes the Temple the central place for Jesus' teaching in Judea (Matt. 21:23, 26:55; Mark 12:35, 14:49; Luke 19:47, 20:1, 21:37; John 7:14, 7:28, 8:2, 18:20). The Third Evangelist emphasizes Jesus' daily teaching in the Temple:

> Every day he was teaching in the Temple, and at night he would go out and spend the night on the Mount of Olives, as it was called. And all the people would get up early in the morning to listen to him in the Temple. (Luke 21:37-38 NRSV)

Jesus' Attack on the Moneychangers: Why?

One of the best-known stories from the Gospels is Jesus' outburst in the Temple. What happened? Why? Too many experts have concluded that Jesus was attacking the Temple itself and its establishment.

Some Christians have told me that they consider Jesus most admirable except once, when he "lost his temper" in the Temple in this incident. I am convinced, to the contrary, that Jesus' actions before the moneychangers was a highlight in his life and proved his high morality. After all, to see a powerful person abuse a weaker one and do nothing is not supported by *halakot* (Jewish rules or moral codes) or moral theology. My understanding is that Jesus became angry at abuse and cheating within the Temple. Before substantiating this interpretation, let us recall Mark 11:15-20 (par. Matt. 21:12-17; Luke 19:45-48; John 2:13-22), a passage often-entitled "Jesus Cleanses the Temple":

> Then they came to Jerusalem. And he entered the Temple and began to drive out those who were selling and those who were buying in the Temple, and he overturned the tables of the money changers and the seats of those who sold doves; and he would not allow anyone to carry anything through the Temple. He was teaching and saying, "Is it not written, 'Is my house shall be called *a house of prayer for all the nations*'? But you have made it *a den of robbers*." . . . the whole crowd was spellbound by his teaching. And when evening came, Jesus and his disciples went out of the city. (Mark 11:15-20, emphasis added)

Too many scholars interpret this passage without recognizing the significance of the second italicized phrase. I understand this phrase to indicate that Jesus aligns himself with many Jews who sometimes perceived corruption, in both operation of the Temple cult and the financial transactions involved in the changing of money. The following passage from the Babylonian Talmud placarded the abuses of some high priests (most likely preserving pre-70 traditions):

> Woe is me because of the House of Kathros,
> Woe is me because of their pens. . . .
> For they are the high priests, and their sons are treasurers,
> And their sons-in-law are trustees,
> and their servants beat the people with sticks.[21]

If power corrupts, then the power in the Temple apparently corrupted some priestly families, like the House of Kathros. Sociologically, we should not resist recognizing the tension caused between wealthy priests and the less fortunate.

Evidence of the Kathros family was found during the excavations of the Upper City of Jerusalem; a weight belonging to "Bar Kathros" was found in an excavated house.[22] This weight, the curse on "the House of Kathros" in the Babylonian Talmud, and with the opulence of the houses of priests in the Upper City of Jerusalem help us imagine why many Jews considered the Kathros family corrupt.

There are many possible reasons why Jesus would have been upset by what was going on within the Temple, but any of these would mean that Jesus was *defending* the sanctity of the Temple, not seeking to abolish it. Jesus' actions in the Temple do not reveal a desire to destroy it; they suggest a zeal for the Temple and its mission.

The Qumranites—those who left us the Dead Sea Scrolls—considered the Temple institution polluted (see 1QpHab 8 and 9); other Jews, contemporaneously with Jesus, categorized the Temple priests as consumers of the poor's food, exterminators, "completely godless," and criminals. Some criticized the priests for even considering themselves so pure that to be touched causes pollution. Note, for example the *Testament of Moses* (a pre-70 Jewish composition):

---

21. Babylonian Talmud, *Pesahim* 57.1 and Tosefta, *Minhot* 13.21. See N. Avigad, *Discovery Jerusalem* (Nashville: Thomas Nelson, 1983), 130.

22. For a photograph of the weight, see Avigad, *Discovering Jerusalem*, 130.

They [the priests in Jerusalem] consume the goods of the [poor], saying their acts are according to justice, [while in fact they are simply] exterminators, deceitfully seeking to conceal themselves so that they will not be known as completely godless because of their criminal deeds [committed] all the day long, saying, "We shall have feasts, even luxurious winings and dinings. Indeed, we shall behave ourselves as princes." They, with hand and mind, will touch impure things, yet their mouths will speak enormous things, and they will even say, "Do not touch me, lest you pollute me in the position I occupy." [TMoses 7:6-10 in *OTP* 1.930]

In light of the comments made above, it now appears much clearer that Jesus' enraged response took place outside the Holy Place of the Pre-Herodian Temple and in the area of the Sanctuary extended southward by Herod the Great. Jesus knew that those demanding "entrance fees" were often overcharging Jews who wished to enter the Temple and to worship the only God. In light of historical reflections, Jesus' actions in the Temple courts seem to be an honorable and moral act of opposition to the exorbitant entrance fees being charged to the people. It is not an aspect of anti-Judaism in the New Testament. Jesus sought to restore honorable transactions and allow more Jews to enter the Sanctuary. Jesus contended that the Temple was not reserved only for priests and other wealthy Jews. In light of his actions and teachings, Jesus would have judged some rules to exclude the blind, lame, and impure from entering the Temple to be an unacceptable and excessive interpretation of Leviticus (cf. *Some Works of the Torah* [4QMMT]).

Some attention should be drawn to Jesus' quotation of the scroll (book) of Jeremiah (the reference to a "den of robbers" in Mark 11:17b is a quotation of Jer. 7:11). Jesus most likely had Jeremiah memorized. The pre-exilic prophet is exceptional in the history of prophecy. Later Jews honored Jeremiah and his scribe, Baruch, by composing a cycle of documents bearing their names (e.g. *4 Ezra* and *2 Bar.*). Jeremiah claimed that the Temple would be destroyed because of the sins of the Israelites (Jer. 7:1-34). Israelites and subsequent Jews had sinned and rejected God. Jeremiah's prediction of the Temple's destruction (Jer. 7:12-15) was fulfilled in the early sixth century BCE. The similar prediction that the Synoptic Gospels attribute to Jesus (Mark 13:1-2; Matt. 24:1-2; Luke 21:5-6), influenced by Jeremiah's prophecy, was fulfilled in 70 CE when Titus's troops burned the Temple. If Jesus' own thoughts are represented by Mark 13, they are not anti-Jewish; Jeremiah was not anti-Jewish and, as we have seen, many leading Jews agreed that there was corruption in the house of the Lord.

Jesus' reference to "a den of robbers" is multidimensional. According to Mark, Jesus quotes and derives authority for his words, not from a rabbi but from one of the greatest of the prophets. Jeremiah had characterized the Temple priests as those who turned God's house into a "den of robbers." According to Jeremiah, the priests in Jerusalem gave to themselves what the Torah had given solely to God. Jesus alludes to Jeremiah's depiction of priests who say, "we are safe" (Jer. 7:10). They are not; they are replacing the Creator's will with the presumption that a building will keep them safe.

Following Jeremiah and influencing Mark, Jesus indicates that the Temple is a "den" in which priests rob God's faithful and then retreat to hidden places, as into a robber's cave, to hide from others and plot further crimes. The priests are those who rob faithful Jews by converting a place of prayer into an emporium; they rob pilgrims and the poor, monopolizing exchanges of money, excessively charging to change bronze Jewish coins into silver, and relying on pagan silver that is (in Jesus' eyes) idolatrous.

Let me expand and explain this claim. Quite alarming to Jews who strictly believed the second commandment (not to make an image of God), and most likely to Jesus, was the fact that no coins, even Jewish coins that observed the second commandment, were allowed for payment of the entrance fee. All coins had to be exchanged for Tyrian shekels, which alone were valid for transactions in the Temple. While Herod the Great and his successors did not put an image on the coins they minted, both the Tyrian shekel and half-shekel depicted the King of Tyre, a pagan city on the Syrian coast of the Mediterranean. The coins show King Melkart portrayed as Hercules with this inscription: TYROU IERAS KAI ASYLOU, "[belonging] to inviolable and holy Tyre." Although the Temple authorities were apparently content to use the coins, presumably for economic or political convenience, it is quite conceivable that some Jews—in particular, apparently, Jesus—would have considered that the image of Melkart broke the Second Commandment and brought idolatry into the Temple. For Jesus, the Temple, not Tyre, was "inviolable" and "holy."[23]

Today, thousands of pre-70 coins have been found in and near Jerusalem; some of them are Tyrian shekels and half-shekels. All payments required the shekel and half-shekel; with the census, each Israelite male paid a half-shekel (Exod. 30:11-16; cf. mShekalim 2:4). According to Nehemiah 10:32, the levy

---

23. See P. Richardson, "Why Turn the Tables? Jesus' Protest in the Temple Precincts," in E.H. Lovering, Jr., ed., *Society of Biblical Literature Seminary Papers* 31 (1992): 507–23; U.C. von Wahlde, "Archaeology and John's Gospel," in *Jesus and Archaeology*, ed. J. H. Charlesworth (Grand Rapids, MI: Eerdmans, 2006), 521–84.

Figs. 6.1. Front of a Tyrian Half-Shekel; coin and photograph from the personal collection of J. H. Charlesworth.

was collected annually. Jesus paid this census tax, which is highlighted in the story of how at Jesus' instructions Peter found a silver coin (στατήρ, *statēr*) in a fish; Jesus told him to pay the Temple tax with it (Matt. 17:24-27).

Tyrian shekels and half-shekels are idolatrous. They break the second commandment, not to make any image, by displaying the face of Melkart, a pagan god. Moreover, the inscription on the coins celebrate Tyre as the holy city, not Jerusalem. One of the reasons for Jesus' rage in the Temple most likely was seeing these idolatrous coins that had to be bought by Jews, using Jewish bronze coins that were carefully minted not to break any commandment.

THE TEMPLE AND WHY JESUS WAS CRUCIFIED

The clearest fact about Jesus' life is that he was crucified. Why? There are many answers. We may begin with an aspect of Jesus' personality.

Despite the portraits of the nineteenth century Romantics, Jesus was not "mild" and "meek." He saw evil and became angry; that is wise. He saw corruptions within the Temple and was confrontational. He saw the powerful priests abuse the poor and became irate. Jesus could be confrontational, aggressive, and subversive to all in abusive power.

Figs. 6.2. Reverse of a Tyrian Half-Shekel; coin and photograph from the personal collection of J. H. Charlesworth.

Scholars have shown that Jesus' parables were not just literary means of pictorially making his message simple and memorable. His parables could be subversive and were often couched cryptically to avoid prosecution, but they were embodied political messages. At least one of his parables was directed against the High Priest and the sacrificial cult in the Temple.

Recall the well-known Parable of the Wicked Tenants taught by Jesus (Mark 12:1-12; Matt. 21:33-46; Luke 20:9-19). The parable derives from Jesus: It does not serve the needs of the post-Easter community and its proclamations (the *kerygmata*). Archaeologists have unearthed ancient structures exactly as Jesus describes them, including watchtowers (*Shomerim*). The parable reflects his time, and not the time either before or after him. During his life, Jewish farmers were losing their farms because of taxations by Romans, their collaborators, and priests. They were becoming tenants on a land that held their ancestors' bones, and in the land promised to them. Recall Mark 12:1-12 (RSV):

> Then he [Jesus] began to speak to them in parables. "A man planted a vineyard, put a fence around it, dug a pit for the wine press, and built a watchtower; then he leased it to tenants and went to another country. When the season came, he sent a slave to the tenants to collect from them his share of the produce of the vineyard. But they seized him, and beat him, and sent him away empty-handed. And again he sent another slave to them; this one they beat over the head and insulted. Then he sent another, and that one they killed. And so it was with many others; some they beat, and others they killed. He had still one other, a beloved son. Finally he sent him to them, saying, 'They will respect my son.' But those tenants said to one another, 'This is the heir; come, let us kill him, and the inheritance will be ours.' So they seized him, killed him, and threw him out of the vineyard. What then will the owner of the vineyard do? He will come and destroy the tenants and give the vineyard to others. Have you not read this scripture:
>
> 'The stone that the builders rejected
> has become the cornerstone;
> this was the Lord's doing,
> and it is amazing in our eyes'?"
>
> When they realized that he had told this parable against them, they wanted to arrest him, but they feared the crowd. So they left him and went away. [my translation]

Note the following five points.

First, Mark sets this parable in the Temple, where Jesus has been walking when he becomes embroiled in heated discussions with "the chief priests, the scribes, and the elders" (Mark 11:27-33). His words cause them to argue with each other; then Jesus tells the parable.

Second, the learned group perceives that Jesus "had told this parable against them" (Mark 12:12). We should not dismiss the possible historical accuracy of this tradition; it may not be an editorial expansion, since Mark's interests do not seem to shape the words. They seem to be historical: Many of these men were the finest scholars in antiquity. They knew Hebrew (in various scripts), Aramaic, and certainly some Latin and Greek. They represent the circles that knew and produced Targumic interpretations; that is, they not only translated Hebrew Scriptures to learned and simple Jews but also interpreted the texts. They were consummate teachers and not only priests who officiated in the Temple.

Third, the parable is highly metaphorical and quasi-allegorical. The "slaves" or servants are the prophets. The authors of the Dead Sea Scrolls show us that in Second Temple Judaism, the prophets are defined as "servants" (cf. 1QpHab 7). Thus, Jesus is referring to those servants and prophets, like Jeremiah and Isaiah, whom God sent to Israel, notably to the Temple priests, to accuse them of disobeying God. The "chief priests, the scribes, and the elders" had memorized the passages that Jesus quotes. They had developed an interpretation of this memorable passage; Jesus confounds them with his own biblical knowledge.

Evidence from the Dead Sea Scrolls confirms this exegesis. Jesus had developed the imagery of God's vineyard from Isaiah 5. Isaiah had compared Israel to "a vineyard," with God as "the owner of the vineyard." In Jesus' saying and in a Qumran manuscript (4Q500), Isaiah's image of "the vineyard" is linked to the Temple.

The author of 4Q500 apparently knew an exegesis of Isaiah in which "the vineyard of the Lord" was perceived to refer to the Temple. Only six lines are extant:

Text	Parallels in:
2 . . . your baca trees will blossom and . . .	
3 . . . a wine vat [bu]ilt among stones . . .	Isa. 5:1-7
4 . . . to the gate of the holy height . . .	*Tg. Isa.* 5:1 ["high hill"]
5 . . . your planting and the streams of your glory . . .	t*Sukkot* 3:15
6 . . . the branches of your delights . . .	
7 . . . your vine[yard . . .]	Isa. 5:1-7

Document 4Q500, line 5, frg.1, ("streams of your glory"), is in harmony with a rabbinic interpretation of Isaiah 5:1-2, as for example in the Tosephta (*t. Sukk.* 3:15); and this passage identifies the "tower" and "wine vat" of Isaiah with the "Temple" and "altar" (cf. *t.Me'il.* 1:16). J.M. Baumgarten first observed the importance of the Isaiah Targum and Rabbinic scriptural exegesis for 4Q500.[24] Subsequently, more scholars have agreed with his research and conclusion.[25] Thus, the text found at Qumran strengthens the claim that Jewish exegesis connected vineyard and Temple.

Fourth, the parable represents Jesus' high self-esteem. He is the last of the prophets sent by God, and he is God's son. The description of the son's death is not crucifixion; this indicates another reason why this parable originated prior to 30 CE (when Jesus was crucified) and that it is, ultimately, from Jesus, not a later tradent. Perhaps, about forty years later, just before or just after the destruction of Jerusalem and the Temple by Roman soldiers, Mark may have added: "He (God) will come and destroy the tenants and give the vineyard to others." But such a conceivable addition proves the tradition existed and was available for editing.

Fifth, Jesus (and not Mark, as many commentators claim) adds an explanatory comment that is on target with Jesus' polemics against the Temple establishment. Note these words:

> "The stone that the builders rejected
> has become the cornerstone;
> this was the Lord's doing, ..." (12:10-11)

The Targumim help us understand the well-couched double meaning (*double entendre*) and use of paronomasia or pun, probably by the linguistic genius Jesus (Mark was a poor writer). Jesus spoke in Aramaic but he may, in this parable spoken in the Temple, have used some Hebrew subtleties, since Psalm 118 was composed and probably memorized in Hebrew. In that language, *ben* is "son"

---

24. J.M. Baumgarten, "4Q500 and the Ancient Exegesis of the Lord's Vineyard," *Journal of Jewish Studies* 40 (1989): 1–6.

25. Notably, see G.J. Brooke, "4Q500 1 and the Use of Scripture in the Parable of the Vineyard," *Dead Sea Discoveries* 2 (1995): 268–49; B.D. Chilton, *A Galilean Rabbi and His Bible: Jesus' Use of the Interpreted Scripture of His Time,* Good News Studies 8 (Wilmington, DE: Michael Glazier, 1984), 111–16; C.A. Evans, "Jesus and the Dead Sea Scrolls," in *The Dead Sea Scrolls After Fifty Years: A Comprehensive Assessment,* ed. P.W. Flint and J.C. VanderKam, 2 vols. (Leiden: Brill, 1999), 2:573–98, esp. 588–91; Evans, "On the Vineyard Parables of Isaiah 5 and Mark 12," *Biblische Zeitschrift* 28 (1984): 82–86.

and *eben* is "stone." Priests who lived in Jerusalem and spoke Hebrew would perceive Jesus' pun; and it is possible Jesus crafted and spoke this parable in Hebrew, to make clear he was targeting the priests who comprehended spoken Hebrew or Aramaic (where the paronomasia is also obvious). N.T. Wright offers important insights: "In case it may be thought that the interpretative thread has now been stretched beyond breaking point, we may note finally that the 'stone' is in fact also closely linked with the 'son' of the parable. The Aramaic for 'stone' in Daniel 2 is *eben* (the word is the same in Hebrew); the normal Hebrew for 'son', as for instance in 2 Samuel 7, is *ben*. It did not take much skill in biblical interpretation for the pun (*eben* is *ben*) to be observed and exploited."[26]

As the stone had been "rejected," so Jesus is rejected by the supposed builders of God's Kingdom.[27] Yet, the Lord has been "doing" (Ps. 118) and creating; he has made the *son* (*ben*), Jesus, "the cornerstone (*eben*)." This building symbolism is rich; the cornerstone was the principal stone, the focal point of a major building, and its foundation. Most likely, Jesus made wordplay between the "son" (*ben*), the "stone" (*eben*), and the integrity of the building, the Temple. The historicity of this confrontation seems likely; Jesus and the priests knew they were moving towards a tragedy.[28]

Were there messianic overtones to Jesus' parable? Jesus is not the only Jew who interpreted Psalm 118 in terms of messianism and Davidic imagery. In the Targum to the Psalms (*TgPsalm* 118:23-26), Jews paraphrased the Psalm and added clear royal imagery and Davidic, messianic meaning. Note the latter Targum (which may preserve ancient traditions): "The young man which the builders abandoned is among the sons of Jesse and is worthy to be appointed to kingship and rule" (*TgPsalm* 118:23-26). What bearing has this messianic interpretation of a Psalm passage, cited by Jesus, upon Jesus' claim?

The priests in the Temple had, for centuries, beginning with the Hasmoneans in the second century BCE, defended their legitimacy against others who claimed to be in fact the legitimate priests, "the sons of Aaron," of whom some were exiled to Qumran. The priests in the Temple were so

---

26. N.T. Wright, *Jesus and the Victory of God* (London: Society for Promoting Christian Knowledge, 1996), 501.

27. See the reflections by F.F. Bruce, "New Wine in Old Wine Skins: III. The Corner Stone," *Expository Times* 84 (1972–1973): 231–35; and J.D.M. Derrett, "'The Stone That the Builders Rejected,'" in *Studia Evangelica IV*, ed. F.L. Cross, Texte und Untersuchungen 102 (Berlin: Akademie, 1968), 180–86.

28. See the helpful discussion by B. Randall and B. Kvasnica, "Temple Authorities and Tithe-Evasion: The Linguistic Background and Impact of the Parable of the Vineyard, the Tenants and the Son," in *Jesus' Last Week: Jerusalem Studies in the Synoptic Gospels*, vol. 1, Jewish and Christian Perspectives Series 11 (Leiden: Brill, 2006), 53–80, emphasis in original.

inflamed that "they wanted to arrest" Jesus. Why? Why would a simple story so enrage them? Because they understood not only that the parable was targeted against them but also that their legitimacy—as well as power, prestige, and purse—were being eroded by someone who blasphemously insinuated, within the Temple, that he was the son, the heir, and the cornerstone.

Moreover, Jesus had quoted Psalm 118:22: "The stone that the builders rejected has become the chief cornerstone" (NRSV). The Temple authorities who knew this Psalm probably heard echoes of it in Jesus' words. Most of them could not prove or claim that they descended from "the house of Aaron" (118:3), and were now confronted by one who has the audacity to be he "who comes in the name of the LORD" and receives blessings from the crowd within "the house of the LORD" (118:26).

Such reflections bring to mind a collage of biblical passages and their ancient interpretations for our contemplation. Had Jesus mimicked Solomon riding on a donkey through the Kidron (1Kgs. 1:38) and up into the Holy City, acting out Zechariah's prophecy (Zech. 9:9)? Later, did he imagine a scenario in the Temple by which priests and an heir—indeed the Davidic Messianic King—would chant Psalm 118? Had the crowd's "Hosanna" encouraged Jesus to imagine that his interpretation was divinely inspired? Did that euphoria exacerbate Jesus' disheartening reception when he ascended into the Temple? Had Jesus planned to suggest he could be the Messiah sent by God? Had he hoped that the priests would acknowledge his destiny as "son"? Biblical interpretation represented by the Dead Sea Scrolls (not limited to Qumran), Mark, and Targumic evidence converge to help shine a clearer light on Jesus' attitude to the ruling priests and the Temple and also suggest a possibility for Jesus' self-understanding.

This reconstructed scenario of Jesus' entry into Jerusalem and ascent to the Temple seems to be historical. Before affirming it, one should remember that Jesus, from months of debating in Lower Galilee with those sent out from Jerusalem, knew that the source of the opposition to him came from Jerusalem and from within the Temple. Perhaps Jesus was hoping all was changing at Passover, the time when Jews were joyous about God's past acts of salvation and expectation of a new deliverance from bondage (now by Rome). To assume that this event is not historical and that the Evangelists created it to show Jesus' superiority over priests is undermined by evidence of corruption among first-century priests, such as Josephus's report that the chief priests were stealing the tithe from other priests; some of the later then died of starvation (*Ant* 20.205-07).

JESUS' RELATION WITH PRIESTS AND SCRIBES

Again, it is easy to commit the "all fallacy," and assume that Jesus despised *all* priests. We could compound the error and claim that *all* priests rejected the teachings of a simple Galilean who misled Jews. Against these unperceptive and sweeping claims lies an appreciation of Jesus by many priests and scribes. In the Temple, an anonymous scribe admires Jesus' wisdom and right teachings. The passage is found only in Mark:

> Then the scribe said to him, "You are right, Teacher; you have truly said that 'he is one, and besides him there is no other'; and 'to love him with all the heart, and with all the understanding, and with all the strength,' and 'to love one's neighbor as oneself,'—this is much more important than all whole burnt offerings and sacrifices." When Jesus saw that he answered wisely, he said to him, "You are not far from the kingdom of God." After that no one dared to ask him any question. (Mark 11:32-34)

Perhaps Jesus had many friends among the scribes and priests. One name looms large, that of a man who was certainly a powerful priest: Joseph of Arimathea. Joseph was "from the Jewish town of Arimathea" (Luke 23:50); he was "a respected member" of the Jewish council (Mark 15:43), "a good and righteous man" (Luke 23:50) and a "disciple of Jesus" (John 19:38). This report and the debates within the Temple indicate that some priests favored Jesus' position; clearly not all wanted him arrested.

JESUS' PREDICTION OF THE TEMPLE'S DESTRUCTION AND THE PROPHETS

Mark, who wrote close to 70 CE, knew about the destruction of Jerusalem and the Temple, either impending or recent. Conceivably, he altered Jesus' original words (which would have antedated 30 CE). But Jesus himself, perceiving the growing hatred against the Romans, could have predicted the destruction of the Temple. If so, he might have been influenced by Isaiah, Jeremiah, Ezekiel, and the authors of Lamentations and Daniel. For these prophets and authors, God willed the destruction of the Temple or Sanctuary. Why? They believed that Israel had been unfaithful (see Ps. 118). Only a selection of these ancient traditions, known to Jesus, should suffice now:

- "I will make this house like Shiloh" (Jer. 26:6, 26:9);
- "I will do to the house called by my name as I did to Shiloh" (Jer. 7:14);
- "I am about to profane my Sanctuary (*mqdš*)" (Ezek. 24:21);

- "the people … will destroy the city and the Sanctuary (*mqdš*)" (Dan. 9:26);
- "the Lord has abandoned his Sanctuary (*mqdš*)" (Lam. 2:7);
- "vengeance for his Temple" (Jer 50:28)
- "it is the vengeance of the Lord for his Temple (*hykl*)" (Jer. 51:11).

Another memorable passage opens the Book of Isaiah. The prophet reports that God rejects the sacrifices made in the Temple because of the unfaithfulness of God's people. Sacrifices in the Temple are now worthless until the people repent and have their sins forgiven:

What to me is the multitude of your sacrifices?
says the Lord;
I have had enough of burnt offerings of rams
and the fat of fed beasts;
I do not delight in the blood of bulls,
or of lambs, or of goats.
When you come to appear before me,
who asked this from your hand?
Trample my courts no more;
bringing offerings is futile;
incense is an abomination to me.
New moon and sabbath and calling of convocation—
I cannot endure solemn assemblies with iniquity.
Your new moons and your appointed festivals
my soul hates;
they have become a burden to me,
I am weary of bearing them.
When you stretch out your hands,
I will hide my eyes from you;
even though you make many prayers,
I will not listen;
your hands are full of blood.
Wash yourselves; make yourselves clean;
remove the evil of your doings
from before my eyes;
cease to do evil,
learn to do good;
seek justice,

> rescue the oppressed,
> defend the orphan,
> plead for the widow.
> Come now, let us argue it out,
> says the Lord:
> though your sins are like scarlet,
> they shall be like snow;
> though they are red like crimson,
> they shall become like wool.
> If you are willing and obedient,
> you shall eat the good of the land;
> but if you refuse and rebel,
> you shall be devoured by the sword;
> for the mouth of the Lord has spoken.
> (Isa. 1:11–20, NRSV emphasis added)

Since Jesus was profoundly influenced by Isaiah, and knew this passage, it seems to follow that Jesus also affirmed that sacrifices were acceptable to God only by priests who were pure and worthy to make such sacrifices. Jesus may have admired the high priest office, but he did not approve of the corruption in some aspects of the Temple cult. Jesus admired the small offering of a widow in the Temple treasury; thus the words of Isaiah help us imagine the mind of Jesus. Recall some of Isaiah's words:

> your hands are full of blood.
> Wash yourselves; make yourselves clean;
> remove the evil of your doings
> from before my eyes;
> cease to do evil,
> learn to do good;
> seek justice,
> rescue the oppressed,
> defend the orphan,
> plead for the widow.
> Jesus did plead for the widow in the Temple.

Comparing Jesus and His Contemporary, Yohanan ben Zakkai

The probability of what has been concluded about Jesus and the Temple is strengthened and put into a meaningful context by comparing Jesus (c. 7

BCE–30 CE) with Yohanan ben Zakkai (c. 1–80 CE).[29] The latter was the most famous disciple of Hillel and Shammai (m*Abot* 2:8 and j*Ned* 5:39b), but not a Davidic like Jesus and Hillel. I now choose to emphasize four similarities between these two great teachers, who lived when the Temple defined life for most Jews.[30]

First, both Jesus and Yohanan were from Galilee. Jesus was from Nazareth and Yohanan was from 'Arab (= Gabara). Certainly for Jesus and likely for Yohanan, these Galilean villages were their initial homes for about twenty years. According to traditions, Jesus taught in the Nazareth synagogue, and Yohanan, while in 'Arab, answered questions of a legal nature that concerned the observance of the Sabbath (*Shab.* 16:7, 22:3); this tradition stimulated the tradition that he lived in Galilee for eighteen years.

Second, both were disappointed by the reception received from fellow Galileans. Jesus left Nazareth. Jesus' Galilee ministry was on the northwestern shores of the Sea of Galilee; he is reported to have cursed the villages in which he had centered his ministry, namely Chorazin, Bethsaida, and Capernaum (Matt. 11:2-23; Luke 10:13-15). Likewise, Yohanan was so disturbed by the Galileans' faint religiosity that he reportedly cursed them: "O Galilee, Galilee, you hate the Torah; hence, you will fall into the hands of robbers!" (y. *Shab.* 15d).

Third, both taught in the Temple. The Evangelists reported that Jesus frequently taught in the Temple (e.g. Mark 12:35). A passage reports that Yohanan sat in the Temple's shadow and lectured throughout the whole day (Pes 26a). Jesus may have chosen to teach frequently within the Temple. Yohanan could not choose the Temple for most of his teachings since it had been destroyed. Jesus died long before the Temple was burned. Yohanan lived long after it. Both were teachers with disciples, but Yohanan's were more devoted and attentive to his thoughts. Jesus' disciples were not primarily students and resisted some of his pronouncements.

Fourth, both Jesus and Yohanan loved the Temple and its worship celebrations. Yet, each ostensibly prophesied its destruction. Jesus predicted the demise of the sanctuary (Mark 13:2). Likewise, Yohanan is reported to have exclaimed something of a similar nature. According to one legend, the gates of the Temple had apparently opened of themselves. Thereupon, Yohanan

29. For a definitive treatment of Yohanan ben Zakkai, see Jacob Neusner, *First Century Judaism in Crisis: Yohanan ben Zakkai and the Renaissance of Torah* (Nashville: Abingdon, 1975). See *Encyclopaedia Judaica* 10.148–54.

30. It is surprising that Josephus (who does mention John the Baptizer and Jesus from Nazareth) passes over this famous rabbi, not even mentioning him by name.

denounced the Temple: "O Temple, Temple, why do you frighten yourself? I know of you that you shall be destroyed. Zechariah, the son of Iddo, [Zech. 11:1] formerly prophesied concerning you, 'Open your doors, O Lebanon, that the fire may devour your cedars.'"[31]

Of course, deep differences distinguished Jesus from Yohanan. First, Jesus did not legislate rules for his disciples for life after the destructions of 70; rather, they interpreted his death as salvific and a perfect substitute for the atoning sacrifices. Yohanan, however, developed rules to replace the functions of the Temple. For example, he interpreted the words of Hosea 6:6, "I desired mercy, and not sacrifice," to comfort his followers after the destruction of the Temple and the cessation of the sacrifice for atonement (*Abot R. N.* 4). Thus, he sought to persuade authorities to focus on prayer as a replacement of animal sacrifices; and clearly this advice enabled Rabbinic Judaism to survive with synagogues as houses for prayer.[32] Most likely, it was Yohanan who developed liturgy that allowed Judaism to survive, even thrive, without a sacrificial system.[33]

Second, unlike Yohanan, Jesus was deeply influenced by Jewish apocalypticism, proclaimed the dawning of God's Rule (the Kingdom of God), challenged priestly definitions of purity and rules for Sabbath observance, and most likely held some messianic self-understandings. Unlike Jesus, Yohanan was interested in preparing Jews for life after the destruction of the Temple and its means of praising God, obtaining forgiveness, and ordering daily, monthly, and yearly cycles.

Third, while Jesus was crucified by Roman soldiers, Yohanan attained unparalleled political and religious powers thanks to the ostensible benevolence of a Roman leader. For example, at Yohanan's order, Jews blew a ram's horn (*shofar*) to announce the beginning of New Year's Day in Yavneh (Jamnia), as they had previously done from the Temple in Jerusalem (Mishnah*Rosh ha-Shanah* 4:1, 3).

MIGHT JESUS HAVE TURNED AGAINST THE TEMPLE SACRIFICES IN HIS LAST DAYS?

A caveat: Vast amounts of data thus suggest Jesus appreciated the Temple and worshipped there. During his early ministry, he may have wished that

---

31. *Yoma* 39b; cf. *Abot de Rabbi Nathan*, Recension B, 7.

32. For more discussion, consult "Johanan B. Zakkai," *Jewish Encyclopedia.com*, http://www.jewishencyclopedia.com/view.jsp?artid=362&letter=J#ixzz1EQ3IrN5V.

33. See the brilliant succinct summary of Yohanan by Geza Vermes in *Who's Who in the Age of Jesus* (London: Penguin Books, 2005), 254–55.

the Temple would be reformed. It is possible, however, that during his last visit to Jerusalem, with enthusiastic crowds from many areas of the Jewish world cheering him and hoping for another of God's miracles, and in face of the growing opposition from some in the high priestly family, Jesus uttered a polemic against the Temple and predicted its destruction (as Crossan and Sanders have argued).

It is conceivable, though historians debate its probability, that when Jesus joined his disciples for the last meal he would share with them, during Passover, he uttered the now so familiar words about his body and blood that have subsequently been understood in Christianity as the establishment of the Eucharist. These words have further been understood as evidence that Jesus imagined a movement that did not need the Temple sacrifices. The Gospels, of course, do not distinguish between Jesus' authentic words and words attributed to him over decades. But nowhere in the Gospels does Jesus instruct his disciples specifically about Temple sacrifice and, in the sayings that are recorded in the Gospels, he apparently stressed prayer and not sacrifice. (According to Matthew, Jesus more than once cited Hosea 6:6, to the effect that God required "mercy and not sacrifice": Matt. 9:13; 12:7.) It is conceivable, therefore, that even if Jesus had been devoted to the Temple and its worship, he may at last have concluded that Temple sacrifices were no longer of value. Christopher Rowland offers just this speculation:

> I think it quite possible, therefore, that in the last days and hours of his life the *lack* of success of the Jerusalem expedition led Jesus to form a more reformist position with regard to the Temple (it should be purified for a new age) to a less optimistic, more sectarian and 'rejectionist' position, in which he asserted that its end was in sight and that it might have no part in the divine plan.[34]

Rowland's hypothesis can neither be proved nor disproved; it commands reflection. Might Jesus have changed his mind about the Temple? But how could we know that assuredly? Of course, Jesus, like all humans, could hold conflicting ideas; he could have altered a judgment in light of social hostility. To envision a new eschatological Temple could be categorized as pro-Temple rhetoric or anti-Temple rhetoric. The Jerusalem Temple remains, on either understanding, as the only place in which to worship God. Rowland's hypothesis is plausible in light of the numerous early Jewish texts, most prior to

---

34. Christopher Rowland, "The Temple in the New Testament," in *Temple Worship in Biblical Israel*, ed. John Day (London: T&T Clark, 2007), 472.

or contemporaneous with Jesus, that reject the Temple, considering it corrupt (most of the scrolls composed or edited at Qumran [the Dead Sea Scrolls] and all of the Samaritan traditions and texts that preserve ancient traditions), or envision a new eschatological Temple (viz., Tob. 13:8–14:7; *Jub.* 1:15-18; the *Temple Scroll* and the *New Jerusalem*). After all, within one group, the Enoch group, there is early adoration of the Temple (*1 En.* 25:1-7),[35] and a later negative stance to it (*1 En.* 89:73-77). But Rowland's suggestion remains only plausible.

CONCLUSION

Some leading scholars understandably focus on the famous episode when Jesus cast out those who sold and bought in the Temple and the few sayings that are deemed to be related to this explosive action to conclude that Jesus wished to destroy the Temple. In my judgment, the data in the New Testament that helps us comprehend Jesus' attitude to the Temple cannot be reduced to one action or sayings related to it; rather, a better comprehension of this event depends on setting it in the context of all Jesus' actions and statements, if we wish to arrive at an account that is historical and not theologically driven.

Some questions will remain open to conjecture and honest debate: did Jesus not only frequent the Temple, but offer sacrifice there? To do so would of course have required him to conform to the Levitical purity requirements to enter the Court of the Israelites and to cooperate with—even submit to—the authority of the priests working in the Temple. The Gospels do not depict Jesus in this action.

But we know that we face difficulties relating to the events as they are reported by the Evangelists. The overturning of the moneychangers (Mark 11:15) is separated from the destruction of the Temple (13:2) by the Parable of the Vineyard (12:1-12), and that parable is interpreted by Mark to be a condemnation of some Temple authorities (perhaps the Sadducees who appear in 12:18). Moreover, these traditions are not *bruta facta*, but have been filtered through the transmission and editing of sources—and some of them may be post factum statements after the Temple had been destroyed, or imagined destroyed (e.g., Mark 13:2; ctr. John 2:19).

On the one hand, Jesus' comments about the destruction of the Temple are deeply rooted in the Jeremiah-Baruch traditions that begin in the Old Testament and flow into the Gospels and on into later apocalypses, like 2

---

35. Cf. also Sirach 24:1-12 in which Wisdom finds a home and a resting place in Jerusalem, "the holy tent," and "the beloved city."

Baruch. These traditions are complex. They often predict the destruction of the Temple due to Israel's failure to obey the Covenant, but they also laud the Temple as God's only abode on earth (cf. also the *Temple Scroll*). Likewise, there are many rabbinic traditions harmonious with Jesus' reported actions and sayings; these indicate that some leading Jewish authorities considered aspects of the Temple cult and its business to be corrupt (e.g., Tosefta, Minḥot 13.21 and bTalmud Pesaḥim 57.1)

On the other hand, there are inchoate traditions in the Gospels that suggest Jesus revered the Temple, considered it the House of the Father (John 2:16) and a House of Prayer for all nations (Mark 11:17). To enter the Temple, Jesus must have obeyed the Temple *halakot* (entering a *mikveh* to be purified and paying the Temple tax). He certainly, and frequently, taught and worshipped in the Temple. There is no evidence that he slandered the high priest's office (though he may have spoken critically to influential high priests). He may well have sacrificed as the Levitical traditions demanded.

Thus, we must not attempt to arrange and systematize the Jesus traditions into some coherent norm that ignores many actions and sayings, such as Mark's comment that Jesus did not permit anyone to carry anything through the Temple (Mark 11:16). All attempts to comprehend Jesus' attitude to the Temple should acknowledge that Jesus was in Jerusalem during his last week, not to predict the destruction of the Temple, but to obey the *halakah* that faithful Jews must be in Jerusalem to celebrate Passover and to worship in the Temple, the House of God.

Today can never be yesterday. We are entering a new era in understanding Jesus and his reverence for the Temple, "the Father's house." Part of our contemporary context is the increasing recognition that anti-Jewish attitudes must be rejected, even when they find some apparent basis in the New Testament—but that those apparent bases are often not real. For two millennia, for example, many Christian leaders blamed all Jews for Jesus' death, inflating into theological truth the moment in Matthew's Gospel when the people of Jerusalem cry out that Jesus' blood be on them and their descendants (Matt. 27:25). Increasingly, we recognize that Matthew created this episode for particular purposes, connected to the destruction of Jerusalem in 70. But contextualizing Matthew's story in this way is only part of our responsibility: we must at the same time refuse on principle to generalize from Matthew's story to the sort of sweeping anti-Jewish libel that has so poisoned much of subsequent history. The point has been made, perhaps most memorably in *Nostra Aetate* (1965) but also in numerous formal church statements insisting that Jesus' crucifixion cannot and must not be blamed on the Jewish people.

Contextualizing the question of "Jesus and the Temple" means setting Jesus in the context of first-century Judaism, and that inevitably involves more than a narrow focus on the conflicts in Jerusalem in Jesus' last days. Torah, prophets, Psalms, all alike speak to the significance of the Temple; and if a number of Jewish writings show us a variety of heated judgments regarding the legitimacy of the priests offering sacrifice or the officials controlling its function, those judgments are indications of the importance attributed to the Temple.

Many who composed the chapters in this book have seen the snow on Mount Hermon, the cascading waterfalls near Dan, the fresh water pouring into the Sea of Galilee, and then the Jordan River winding its way southward. They can put themselves imaginatively alongside Jews centuries ago who would have traveled along that water's route. Along with many devout Jews from Galilee, Jesus, his disciples, and his band of followers would have moved southward, and then, joining Jews from Parthia, ascended up the Wadi Kelt towards Jerusalem. Cresting the Mount of Olives, the pilgrims would have seen the Holy City below, cradled by treacherous valleys on the East and West. Approaching the city from the East and early in the morning, one who had made a long and exhausting journey would have been mesmerized by the scene below as the marble and gold sparkled from the Temple and the dark cloud from the sacrifices wound its way heavenward, symbolizing the *axis mundi*.

Having seen images of that marvelous Temple and having heard how formative it was for Jews, we may imagine what Jesus and other Jews would have experienced when they saw the wonder of the Holy City and its prize glistening on the horizon. Pondering the awesome scene, many of those who lived so long ago may well have chanted or remembered words cherished since youth:

> How lovely is your dwelling place,
> O Lord of hosts!
> My soul longs, indeed it faints
> for the courts of the Lord;
> my heart and my flesh sing for joy
> to the living God.
> Even the sparrow finds a home,
> and the swallow a nest for herself,
> where she may lay her young,
> at your altars, O Lord of hosts,
> my King and my God.
> Happy are those who live in your house,

ever singing your praise. *Selah* . . .
For a day in your courts is better
than a thousand elsewhere.
I would rather be a doorkeeper in the house of my God
than live in the tents of wickedness. (Ps. 84:1-4, 10 NRSV)

7

The Temple and Jesus' Followers

James H. Charlesworth

Did Jesus' Followers Worship in the Temple?

Many Christians contend that although the Book of Acts portrays Jesus' followers as frequenting Jerusalem's Temple after his death, they never worshipped there; that is, they did not participate in the Temple cult and offer sacrifices.[1] People holding such views may have been influenced by sermons that stress how Jesus replaced the Temple for his followers. Some readers of the Gospels may assume that Jesus' followers hated the Temple priests, because the Gospels present the latter as in collusion with the Roman governor in Jesus' death and as being behind Stephen's stoning. Thus, many might conclude that Jesus' followers would have avoided the Temple and the cultic activity that was conducted there. Due to recent archeological research, we now know that many Galilean Jews belonged to families who had migrated to Galilee from Judea after the Hasmonean conquests.[2] Thus, the area in which Jesus centered his ministry had been settled and repopulated by these people. All observations indicate that most of these people were Torah-observant Jews who revered the Temple,[3] as we may judge from the objects they left behind. They used knife-cut oil lamps and large stone vessels made in Jerusalem, both of which have ties to both Temple worship and the purity laws of the Torah.[4] In the pre-70 CE

---

1. The present chapter presupposes and builds upon the preceding one on "Jesus and the Temple."

2. J.H. Charlesworth, review of *Settlement and History in Hellenistic, Roman, and Byzantine Galilee*, by Uzi Leibner, *Journal for the Study of the Historical Jesus* 8 (2010): 281–84.

3. Charlesworth, "Jesus Research and Near Eastern Archaeology: Reflections on Recent Developments," in *Neotestamentica et Philonica: Studies in Honor of Peder Borgen*, ed. D.E. Aune, T. Seland, and J.H. Ulrichsen, Supplements to *Novum Testamentum* 106 (Leiden: Brill, 2013), 37–70. Charlesworth, "Gesù, L'Archeologia e la Fede Cristiana," in *Archeologia e Fede* (2003), 9–36. Charlesworth, ed., *Jesus and Archaeology* (Grand Rapids, MI: Eerdmans, 2006), esp. xxii–xxv, 11–63; 692–95.

Migdal synagogue unearthed by archaeologists, a large carved stone was found, the images on which highlight the architecture of and festivals in the Temple. Thus, these Galilean Jews celebrated the centrality of worship in the Temple.[5] It seems reasonable to assume that many of Jesus' Jewish followers who came to acknowledge him as Messiah, Son of God, or Son of Man might have continued to observe the Torah rules about worshipping and sacrificing in the Temple. If we may trust the depictions of Jesus in the Gospels, some of these Jews may have remembered how Jesus had centered his Judean ministry in the Temple and also worshipped there as a faithful Jew.

Following his death, Jesus' followers began to develop a conception of "the church" as "the H\house of God" (1 Cor. 3:9; Heb. 3:6; 1 Pet. 2:5; 4:17). Some of Jesus' followers developed the belief that God dwelt within the community of Jesus' believers and not exclusively in buildings made by humans (see Acts 7:48). Nicholas Perrin has gone farther, arguing that Jesus and his followers, and not just the post-70 Evangelists, believed that Jesus embodied and thus replaced the Temple built by Herod in Jerusalem.[6]

One can easily present a Markan view that portrays the Temple as negative. So, for example, Mark seems to present Jesus' cursing of the fig tree as a symbolic demonstration of the destruction of the Temple (Mark 11:13-14, 20-21). As the fig tree failed to produce what is expected from it, likewise the Temple failed to fulfill its purpose as the house of prayer (cf. Mic. 7:1-2). Scholars have rightly pointed out that, according to Mark, Jesus seems to envision a future Temple: "My house *shall be called* a house of prayer" (Mark 11:17, emphasis added).[7] It is conceivable that Mark thought the Temple was not presently "a house of prayer."

Moreover, Mark seems to propose that the true purpose of the Temple as the house of prayer calls for fulfillment not in a building, but in a community

---

4. Charlesworth, "Hat die Archäologie Bedeutung für die Jesus-Forschung?" *Evangelische Theologie* 68 (2008): 246–65. Charlesworth and M. Aviam, "Überlegungen zur Erforschung Galiläas im ersten Jahrhundert," in *Jesus und die Archäologie Galiläas*, ed. C. Claussen and J. Frey, Biblisch-Theologische Studien 87 (Neukirchen-Vluyn: Neukirchener Verlag, 2008), 93–127. Also, see Charlesworth and Aviam's chapters in *The Tomb of Jesus and His Family? Exploring Ancient Jewish Tombs Near Jerusalem's Walls* (Grand Rapids, MI: Eerdmans, 2013).

5. See Charlesworth's and Aviam's chapters in *Parables of Enoch: A Paradigm Shift*, edited by Charlesworth and D. L. Bock, T&T Clark Jewish and Christian Texts Series 11 (London: Bloomsbury, 2013), 37–57, 173–217; see esp. 159–69 and the images of the stone on 165–67.

6. I am appreciative of J.P. Sweeney's overview and critique of N. Perrin's *Jesus the Temple*. Sweeney presented his paper during the 2011 annual meeting of the Evangelical Theological Society's meetings in San Francisco.

7. The verb is a future Greek tense: "it shall be called" (κληθήσεται).

of the New Covenant of Jesus' followers. Mark may allude to the fulfillment of true Temple worship by the replacement of the Temple with Jesus' disciples (cf. Mark 11:20-25). Perhaps, as discussed in the preceding chapter, we find a prediction of the replacement of the Temple by the "Christian community" in the "Parable of the Vineyard," which concludes with the vineyard being given "to others" (Mark 12:8-9).

Mark preserves a tradition that indicates the Temple is a building built by human hands, and declares that it will be replaced with one "not made with hands" (14:58; compare 15:29). These accusations are not attributed to Jesus; possibly they do not represent Mark's own view. But they do indicate the destruction of the Temple and the erection of a "new Temple." And Mark's report that the Temple curtain was torn in two––"from top to bottom"––at the moment of Jesus' death seems to indicate a negative judgment on the Temple in Mark's story (15:38).[8]

Turning to Matthew, the author seems to suggest that the Temple has been defiled through the collusion of the "chief priests and elders" in the death of Jesus (Matt. 27:3-10). The author also suggests that Jerusalem is full of Jews guilty of killing God's Messiah and that they are destined for destruction (Matt. 22:7, 23:37-39). It appears that Matthew implies that the Temple sacrifices were no longer important to Jesus, since he would have had no use for a corrupt Temple. Did Matthew not transfer the symbolism of the Temple to the "church," a noun used by him but by no other Evangelist (16:17-19)?

For centuries, scholars have argued that Jesus was persecuted by Sadducees, like Caiaphas, and that he and his followers were opposed by many Temple priests and Pharisees, like the early Saul. It appears that these high priests, namely Annas and Caiaphas, were, according to the Gospels, instrumental in Jesus' death. Moreover, the stoning of Stephen seems to be due to his supposed defamation of the Temple according to the priests who were accusing him. How could one deny that these events are described in the New Testament? Would it then not seem to follow, at least by inference, that Jesus' followers would have avoided, perhaps even despised, the Temple? Did not Jesus' followers flee Jerusalem after the crucifixion and never return, as seemingly implied in John 21?

Numerous passages in the New Testament need to be read historically and in light of what we know from pre-70 Jewish culture in ancient Palestine.

---

8. These issues are very complex. Some passages in Mark, about the Temple, seem to derive from Jesus, others from traditions prior to Mark, others from Mark himself, and some are attributed to antagonists to Jesus in the Marcan rhetoric. I refer the reader to the many good discussions of these issues that have been published.

For example, the tradition that Jesus' followers are to return to Galilee after his death and that there, after his resurrection, they would see him again (Mark 14:28; 16:7) does not require that the Temple has been replaced by a Galilean type of "Christianity." Likewise, the compiler of John 21 indicates that Jesus' followers again took up fishing on the Sea of Galilee, but this does not mean that Jesus' disciples left Jerusalem, returned to Galilee, and no longer visited Jerusalem. Such texts were once read to imply that Jesus' followers and disciples left Jerusalem, leaving the Temple behind. Today, many scholars are more likely to accept the account in Luke-Acts, according to which Jesus centered his ministry in Jerusalem and his Torah-observant followers continued to frequent the Temple. Did they also participate in the sacrifices offered there?

Christian theologians, for most of two millennia, have understandably argued that Jesus eventually becomes the cornerstone of the "New Temple." They suggest that if Jesus is the *axis mundi,* then the Temple is redundant. They observe that the author of Revelation portrays the New Jerusalem without a Temple, and contend that it has become obsolete. They note that the logic of the letter to the Hebrews is that something better than the sacrifices repeatedly offered in the Temple has now arrived in the sacrificial death of Jesus. Many Christians today throughout the world hold such impressions. Such hermeneutical moves are often based on sophisticated and sane exegesis of later writings, but what Christians thought about the Temple after 70 is not our main focus here.

PERCEIVING AND CHALLENGING ASSUMPTIONS

It is important to be clear about the question we are asking. We are not asking what Mark or another Evangelist thought about Jesus' teachings and perception of the Temple. We wish to explore what can be known about Jesus' earliest followers: Did they not only frequent the Temple but also worship and perhaps sacrifice there? Three chronological periods should be distinguished:

I   Before 30 CE: when Jesus and his followers went together to the Temple

II   30 to 70 CE: when some of Jesus' followers lived in Jerusalem and when Paul wrote to his congregations in the Diaspora

III   70 to 150 CE: after the Temple's destruction; the period of the composition of the Gospels

History seldom can be divided into such distinct periods; yet, if we keep these historical periods clearly before us, we will perceive changes from the time of Jesus until the time when his brother, James, was active in the Jerusalem church and, later, until the time of the author of Revelation (at the end of the first century). Obviously, after the burning of the Temple in 70 CE, Jews and "Christians" needed to find a substitute for the Temple.[9]

I. BEFORE 30: WHEN JESUS AND HIS FOLLOWERS WENT TOGETHER TO THE TEMPLE

Numerous early and reliable historical texts indicate that Jesus' first disciples revered the Temple; some of them, even those from Galilee, revered the Temple as much as Jesus (as I indicated in a previous chapter). As E.P. Sanders rightly notes, the early apostles accepted Temple worship. They did not consider the Temple impure (Acts 2:46; 3:1; 21:26).[10]

According to Oxyrhynchus Papyrus V 850, Jesus and his disciples frequented the Temple court.[11] This pre-fourth century text reports how Jesus, "along with the disciples," enters the Holy Court of the Temple.[12] They walk "about the Temple." It is clearly the "place of purification" and contains "holy vessels." This text correctly reports that before one enters this "pure place," one must immerse himself in a *mikveh* (Jewish bath for ritual purification) and change clothes. Many pre-70 CE *mikvaot* have been discovered south, west, and north of the Temple Mount. These baths for purification are habitually constructed with a plastered division running down the middle of two sets of steps. Thus, one who descends on the right and ascends on the left is protected from another Jew who is impure as he begins to enter the bath. Subsequently the purified Jew may enter the Temple area; and the discovery of *mikvaot* near the Migdal synagogue indicates that at least some Jews would enter a synagogue or another sacred place of study to read God's Word only after immersing themselves in a *mikveh*.

9. For a general discussion, see H. Rosenau, *Vision of the Temple: The Image of the Temple of Jerusalem in Judaism and Christianity* (London: Oresko Books, 1979) and R.J. McKelvey, *The New Temple: The Church in the New Testament,* Oxford Theological Monographs (London: Oxford University Press, 1969).

10. E.P. Sanders, *Jesus and Judaism* (Philadelphia: Fortress Press, 1985), 76.

11. See Joachim Jeremias and Wilhelm Schneemelcher in *New Testament Apocrypha,* trans. and ed. R. McL Wilson, vol. 1 (Louisville: Westminster John Knox, 1991), 94–95. Also see, J.K. Elliott, ed., *The Apocryphal New Testament* (Oxford: Clarendon, 1993), 33–34. The original composition is of unknown date. Conceivably, the miniature work is a copy of an earlier work; perhaps the copy was intended as an amulet.

12. The anti-Jewish rhetoric and the reference to Jesus as "Savior" indicates that a late, and not an early, date should be assigned to the work. Perhaps it was composed in the late second century ce. For the latest study, see Christoph Markschies and Jens Schröter, eds., *Antike christliche Apokryphen in deutscher Übersetzung,* vol. 1 (Tübingen: Mohr Siebeck, 2012), 357–59.

Behind this highly edited and anti-Jewish text lies a surprisingly reliable source for the requirements that must be met before one enters the Temple. Note the words of the Pharisee, Levi, whom Jesus meets in the Temple: "I am purified, for I have bathed in the pool . . . and have descended by one staircase and ascended by the other." Before entering the Temple, Jesus and his Jewish followers had to enter a *mikveh* (see Mishnah *Hagigah, Middot*, and esp. *Mikvaot*).

In the previous chapter, I suggested that Jesus not only worshipped in the Temple but might have offered sacrifices there. No New Testament canonical text makes such a claim, although many passages in the Gospel may imply its possibility when they refer to Jesus in the Temple. In the *Acts of Thomas* 79, however, we read explicitly that Jesus "offered sacrifice in the Temple." Why does the author make this claim? It is to prove that Jesus wished "to show that every offering is hallowed."[13] The *Acts of Thomas* was most likely composed in Edessa in the third century CE. Christianity in the East was heavily influenced by synagogal worship and frequently had a close relation with Judaism. Hence, such a claim that Jesus offered sacrifices in the Temple should neither be assumed to be historical nor dismissed as pure legend. It is clear that some of Jesus' followers in that place and time believed that he sacrificed in the Temple.

According to the Gospels, when in Judea, Jesus customarily and frequently taught in the Temple. Hence, his disciples and others would congregate around him in the Temple. Thus, we may conclude that before 30 CE, Jesus' earliest followers frequented the Temple with him. They would obviously have agreed with Jesus' assessment that the Temple was the Father's House. It was the hallowed place to worship and to study. The disciples did hear debates between Jesus and many priests and Pharisees in the Temple, but debates within Judaism are almost always signs of respect and a desire to discuss the meaning of Torah.

II. 30 TO 70: WHEN JESUS' FOLLOWERS LIVED IN JERUSALEM AND WHEN PAUL WROTE

According to the author of Acts, Peter and John ascended to the Temple after Jesus' death. Why? Although sermons and publications often focus only on their power to heal a man near the gates of the Temple, the text specifies the hour and thus the reason Peter and John went to the Temple: "Now Peter and John were going up to the Temple at the hour of prayer, the ninth hour" (Acts 3:1). According to this text, Peter and John ascended the Holy Mountain at the specified time for prayer; thus, they most likely intended to enter the Temple to pray.

---

13. See Elliott, *The Apocryphal New Testament*, 478.

According to Acts 7, Stephen, a Diasporic Jew, is stoned by other Jews outside the walls of Jerusalem. Why? He may have more harshly criticized the Temple than Jesus.[14] He may have merely represented some of the thoughts attributed to Solomon, that God does not dwell in houses built by humans. Timothy Wardle rightly points out that Stephen's death did not follow immediately upon his speech; the council became enraged after Stephen made accusations about the complicity of the Sanhedrin in Jesus' death, thereby attacking the leadership of the priests.[15] To explain why Stephen was stoned would demand discerning how much of what is attributed to him is authentic or an editorial alteration by Luke, and also how much of what Stephen said was actually against the Temple and not more narrowly against some aspects of the Temple cult. Further, though Stephen's high evaluation of Jesus, the Son of Man, standing in heaven beside God occurs in a vision after his condemnation (Acts 7:55-56), it is consistent with the accusations earlier in the Gospel that, according to Luke, were regarded as evidence of blasphemy on the part of Jesus by priests perhaps centered in the high priestly dynasty of Ananus. If "a great many of the priests" came to believe in the claims of Jesus (Acts 6:7), then one should avoid a clear dichotomy between Jews supporting Jesus' claims and priests standing against Jesus. Most likely, Stephen was trying to argue, within a polemical confrontation, that God's presence may be found in the Temple, but God cannot be limited to any one location.[16]

The author of Luke and Acts emphasizes that after Jesus' death, his followers frequented the Temple.[17] Jesus' followers were reported teaching in the Temple (Acts 5:25), and proclaiming his message throughout Jerusalem (Acts 5:28). They were in the Temple continually, praising God (Luke 24:53) and meeting daily in the Temple (Acts 2:46; cf. Acts 5:42—6:1, nrsv). Recall Acts 5:42: "And every day in the Temple and at home they did not cease to teach and proclaim Jesus as the Messiah." According to Luke, Jesus and his disciples frequented the Temple: "And every day he [Jesus] was teaching in the Temple, but at night he exited to lodge on the mount called Olivet. And early in the morning, all the people came to him to hear him in the Temple"

---

14. See James D.G. Dunn, *Beginning from Jerusalem* (Grand Rapids, MI: Eerdmans, 2009), 261–63.

15. Timothy Wardle, *The Jerusalem Temple and Early Christian Identity*, WUNT 291 (Tübingen: Mohr Siebeck, 2010), 197–202.

16. See B. Witherington, *Acts*, 273; and Wardle, *The Jerusalem Temple and Early Christian Identity*, 199–201.

17. Note the brilliant insights by C.K. Barrett, "Attitudes to the Temple in the Acts of the Apostles," in *Templum Amicitiae: Essays on the Second Temple Presented to Ernst Bammel*, ed. W. Horbury, Journal for the Study of New Testament Supplement Series 48 (Sheffield: JSOT, 1991), 345–67.

(Luke 21:37-38). Such summaries are obviously from the hand of Luke, but most likely they represent reliably that Jesus and his disciples frequented the Temple.

The author of Acts witnesses to tensions and problems within Jerusalem among the followers of Jesus in the first decades after the crucifixion. But there is no evidence that the rival groups in his narrative, namely the Hebrews or Hellenists (Acts 6), advocated a negative attitude to the Temple.[18]

Apparently, according to John, Jesus liked to center his teaching near the eastern wall of the Temple, in a place called Solomon's Portico (John 10:22). Likewise, Peter, John, and other followers, before 70 CE, would gather "in the portico called Solomon's" (Acts 3:11). The author of Acts reports that many signs and wonders were done by Jesus' apostles in Solomon's Portico (Acts 5:12). We are then told that many people held Jesus' followers "in high honor" in the Temple (Acts 5:13). There is far more harmony in the Temple among priests and Jesus' followers than some popular assessments have allowed.

A cursory reading of Paul's letters often gives readers the opinion that he rejected the earthly Temple in Jerusalem and substituted a heavenly Temple for it. This is conceivable if we compare his letters with early Jewish texts do mention the Heavenly Temple; notably among them are *1 Enoch* 14 (implicitly), the *Testament of Levi* 3 (explicitly), the Qumranic *Songs of the Sabbath Sacrifices*, Philo (esp. *SpecLeg* 1.66), and Rabbinic writings (viz., b*Hag* 12b; *GenRab* 55.7, *Midrash on Song of Songs* 4.4).[19] Reflections on the Heavenly Temple were frequently prompted by reading biblical texts, especially Isaiah 6, Ezekiel 1, and Daniel 7. Thus, almost always, contemplating the Heavenly Temple was a way of celebrating the Jerusalem Temple, which in terms of biblical geography was customarily assumed to be beneath it.

In his epistles, Paul seems to transform the Jerusalem Temple into the Body of Christ. He clearly stressed that those who believe Jesus is the long-expected Messiah are the Temple: "What agreement has the Temple of God with idols? For *we are the Temple of the living God*" (2 Cor. 6:16, emphasis added).[20] This section of 2 Corinthians mirrors Qumranic thought, and may be a portion of the letter Paul mentions in 1 Cor. 5:9 ("I wrote to you in my letter not to

---

18. Note Catchpole's similar judgment: "[N]either of the two groups, Hellenists or Hebrews, had a negative attitude to the Temple in principle, though their conduct would not be inconsistent with the view that the present Temple could be vulnerable." Catchpole, *Jesus People*, 231.

19. See Avigdor Aptowitzer, "The Heavenly Temple in the Agada," *Tarbiz* 2 (1931): 137–53, 257–58.

20. On *naos*, see Otto Michel, "ναός," *Theologische Wörterbuch zum Neuen Testament* 4 (1942): 884–95; ET = *TDNT* 4 (1967): 880–90.

associate with immoral men"). He then quotes Lev. 26:11-12, mixing Hebrew and the Greek version that he normally cites:

"As God said,
I will live in them and move among them,
and I will be their God,
and they shall be my people . . ."

As W.D. Davies pointed out, for Paul "the whole community constitutes the shrine or temple (*naos*) of God."[21] By altering the mt and lxx from "among you" to "among them," and especially "in them," Paul, as Davies states, "seems anxious to emphasize that God no longer dwells *with* his people in a tent or temple, but actually dwells *in* them."[22] Such exegetical methods would indicate that Paul rejected the Jerusalem Temple; it reappears as the presence of the living God within the messianic community. The point is clear in 1 Cor. 3:16: "Do you not know that you are God's Temple and that God's Spirit dwells in you?" Similar thoughts reappear in 1 Cor. 6:19 and 2 Cor. 6:16. They are not unprecedented in the history of Jewish thought. Philo argued that the human body is "a sacred dwelling-place or shrine"[23] fashioned "for the reasonable soul" (*On Creation* 137). And at Qumran, the Holy Ones guided by the Holy Spirit believe that, although the Sanctuary remains in Jerusalem, they constitute God's Temple in the House of Holiness (namely the Yahad); note the following alteration of the concept of "offering": "I will shout (for joy) to him. And I will praise him with the offering of the utterance of my lips" (1QS 10.14).[24]

Thus, one can appreciate (if not necessarily endorse) the position advocated by James D. G. Dunn, who concludes that Paul "abandoned wholly or almost completely" the fourth pillar of Second Temple Judaism: the central importance of the Temple.[25] Dunn is convinced that for Paul "the people of the holy land seem to have been replaced by the image of the body of Christ" (721). Note his conclusion: "Categories of temple and priesthood, of holiness and purity remain elements in his theologizing, but appear only in a communalized or desacralized

---

21. W.D. Davies, *The Gospel and the Land: Early Christianity and Jewish Territorial Doctrine* (Berkeley: University of California Press, 1974), 186.

22. Ibid., 187.

23. οἶκος γάρ τις ἢ νεὼς ἱερός. See F.H. Colson and G.H. Whitaker, *Philo I*, Loeb Classical Library 226 (London: Heinemann, 1929, and Cambridge, MA: Harvard University Press, 1971), 108.

24. My translation.

25. James D.G. Dunn, *The Theology of Paul the Apostle* (Grand Rapids, MI: Eerdmans, 1998), 721.

form—all believers as 'holy ones,' as temple, as priests in service of the gospel" (721). As Dunn writes,

> But with Paul at least the implication is that of a temple constituted by the immediate indwelling of God in individual and people, rather than mediately through a temple as such (2 Cor. 6.16), and of such a direct indwelling that it made redundant any continuing (or for Gentiles converts, new) loyalty to the Jerusalem temple.[26]

I would agree that Paul takes cultic language out of the cult and moves sacred space from Temple to the individual, but that does not mean the Temple and the sacred cult ceased to be important for Paul. Dunn certainly knows Paul's mind and he has presented a sane and clear assessment of Paul's views on the Temple. While Dunn has clearly contributed to the scholarly dialogue, I have the impression that he has been far clearer than the complex evidence given to us by and about Paul suggests.

J. Louis Martyn argues that when using the term "Jerusalem" that "Paul thinks in the first instance of the Jerusalem church, not of the city as such, and certainly not of the Jewish cultus with its temple, its priests, and its traditions."[27]Martyn makes a good point when focusing on Galatians, but his judgment cannot be extended to the full range of Pauline traditions. In his letters, all of which antedate 70 CE, Paul uses a term that usually means "temple," *naos* (ναός), as a metaphor for people or a body. In the process, he displays his acquaintance with the Jerusalem Temple (1 Cor. 3:17, 2 Cor. 6:16, Eph. 2:21; cf. John 2:19, 21). Once, Paul uses the term "*hieros*," which often means "temple."[28] In 1 Cor. 9:13, *hieron* (ἱερόν) is a general term for the Temple service or cult: "Do you not know that those who are employed in the Temple service [lit., "holy places"] get their food from the Temple, and those who serve at the altar share in the sacrificial offerings?" Thus, Paul, as a faithful Jew, seems to have a very positive view of the Holy Place, the Temple. He apparently distinguished between the priests who opposed him and the House of God. Again, Davies is a good guide: "Actual Temple practice is not frowned upon, but supplies a model for Christian forms. There is no hint of criticism of the priesthood or the Temple system."

---

26. Ibid., 545.

27. J. Louis Martyn, *Theological Issues in the Letters of Paul* (Nashville: Abingdon, 1997), 26.

28. Gottlob Schrenk, "ἱερός [and cognates]," *Theologische Wörterbuch zum Neuen Testament* 3 (1938): 221–84; ET = *TDNT* 3 (1965): 221–83.

Moving from Paul's epistles to Acts, no one should doubt that Paul frequented the Temple.[29] According to Acts 21:26, Paul enters the Temple to purify himself with followers who wish to complete the strict Jewish Nazirite vow for purification. They must offer the required sacrifices on the eighth day after shaving their heads (Num. 6:9-12). Paul makes offerings in the Temple on behalf of the four Nazirites (Acts 21:26). He also purifies himself, perhaps to win support (or diminish rejection) from Jews (and "Jewish Christians") who thought he had contaminated himself by being with non-Jews. This report cannot be a creation by Luke as it goes against his usual tendencies; it must be a source.[30]

According to Acts 21:27-36, Paul is in the Temple. It appears that the Jews from Asia, who accused Paul incorrectly, thought that he had brought a Gentile into the Temple. According to Acts 22:17-21, Paul is praying in the Temple. He falls into a trance (*en ekstasei*) and sees Jesus. The author of Acts places Paul frequently in the Temple, and he actively proclaims his testimony to Jesus Christ there.

DID PAUL NOT EMPHASIZE THE IMPORTANCE OF THE TEMPLE?

Some evidence suggests that the early followers of Jesus constructed a communal Temple identity. They used cultic terminology from the Temple to define their own self-understanding. In ways known from the Old Testament prophets and the Qumranites,[31] the early followers of Jesus replaced sacrifice with prayer, obedience, and other forms of worship that proved efficacious, as had the animal sacrifices.[32] Note the Qumran perspective:

29. Using Acts to understand Paul's thought and life is precarious, but here I follow Davies and Martin Hengel. In seeking to understand Paul's view of the Temple, it is imperative to use Acts. And the traditions in it are harmonious with Paul's own thoughts. Martin Hengel and Anna Maria Schwemer contend that Acts is very early, since it does not know about Paul the letter-writer. See their *Paul: Between Damascus and Antioch: The Unknown Years*, trans. John Bowden (Louisville: Westminster John Knox, 1997), 3.

30. Paul needed to be purified, having come from a long journey abroad. The four poor Nazirites in the Palestinian Jesus Movement needed Paul to pay their expenses for the requisite sacrifices. See Ernst Haenchen, *The Acts of the Apostles: A Commentary* (Philadelphia: Westminster, 1971), 611–12. Hans Conzelmann wisely saw that the source "did not offer a historically accurate picture of Paul." But, it is a source. See Conzelmann, *Acts of the Apostles*, trans. J. Limburg et al., Hermeneia (Philadelphia: Fortress Press, 1987), 183.

31. See esp. Michael Newton, *The Concept of Purity at Qumran and in the Letters of Paul*, Society for the New Testament Studies Monograph Series 53 (Cambridge: Cambridge University Press, 1985).

32. See Elizabeth Schüssler Fiorenza, "Cultic Language in Qumran and in the NT," *Catholic Biblical Quarterly* 38 (1976): 159–77; Joel Marcus, *The Way of the Lord* (Louisville: Westminster John Knox,

When, according to all these norms, these [men] become in Israel a foundation of the Holy Spirit in eternal truth, they shall atone for iniquitous guilt and for sinful unfaithfulness, so that [God's] favor for the land [is obtained] without the flesh of burnt-offerings and without the fat of sacrifices. (1QS 9.3-5)[33]

These words indicate that the Qumranites, predominantly "the Sons of Aaron who alone shall rule over judgment and property" (1QS 9.7), are the only ones who "atone for iniquitous guilt and for sinful unfaithfulness." The Temple cult's sacrifices are rejected; they are polluted by the infidelity of the administering priests.

Many of the earliest followers of Jesus, especially those outside Palestine, in light of tensions with some leaders in the Temple, tended to shift the concept of the holy Temple to Jesus' new covenant community. In *The Jerusalem Temple and Early Christian Identity*, Timothy Wardle argues as follows: "The example *par excellence* of this tendency is Paul, as the ideology and language of sacrifice and cult provided him with important terminology with which to describe the crucifixion of Jesus Christ and the resultant community of believers in Jesus (Rom. 3:25; 1 Cor. 5:7; Rom. 12:1)." For Paul, the physical Temple is recycled as the spiritual temple; he exhorts his readers: "[P]resent you bodies as a living sacrifice, holy and acceptable to God, which is your spiritual worship" (Rom. 12:1). With such thoughts, Paul seems to appreciate the Temple but re-appropriates its cult.

Finally, whether it was composed by Paul or by a Paulinist, 2 Thessalonians is the "one passage" in the Pauline corpus, as Davies perceived, in which the Temple does "seem to remain for Paul a center of eschatological significance."[34] Recall the passage: "Let no one deceive you in any way. For that day will not come, unless the rebellion comes first, and the man of lawlessness is revealed, the son of perdition, who opposes and exalts himself against every so-called god or object of worship, so that he takes his seat in the Temple of God, proclaiming himself to be God" (2 Thess. 2:3-5). The spatial imagery (the eschatological evil man sits) indicates that a specific place is intended; the most likely place is then the Jerusalem Temple. The author claims that the end time will not come until

1992); and the contributions to Beate Ego, Armin Lange, and Peter Pilhofer, eds., *Gemeinde ohne Temple–Community Without Temple: Zur Substituierung und Transformation des Jerusalemer Tempels und seines Kults im Alten Testament, antiken Judentum und Frühen Christentum*, WUNT 118 (Tübingen: Mohr [Siebeck], 1999).

33. Translation by Charlesworth in *The Dead Sea Scrolls*, vol. 1 (Tübingen: Mohr Siebeck, 1994), 39.

34. Davies, *The Gospel and the Land*, 193.

the man of lawlessness appears and desecrates "the Temple of God." The author celebrates the extreme importance of the Jerusalem Temple in the economy of salvation.

In summation, it is not certain what epistles best represent Paul's judgment on the Temple, and it may have evolved. Likewise, it is not evident how reliable are the sources preserved in Acts. It is misleading to bring a synthesis to Paul's disparate thoughts. It is certain that to stress the people of God as the eschatological Temple is not anti-Temple rhetoric. We have learned from Qumran and from related texts that a hatred of some aspects of the Temple cult does not imply that the Temple is not the House of God. Eschatological thinking is notoriously contradictory and a perception of the end time may be only a defamation of the present Temple (as in Jeremiah and the Baruch Cycle) and not a rejection of the Temple as God's own House.

DID THE AUTHOR OF HEBREWS IMAGINE THE TEMPLE AS IMPORTANT?

The author of Hebrews uses Temple imagery to proclaim his belief that Jesus is the "Forerunner" of faith, with a focus on the tabernacle of the wilderness, and the enthroned High Priest, in light of the heavenly Temple.[35] As Ernst Käsemann concluded in his insightful study of Hebrews: "Finally, this has again made clear *that all the utterances in Hebrews culminate in the description of Christ's high priestly office, but take their basis, which supports and purposefully articulates the individual parts, from the motif of the wandering people of God*" (emphasis in original).[36]

While the author imagines a heavenly Temple, he makes no mention of the Temple in Jerusalem being destroyed. He refers to priests who are presently offering sacrifices in the Temple. One can easily get the impression that the work antedates 70 CE.[37] His position would have been enhanced if he had written after 70; then he could have said that *only* those who profess the heavenly High Priest can obtain atonement, since the earthly Temple cult ceased.

If some passages seem to suggest naïve secessionism, Temple imagery nevertheless dominates, suggesting its importance to the author. The primary

---

35. Aelred Cody, *Heavenly Sanctuary and Liturgy in the Epistle to the Hebrews: the Achievement of Salvation in the Epistle's Perspectives* (St. Meinrad, IN: Grail, 1960).

36. Ernst Käsemann, *The Wandering People of God: An Investigation of the Letter of Hebrews*, trans. Roy A. Harrisville and I.L. Sandberg (Minneapolis: Augsburg, 1984), 240.

37. See my arguments for a pre-70 date in *The Old Testament Pseudepigrapha and the New Testament: Prolegomena for the Study of Christian Origins*, Society for New Testament Studies Monograph Series 54 (Cambridge: Cambridge University Press, 1985).

focus of the author of Hebrews is turned to Jesus. He is enthroned in the heavenly Temple as the final sacrifice, the heavenly high priest.[38] As Harry Attridge notes, "The interior reality that the heavenly temple symbolizes is not a principle or virtue generally available to humankind, but a relationship made possible by Christ."[39] Even so, the arguments that state the sufficiency of Christ's sacrifice are not polemical toward continued participation in the cultic participation and sacrificial offerings in the Temple: the work of Christ may be exalted, but the Temple is by no means depreciated. If that were the case, then why would the author of Hebrews have utilized Temple symbolism in the first place? By analyzing Temple symbolisms under a positive light, one learns about the importance of the Temple in developing "Christian" theology. See also the chapter on Hebrews in this volume by Harold Attridge.

WHAT DID THE COMMUNITY BEHIND Q THINK ABOUT THE TEMPLE?

Many scholars assume that behind Matthew and Luke is a "Sayings Source" that preserved Jesus' words. Building on that assumption or discovery, David Catchpole concludes that the Q community represented an intentionally positive view of the Temple, such that the Q community pictured the Temple as something important to the community, though in need of appropriation within the burgeoning Jesus Movement.[40] John S. Kloppenborg disagrees, seeing instead a somewhat indifferent attitude towards the Temple.[41] Thus, using the terminology developed by Kyu Sam Han,[42] Catchpole thinks Q represented a "critical allegiance" to the Temple, but Kloppenborg judges Q to witnesses to an "ambivalent allegiance" to the Temple.[43] In this way, Catchpole

---

38. For more reflections, see Otfried Hofius, *Katapausis: Die Vorstellung vom endzeitlichen Ruheort im Hebräerbrief*, WUNT 11 (Tubingen: Mohr Siebeck, 1970) and A.N. Chester, "Hebrews: The Final Sacrifice," in *Sacrifice and Redemption: Durham Essays in Theology*, ed. S.W. Sykes (Cambridge: Cambridge University Press, 1991), 57–72.

39. Harry W. Attridge, *The Epistle to the Hebrews*, Hemeneia (Philadelphia: Fortress Press, 1989), 224.

40. David R. Catchpole, *The Quest for Q* (Edinburgh: T&T Clark, 1993) and "Temple Traditions in Q," in *Templus Amicitae: Essays on the Second Temple Presented to Ernst Bammel*, ed. W. Horbury, Journal for the Study of the New Testament Supplement Series 48 (Sheffield: Sheffield Academic Press, 1991), 305–29.

41. John S. Kloppenborg, *Formation of Q* (Philadelphia: Fortress Press, 1987); *The Shape of Q* (Minneapolis: Fortress Press, 1994); *Conflict and Invention: Literary, Rhetorical and Social Studies on the Sayings Gospel Q* (Valley Forge, PA: Trinity Press International, 1995).

42. Kyu Sam Han, *Jerusalem and the Early Jesus Movement: The Q Community's Attitude Toward the Temple*, Journal for the Study of the New Testament Supplement Series 207 (London: Sheffield Academic Press, 2002).

43. I refer to the Han's publication for the definition of these terms.

conceives of Q as representing a Temple-supporting community, though one critical of its abuses, whereas Kloppenborg understands the allegiance of Q to the Temple to be *de facto* of the Jewish identity of the authors.

Scholars agree that there are different views of the Temple in Q (it if is a written composition).[44] Perhaps the more lenient view of the Temple, or positive one, found in Luke 4:1-13 (Q 4.1-13) and Luke 11:42 (Q 11.42c), reflects differing views within the community or a later softening of Temple rhetoric.[45] The Temple clearly continues to define the Q community and some within this hypothetical community may have continued to obey Torah and make the required pilgrimage to the Holy City to worship in the Temple. As pointed out in my previous chapter, and by Motti Aviam in his preceding chapter, archaeological evidence is connecting Lower Galilean Judaism (and that would include the Jews attracted to Jesus) with the Temple; the newly unearthed stone in the Migdal synagogue connects that synagogue with the symbolism of the Temple.[46] Perhaps some passages in the alleged source Q indicate that some of Jesus' earliest followers worshipped in the Temple.[47]

Catchpole may accurately assess some of the sayings in Q, stating that the Jews represented by them tend to center their thoughts on Jerusalem and the Temple: "The Q community thus inherited . . . a continuing commitment to the covenant, the law, and the temple." He continues, "The fate of the temple in the future was not taken to imply its religious irrelevance in the present."[48] Again, one cannot ignore evidence that the Temple and its cult continued to define the Palestinian Jesus Movement.

Other traditions and sources known to Matthew, besides Q, should be at least noted. One is found in Matthew 6:1-18. W.D. Davies and Dale C. Allison rightly point out that we cannot determine the attitude to the Temple in this pre-Matthean "cult-didache."[49]

44. Perhaps we should not assume that there is a Q source; see Mark S. Goodacre, *The Case Against Q: Studies in Markan Priority and Synoptic Problem* (Harrisburg, PA: Trinity Press International, 2001).

45. In *Jerusalem and the Early Jesus Movement*, Kyu Sam Han argues that the later view of the Temple in Q "shows that the enmity was resolved as the Q community achieved a new social identity apart from the Temple symbolism" (213).

46. See esp. Motti Aviam, "Reverence for Jerusalem and the Temple in Galilean Society," in this volume.

47. I am impressed with the power and conservative nature of oral traditions. They are usually transmitted within communities that often keep them stable. Until I am more convinced that Q was a written document, I am not persuaded by arguments about its expansion or redaction.

48. Catchpole, *The Quest for Q*, 279.

49. W.D. Davies and Dale Allison, *The Gospel According to Saint Matthew*, International Critical Commentary (Edinburgh: T&T Clark, 1988), 1:575.

DID JESUS' BROTHER JAMES CONTINUE TO WORSHIP IN THE TEMPLE?

The author of Mark 6:3 provides the names of Jesus' brothers (or, in the tradition of Roman Catholic interpretation, half-brothers): James, Joseph, Judas, and Simon (cf. Matt. 13:55). After 30 CE, Jesus' relatives lived in Jerusalem and continued his ministry there for decades; thus, one can appreciate why some experts imagine a Jesus dynasty.[50] What can be known about James, Jesus' brother or half-brother (cf. Gal. 1:19)?[51] Over the past fifteen years, an unprecedented number of books have been devoted to James, Jesus' brother. The most objective and scholarly are the following:

- John Painter, *Just James: The Brother of Jesus in History and Tradition* (1997)[52]
- Pierre-Antoine Bernheim, *James, Brother of Jesus* (1997)[53]
- Bruce Chilton and Craig A. Evans, *James the Just and Christian Origins* (1999)[54]
- Hershel Shanks and Ben Witherington III, *The Brother of Jesus* (2003)[55]

No book focused on James has discussed how James research helps us comprehend the followers of Jesus' attitude to the Temple before 70 and its variegated forms of worship,[56] from the chanting of Psalms to the sacrificing of bulls.[57]

---

50. Harnack, Schoeps, and Stauffer thought there was a Jesus dynasty. H. von Campenhausen argued against the hypothesis. For a discussion of this debate, with support in a looser sense, see Richard Bauckham, *Jude and the Relatives of Jesus in the Early Church* (Edinburgh: T&T Clark, 1990), 125–33. More recently, James D. Tabor argues insightfully and forcefully for the hypothesis; see Tabor's *The Jesus Dynasty* (New York: Simon & Schuster, 2006).

51. The *Gospel of Thomas* highlights James; Jesus passes his power on to his brother (*Gos. Thom.* 12). It is possible that this gospel derives from an early Aramaic source that mirrored the followers of Jesus within Jerusalem. See April D. DeConick, *Thomasine Traditions in Antiquity: The Social and Cultural World of the Gospel of Thomas* (Leiden: Brill, 2005) and DeConick, *Recovering the Original Gospel of Thomas* (London: T&T Clark, 2005).

52. John Painter, *Just James: The Brother of Jesus in History and Tradition* (Columbia: University of South Carolina Press, 1997).

53. Pierre-Antoine Bernheim, *James, Brother of Jesus*, trans. John Bowden (London: SCM, 1997).

54. Bruce Chilton and Craig A. Evans, *James the Just & Christian Origins*, Supplement to Novum Testamentum 98 (Leiden: Brill, 1999).

55. Hershel Shanks and Ben Witherington III, *The Brother of Jesus* (New York: HarperCollins, 2003). Shanks and Witherington's popular and well-written book is full of important data, but it is focused on the ossuary that bears the controversial inscription: "James, the son of Joseph, the brother of Jesus."

56. In *James, Brother of Jesus*, and in "the temple system," Bernheim discusses with great erudition and insight the importance of the Temple in Early Judaism, but in these pages (64–69) he never mentions

Some valued insights on James and the Temple do appear in these books focused on James, sometimes stimulated by the discovery of an ossuary bearing three names: "James, the son of Joseph, the brother of Jesus."[58] The scholars listed and those who contributed to the book edited by Chilton and Evans tend to concur upon and emphasize numerous points.

First, in historical studies, priority is often given to Paul's authentic letters when Paul's comments differ from traditions in Acts. The scholars demonstrate that such a methodology is too simplistic; it fails to acknowledge that Paul was emotionally shaping his accounts.

Second, the documents collected into the New Testament tend to have a bias against James and for Paul. Thus, one needs to consult the following additional sources for James: Josephus, the *Protoevangelium of James*, the *Gospel of the Hebrews*, the *Gospel of Thomas*, Hegesippus, Epiphanius, Clement of Alexandria, Eusebius, the *Apocryphon of James*, the *First and Second Apocalypse of James*, the *Kerygmata Petrou*, the *Epistula Petri*, the *Pseudo-Clementines*, Helvidius, and Jerome.[59] Clearly a myopic focus on the canonical works will be misleading, and we should readily admit that all sources are biased.

Third, according to ancient tradition, James was the first Bishop of the Jerusalem Church. This is stated explicitly by Clement of Alexandria (*apud* Eusebius, *HE* 2.1.2-5).[60]

Fourth, James focused his life and teaching in (not on) the Temple. Most likely, in the Temple he prayed with the eschatological hope that Jesus would return from the East, as reported by angels (Acts 1:6-11).

James. Bruce Chilton and Craig Evans do comment on the importance of the Temple for James in *James the Just & Christian Origins*, 8–9, 258–61, and 233–49.

57. I have not included Robert Eisenman's *James the Brother of Jesus* (New York: Viking, 1997). He does not inform us of how and what ways James Research helps us understand the importance of the Temple within the Palestinian Jesus Movement, fails to engage the fruitful advances by scholars, is idiosyncratic, rejects the correct dates for the *Pesharim* and the first reports of the Righteous Teacher (all antedate Paul and James and thus cannot refer to them), is clearly at variance with the consensus among historical, Qumranic, and biblical scholars, incorrectly imagines that Palestinian messianism before 70 had only one form, and fails to see the vast difference between the Palestinian Jesus Movement before 70 and the complex chaotic world represented by Christianity in the second century ce. Yet, I admire Eisenman's erudition, creative energies, and focus on primary sources too often ignored.

58. See Charlesworth, *Has Jesus' Family Tomb Been Discovered?* [Grand Rapids, MI: Eerdmans, forthcoming].

59. Painter is the best guide to the traditions; and he examines all these diverse and conflicting sources.

60. See esp. Martin Hengel, "Jakobus der Herrenbruder–der erste 'Papst'?" in *Glaube und Eschatologie: Festschrift für Werner Georg Kümmel zum 80. Geburtstag*, ed. E. Grässer and O. Merk (Tübingen: Mohr Siebeck, 1985), 71–104.

The historian can only speculate about what might have been the future of "Christianity" if Western Christianity had not rejected "Jewish Christianity" (however one might define that term). That is, when the Roman legions burned much of the Holy Land, Jerusalem, and especially the Temple, they also undermined James's "Semitic Christianity." The undisputed primacy of James and the Mother Church in Jerusalem was lost forever. Almost all power was passed on to Antioch, Alexandria, and especially Rome.[61] One can find remnants of James' position and thoughts in the New Testament documents, some apocryphal books, the Church Fathers, and notably Syriac Christianity.

The extant sources raise many questions. Are we to imagine diversity in the earliest decades, with Paul and Peter defining Western Christianity while James and Thomas shaped Eastern Christianity? Why are the introductions to Early Christianity so focused on the West? How should the Thomas traditions, known from the evidence about Edessa and justly famous for Christians on the Malabar Coast of India, be integrated into a new reconstruction of Christian origins? Is the world east of Jerusalem so unimportant, as many publications assume, when according to Acts 2 the languages mentioned are predominantly to the East?

If Jesus' followers, Greeks and Jews, believed that the Torah or Law was fulfilled in Jesus, why is the Temple not mentioned in the "council" in Jerusalem (Acts 15)? Why is the Temple seldom mentioned in studies on James? He is clearly is portrayed as one who adhered in extreme fashions to Judaism and the Torah which demanded worship only in the Temple.

The death of James looms large in ancient lore. Most importantly for us, the association with the Temple appears central to each account.[62] The Jewish-Christian author of the *Ascents of James* contends that Jesus rejected animal sacrifice in the Temple (but how reliable is such a claim?), and describes how James was thrown down the steps of the Temple, but survived.[63] Josephus implies that James was stoned (*Ant* 20.197-203). The author of the *Second Apocalypse of James* reports that James was thrown down from the Temple, clubbed, and then stoned to death (61–62).[64] Hegesippus (*HE* 2.23.3-18) and Eusebius (*HE* 2.23.3) state that he was thrown from the top of the Temple

61. See the insightful reflections by Bernheim in *James, Brother of Jesus*, 259–68.

62. As Evans judged, the *Second Apocalypse of James* closely associates Jesus with the Temple; see Evans, *James the Just & Christian Origins*, 249.

63. See Robert E. Van Voorst, *The Ascents of James: History and Theology of a Jewish-Christian Community*, Society of Biblical Language Dissertation Series (Atlanta: Scholars, 1989).

64. See Charles W. Hedrick's translation in *The Nag Hammadi Library*, ed. James M. Robinson (New York: Harper & Row, 1977), 254–55.

(actually the Sanctuary), stoned, and then clubbed apparently once (Clement implies many times).

Hegesippus, a Christian who lived in the second century CE, provides our most important biographical details on James. While his account of James contains some legendary embellishments, one statement has been accepted as fundamentally reliable: James, whom later writers describe as the first "bishop" in Jerusalem,[65] chose to pray not on the Mount of Olives but in the Temple. Note the passage:

> [It was] James, the brother of the Lord, to whom the throne of the bishopric in Jerusalem had been allotted by the Apostles. . . . He alone was allowed to enter into the sanctuary . . . and he used to enter alone into the temple (*eis ton naon*) and be found kneeling and praying for forgiveness for the people, so that his knees grew hard like a camel's because of his constant worship of God, kneeling and asking forgiveness for the people. [*apud* Eusebius, *HE* 2.23.1-7. LCL 153]

James was martyred in 62 CE. A Sadducean high priest, named Ananus (Anan), the son of Anan, convened the Sanhedrin (but without legal support from the governor) and had James condemned. Ananus was responsible for James's death. Ananus was high priest for only three months, perhaps, as Josephus reports, because he was a harsh judge (*Ant* 20.200-293). The Pharisees persuaded Agrippa to remove Ananus from the high priesthood. He was summarily dismissed by King Agrippa (*Ant* 20.200-203).

In summary, it becomes clear that James was a controversial figure in early Christian literature. He is marginalized in the canonical Gospels, portrayed as Jerusalem's authoritative leader in Acts (Acts 15:13-21), seen as an adversary by Paul (Gal. 2), considered a victim by Josephus (*Ant* 20), and hailed as a hero in many apocryphal works and by Hegesippus (*apud* Eusebius, *HE* 2.23).

Behind all these reports rises the importance of the Temple in James studies. Legends do not hide the probability that James did continue to worship (at least, to pray) in the Temple. According to the *Second Apocalypse of James* 60–63, Jesus' brother tells those present to play the trumpets, flutes, and harps. Later that same day, he "arose" "and spoke" in the Temple for a "few hours." He is depicted "standing beside the columns of the Temple."[66]

65. Both Epiphanius and Eusebius list James, followed by Symeon, as the first Jerusalem bishops. Each was a relative of Jesus. See the discussion of the Jerusalem bishops list in Richard Bauckham, *Jude and the Relatives of Jesus in the Early Church*, 70–79.

James may not have participated in the sacrifices led by the high priests. After all, by the sixties the opposition to Jesus' followers had irrupted for decades and much of the source of the explosion was from the high priestly families. Nevertheless, vast amounts of evidence point to the continuing reverence for the Temple by Jesus' apostles, first disciples, James, and others in the Palestinian Jesus Movement.

Earlier we discussed how Paul entered the Temple to perform purification rituals. Most likely, James was behind Paul's willingness to enter the Temple to purify himself. Paul refers to James as one of the "pillars" (*styloi*) of Jesus' movement (Gal. 2:9). Does such an honorific epithet suggest a link with the pillars or porticoes in the Temple?[67] If so, it is possible that James was imagined to be one of the "pillars" in the eschatological Temple in the age to come.[68] Such questions bring us back to see how James' life, death, and adoration are all related to the Temple and its veneration.

A caveat needs emphasizing; we should not try to systematize complex data. On the one hand, we should resist concluding, using Qumran polemics, that all Jesus' followers rejected the Temple and judged the high priests, especially those related to Annas in 30 and Ananus in 62, as evil priests. On the other hand, it is obvious that some of Jesus' followers, from Peter to James, revered the Temple and hallowed it as the House of God, the center of Jewish worship. Did Jesus' followers, after his crucifixion in 30, abandon worship, as prayer, in the Temple, and did all of Jesus' Torah-observant followers refuse to sacrifice in the Temple? The answer is clearly: "No." Did Jesus' brother, James, continue to pray in the Temple? In light of numerous independent sources, the answer is obvious: "Yes."

With some followers of Jesus before 70, especially Paul and the author of Hebrews, we perceive Temple imagery being shifted from cult to community. The sacred is moved from a particular building to a universal creation, the individual and the corporate "Body of Christ." These developments pave the road for the way ahead. After 70, as with Rabbinic Jews,[69] "Christians" felt

---

66. Such positive images of the Temple appear in this text although its author claims that the House was doomed to destruction (*Second Apocalypse of James* 60).

67. The author of 1QSa 1.12-13 refers to "the pillars (or "foundations," "units") [יסודות] of the holy Congregation," and that concept is eschatological.

68. C.K. Barrett published that argument: "Paul and the 'Pillar' Apostles," in *Studia Paulina in Honorem Johannis de Zwaan Septuagenarii*, ed. J.N. Sevenster and W.C. van Unnik (Haarlem: Erven F. Bohn, 1953), 12–13.

69. Generally speaking, the early rabbis harbored the hope that the Temple would be restored. In contrast, after 70, Jesus' followers felt it had been replaced by a spiritual temple, the Body of Christ.

a need to replace the Temple after it was destroyed. Both groups provide spotlights that throw light back onto the paradigmatic importance of the Jerusalem Temple for followers of Jesus.

III. 70 TO 150: AFTER THE TEMPLE'S DESTRUCTION; THE TIME OF THE COMPOSITION OF THE GOSPELS

Before 70 CE, there were over twenty types of Palestinians Jews;[70] only two types survived the conflagration of Jerusalem and the Temple: The followers of Hillel (and Shammai), who developed Rabbinic Judaism, and the followers of Jesus, who would eventually be called "Christians." Obviously, as with Rabbinic Jews, "Christians" after 70 were forced to find substitutes for the Temple's functions and place in the cosmos. In this chapter, our reflections must remain simple and focused.

Perceptions of post-70 phenomena and theological ideas should not blind us to a perception of the beliefs and habits of Jesus' disciples and followers prior to 70. If Mark is judged to be Peter's scribe who wrote the first Gospel about 70, he was not one who had known Jesus, and he probably knew virtually nothing about or showed no interest in the question that is now in focal view. Mark put an emphasis upon following Jesus as Messiah and being willing to carry a cross in life's struggles. His interest was not upon the Temple in far away Jerusalem. Let us briefly review some of the influential publications on Mark.

Willi Marxsen paved the way to see the theological creativity of Mark. According to Marxsen, Judea and the Temple are no longer important for Mark: "Galilee establishes the identity of the now Risen Lord with the earthly Jesus, just as the awaited Parousia, likewise in Galilee, secures his identity with the one who is to return."[71] Eduard Schweizer argued that Mark believed Jesus' actions in the Temple (the incident with the moneychangers) symbolized the abolition of an institution. The Temple had been "restricted entirely to Jews"; now Mark's Jesus offers a New Temple that is open to everyone.[72] Hugh Anderson rightly showed that for Mark, Jesus appears in the Temple as "the supremely authoritative Teacher." He contends that for Mark, the cursing of

---

70. The list is long. It includes Hillelites, Shammaites, other more apocalyptically oriented Pharisees, Sadducees, Samaritans, Baptist groups, the various Enoch groups, the Essenes at Qumran, the Essenes elsewhere, the revolutionary groups that were numerous, the various groups within the Temple, and the numerous groups that claimed to be followers of Jesus.

71. Willi Marxsen, *Mark the Evangelist*, trans. James Boyce et al. (Nashville: Abingdon, 1969), 215.

72. Eduard Schweizer, *The Good News According to Mark*, trans. Donald H. Madvig (Atlanta: John Knox, 1970), 233. He later suggests that institution is the church (32).

the fig tree illustrates that "the Temple and all it stands for comes under the withering blast of his [Jesus'] prophetic word."[73]

Among the Evangelists, only Mark mentions that Jesus prohibited anyone carrying a vessel through the Temple (11:16). This tradition preserves a deeply Jewish perspective (cf. Mishnah Berakoth 9:5). Vincent Taylor judges this prohibition to signify "a respect for the holiness of the Temple"; it "was not an attack upon the sacrificial system." While Marxsen throws the spotlight on Mark, Taylor shifts it to the historical Jesus. Yet it seems clear that he would agree with other commentators, such as John Painter,[74] that we are also hearing Mark's viewpoint; Mark would have been pleased with the reference to the Temple being "a house of prayer for all the nations" (Mark 11:17).[75] Thus, Mark carries forward, in places, a positive appreciation of the Temple.

Matthew, who writes after 70 CE, claims that God's glory is not to be found in the Temple. It is to be found in Jesus (Matt. 1:23; 18:20; 28:19). Matthew alone has Jesus exclaim that priests in the Temple have profaned the Sabbath and that "One greater than the Temple is here" (12:6). Matthew concludes Jesus ministry in Jerusalem. However, he adds to the Passion Narrative vitriolic polemics so that the Jews claim that they and their descendants are responsible for Jesus' crucifixion. It is easy, with regard to Matthew, to see mainstream Judaism and the Jesus' Palestinian Movement, once closely related, as the traditions of Hillel prove,[76] moving in different directions. In the process the Temple no longer remains in focus for Jesus' followers. W.D. Davies and Dale Allison judge that for Matthew the old Temple is passé; "its place is taken by the ecclesia."[77] For Matthew, the new Temple reappears as the Christian community.

In Luke-Acts, one-and-the-same author begins by emphasizing Jerusalem as the Holy City and then concludes his narrative with Paul in Rome.[78] The rhetoric seems to move the "Good News" from the Holy Land to the world stage. In the process, the Temple is portrayed not only as the place of worship for Jesus, Peter, John, and Paul but also the source of opposition to this new messianic movement. Eventually, any focus on the Temple is lost as Luke

73. Hugh Anderson, The Gospel of Mark (London: Oliphants, 1976), 264–65.

74. John Painter, Mark's Gospel (London: Routledge, 1997), 159.

75. Vincent Taylor, The Gospel According to St Mark, 2nd ed. (London: Macmillan, 1966), 463.

76. See the discussions in Charlesworth and L.L. Johns, eds., Jesus and Hillel: Comparative Studies of Two Major Religious Leaders (Minneapolis: Fortress Press, 1997).

77. Davies and Allison, The Gospel According to Saint Matthew, 3:154.

78. J.B. Green, "The Demise of the Temple as 'Culture Center' in Luke-Acts: An Exploration of the Rending of the Temple Veil," Revue Biblique 101 (1994): 495–515.

portrays the Palestinian Movement moving away from its motherland. For Luke, traditions are edited so that Paul, and not his rivals Peter or James, becomes dominant. The Kingdom of God is announced to exist within Jesus' group ("within all of you"; unique to Luke 17:21). The Temple remains a remnant of previous history; it becomes a catalyst for Christian liturgy.[79]

Surely the Temple is in view in the earliest Christian hymnbook, the *Odes of Solomon*, especially in Ode 4, which antedates 125 CE and was probably composed earlier. Note the moving poetic imagery in "God's Sanctuary." The Odist focuses on the Temple, the Sanctuary, which cannot be desecrated, altered, or moved because it is "the ancient one" that was designed before God made all the special places in which to worship:

> No man can desecrate Your holy site, O my God;
> Nor can he alter it, and put it in another site.
>
> Because (he has) no power over it;
> For Your sanctuary You designed before You made special sites.
>
> The ancient one shall not be desecrated by those inferior to it.
> You have given Your heart, O Lord, to Your faithful ones. (Ode 4:1-3)[80]

As we move to focus on Luke-Acts, observe the comments by leading Lukan scholars. Hans Conzelmann published a major and influential book that is neither concerned with the historical Jesus nor with the earliest community of Jesus' followers. Conzelmann focuses on Luke as a theologian. He argued that for Luke, Jesus' action against the Temple cult had one "sole purpose": it was to illustrate how Jesus took possession of the Temple (Luke 19:45). He wrote, "In Luke it is not a question of the eschatological end of the Temple, but of its cleansing; in other words, Jesus prepares it as somewhere he can stay, and from now on he occupies it as a place belonging to him."[81]

---

79. Daniel K. Falk rightly notes that the destruction of the Temple in 70 was "the single most formative factor in the development of Jewish liturgy." Could it have been less important for "Christians" living in the Levant? Too often, the faithful followers of Jesus within ancient Palestine are lost to view as scholars focus on the movement westward with Peter and Paul. See Falk in *The Book of Acts in its First Century Setting*, ed. Richard Bauckham, vol. 4 (Grand Rapids, MI: Eerdmans, 1995), 268. Also see Margaret Barker, *The Great High Priest: The Temple Roots of Christian Liturgy* (Edinburgh: T&T Clark, 2003).

80. Translated by Charlesworth in *The Earliest Christian Hymnbook* (Eugene, OR: Cascade Books, 2009), 7.

Far more than the other Evangelists, Luke emphasizes geography,[82] and is preoccupied with Jerusalem and the Temple.[83] These two places seem to conflate for Luke; Jerusalem is the goal of Jesus' earthly itinerary (13:31-35). The Temple begins the final chapter in the story of salvation with Zechariah burning incense in the Temple (1:9). It is the center of Jesus' bar mitzvah (2:41-52). The story demarcates Jesus as one who is destined to be preoccupied "with things of my Father"; that is a euphemism for "in the House of My Father" (2:49) because Jesus is in the Temple (2:46). Luke places Jesus' first discussion with the wise men in Israel not in Nazareth or in Capernaum; it is in the Temple at Passover.[84]

The Temple is also where the Eleven, with others, return from Bethany. While Luke knows the early traditions about the resurrection appearances of Jesus in Galilee, since he depends on Mark, he records only those centered near Jerusalem and the Temple (Luke 24). In fact, the last words in Luke signify the importance of the Temple for him: "And they returned to Jerusalem with great joy, and were continually in the Temple (ἐν τῷ ἱερῷ), praising God" (24:52-53). Customarily, conclusions define the meaning of a literary masterpiece; thus, Luke's ending, with a view upon Temple worship, is exceptional. By the time of the Third Evangelist, as Bovon notes, "the synagogues have closed their doors to the Christian gospel."[85]

As Daniel K. Falk states, "Acts portrays Palestinian Christians praying in only two specified venues: the Temple (Acts 3:1; 22:17; perhaps 2:42, 46–47?) and homes (Acts 4:24-31; 12:5, 12; perhaps 1:14, 24–25?)."[86] He also rightly adds, "According to Luke, the first Jerusalem Christians continued their devotion to the Temple and its service (Acts 21:15-26) and maintained a distinctive presence there with preaching (Acts 5:20-21, 42) and regular assembly in Solomon's portico (Acts 3:11; 5:12-13) so that even many priests believed (Acts 6:7)."[87] That is before 70 CE. In summation, I am convinced Luke thought that for his time, the Temple was an institution of the past, belonging

---

81. Hans Conzelmann, *The Theology of St. Luke*, trans. Geoffrey Buswell (New York: Harper & Row, 1961), 77.

82. See Michael Bachmann, *Jerusalem und der Tempel: Die geographish-theologischen Elemente in der lukanischen Sicht des jüdischen Kultzentrums*, BWANT 9 (Stuttgart: W. Kohlkammer, 1980).

83. This well-known fact about Luke is succinctly and brilliantly discussed by Joseph A. Fitzmyer, *The Gospel According to Luke*, Anchor Bible (New York: Doubleday, 1981), 1:164–71.

84. See the reflections by François Bovon, *Luke 1*, Hermeneia (Minneapolis: Fortress Press, 2002), 112.

85. Bovon, *Luke 1*, 10.

86. Falk, *The Book of Acts in its First Century Setting*, 4:269.

87. Falk, *The Book of Acts in its First Century Setting*, 4:270.

to the Baptizer and the earthly Jesus, and grudgingly to Paul, but not to the emerging *ecclesia pressa*. After all, it was not possible to worship in the Temple as before 70.[88]

The Gospel of John, which took its final and present form long after 70, portrays Jesus on Mount Gerizim, the holy mountain of the Samaritans. He is depicted engaged in conversation with a Samaritan woman. He tells her, "Woman, believe me, the hour is coming when neither on this mountain nor in Jerusalem will you worship the Father" (4:21). This claim rejects the Jerusalem Temple. Such a claim harmonizes with the Johannine emphasis that Jesus has become the Temple; Jesus answered some Judean leaders: "Destroy this temple, and in three days I will raise it up" (2:19). When these Jews misunderstand him, the author adds an explanatory gloss: "But he spoke of the temple of his body" (2:21). Christopher Rowland succinctly summarizes the Fourth Evangelist's perspective of the Temple:

> The manifestation of divine glory exemplified by the sign at Cana in Galilee means that the locus of that divine glory is now focused pre-eminently, and perhaps exclusively, in the Word become flesh and in the demonstration of glory in the lifting up of Jesus on the cross (Jn 3.14; 12.32-33). As Jesus tells the Samaritan woman, Gerizim and Zion have had their day. True worship is worship in spirit and truth (Jn 4.20-24). The Temple has to take second place to this definitive manifestation of divine glory. The divine presence continues in the community of believers and the Father and the Son make their home with the faithful disciple (Jn 14.23).[89]

WHY DID THE AUTHOR OF REVELATION HAVE NO TEMPLE IN THE NEW JERUSALEM?

Inheriting the Jewish concept of two Temples (one on earth and one in heaven), usually the author of Revelation imagines the heavenly Temple in heaven (eleven times). In Rev. 3:12, he intends to depict the relationship of the community with God. In the New Jerusalem that descends from heaven, there is no Temple. For him, no temple will be required. God and the Lamb (who represents the crucified and resurrected Jesus) replace the Temple (21:22a, b). One no longer needs to look up to heaven for God and the Temple. God is now fully on earth with his elect, as he had promised through the prophets and

---

88. Kenneth W. Clark, however, rightly pointed to traditions that indicated some worship continued in the ruins of the Temple. See Clark, *The Gentile Bias*, ed. John L. Sharpe III (Leiden: Brill, 1980).

89. Rowland, "The Temple in the New Testament," in *Temple and Worship in Biblical Israel*, 472.

the Psalms. The Lamb's self-sacrifice replaces any need for continuous sacrifices of animals.[90] Thus, as Karl Barth (who spoke of the Temple as "the church'") pointed out in 1925, "In the heavenly Jerusalem of Revelation nothing is more finally significant than the church's complete absence: 'And I saw no Temple therein.'"[91]

Following the method and perspective of apocalyptic eschatology, all phenomena are redefined and all hope is transferred to a future time or transcendent realm.[92] The rhetorical development of Temple in Revelation should be recognized; eventually, as Andrea Spatafora noted, the "temple of God" (11:1) evolves from God's heavenly abode to a metaphor for the church; in John's theology the Temple "is a vehicle for his ecclesiology."[93]

In *The Apocalypse in the Light of the Temple*, John and Gloria Ben-Daniel seek a new approach to Revelation by examining it in light of ancient traditions regarding the Temple.[94] They contend that the organizing principle in Revelation is "the theme of the Temple" (4). They are convinced that the "Temple revealed to John and described in the Apocalypse is the same heavenly Dwelling that was revealed to Moses with the purpose of building the Tent or Dwelling of God on earth" (10). One fundamental difference is caused by the advent of the Messiah. While scholars may consider that such a conclusion is tendentious and that metaphors are taken too literally, it is imperative to observe how important the Temple continued to be for many who believed Jesus had been the Messiah.

---

90. See esp. Loren Johns, *The Lamb Christology of the Apocalypse of John*, WUNT 2. Reihe, 167 (Tübingen: Mohr Siebeck, 2003).

91. Karl Barth, "Biblische Fragen: Einsichten und Ausblicke," in *Das Wort Gottes und die Theologie* (Munich: Chr. Kaiser, 1925), 70–78; Barth, "Biblical Questions: Insights and Vistas," in *The Word of God and the Word of Man* (London: Hodder & Stoughton, 1928), 51–96; the quotation is on p. 72. As Rowland points out, Barth wisely gave priority to Kingdom over institution (*Temple and Worship in Biblical Israel*, 480).

92. See Charlesworth, *The New Testament Apocrypha and Pseudepigrapha*, American Theological Library Association Bibliography Series 17 (Methuchen, NJ: Scarecrow, 1987),19–30.

93. Andrea Spatafora, *From the "Temple of God" to God as the Temple: A Biblical Theological Study of the Temple in the Book of Revelation*, Tesi Gregoriana Serie Teologia 27 (Rome: Editrice Pontificia Università Gregoriana, 1997), esp. 9.

94. David and Gloria Ben-Daniel, *The Apocalypse in the Light of the Temple: A New Approach to the Book of Revelation* (Jerusalem: Beit Yochanan, 2003).

Other Early Witnesses

According to the extant fragments of the *Gospel of the Ebionites*,[95] Jesus came "to abolish the sacrifices."[96] This rhetoric, however, that informs us of attitudes to the Temple by Christians who lived after the first century CE (see also the *Acts of Pilate* 4 [contrast ch. 16). In the pre-fourth-century *Acts of Andrew*,[97] Jesus and the Twelve enter the Temple, but it is now labeled "the temple of the Gentiles." They enter not to worship but to observe "the devil's ignorance." The high priests and their cohorts are pilloried as "the priests of the idols." Such later anti-Jewish rhetoric should be dismissed as "heretical," using the words of Eusebius (*HE* 3.25.6). These "gospels" inform us neither of Jesus' attitude nor of his disciples' attitude. The compositions also do not represent the attitude of the emerging Church. To observe documents that claim Jesus Christ and his community replaces the Temple is not necessarily anti-Jewish. After all, Jews had to find ways to replace the Temple and its cult.

The Temple was widely recognized as a Temple by Gentiles. Maybe Alexander the Great did not offer sacrifices in the Temple as Josephus claimed (*Ant* 11.329-30), but other Gentiles did. The most famous were the Egyptian Ptolemy III (*Against Apion* 2.48), the Syrian Antiochus VII (*Ant* 13.242-43), and the Romans Marcus Agrippa (*Ant* 16.14) and Lucius Vitellius (*Ant* 18.122).[98] It is thus conceivable that some Gentile "Christians" offered sacrifices in the Temple, as implied by Lev. 22:25. Clearly many early Jews believed that at the end time, Gentiles would flood into the Temple, as we know from many texts (viz., Isa. 2:3; *1 En.* 90:29). Recall Mic. 4:1-2: "Peoples shall stream to it, and many nations shall come and say: 'Come, let us go up to the mountain of the LORD, to the house of the God of Jacob; that he may teach us his ways and that we may walk in his paths'" (NRSV). The streets in the new Jerusalem that are reflected in the *Temple Scroll* are most likely expanded to make room for the influx of the righteous Gentiles.

Above, we asked one central question: "Did Jesus' followers frequent the Temple and worship there?" For the period before 70 CE, the answer is "yes."

95. Epiphanius, *adv. Haer* 30.16 (ed. Holl, *GCS* 25, 335–56).

96. Elliott, *The Apocryphal New Testament*, 15.

97. Papyrus Utrecht 1 is a Sahidic Coptic fragment of the fourth century; the original Greek would be older.

98. I am indebted for this information to Jerome Murphy-O'Connor, *Paul: A Critical Life* (Oxford: Oxford University Press, 1997), 342–43.

Conclusion: The Palestinian Jesus Movement and the Temple

We have reviewed the New Testament evidence focused on one question: Did Jesus' earliest followers frequent the Temple and worship there? We have noted that the apostles and many of the earliest followers of Jesus continued to worship regularly in the Temple. Note in Acts 2:46, they were "attending the Temple together" and in Luke 24:53, Jesus' disciples "were continually in the Temple, praising God." While these summaries reflect Luke's editorial hand, they also are reliable historically, as other passages indicate. Jesus, his disciples, and followers frequented and hallowed the Temple. For Jesus and the Twelve, the Temple often became the focal point for ministry and preaching (see, e.g., Acts 3:11-12; 5:12-16; 21, 42). Paul also participated in Temple rituals and taught there (Acts 21:26-36; 22:17). Paul's statement, "For Christ, our paschal lamb, has been sacrificed" (1 Cor. 5:7), does not replace the Temple; it hallows it.

Theological reflections help us understand that Temple language evolved into a new symbolical world for Jesus' followers. The polished stones (ashlars) of the Temple in Jerusalem were recycled symbolically into believers as "living stones" (1 Pet. 2:5) within a temple built by God for his Son so that the author of Hebrew may claim "we are His house" (Heb. 3:1-6).

Sociological reflections on the Temple and worship by Jesus' followers help us perceive a shift from "the House" to the "house church." The best example of the latter is "Peter's House" in Capernaum, as attested by the inscriptions in many ancient languages and the plastered interior of a public room. Most likely before, and definitely after, the loss of the Temple, Jesus' followers met in the homes of patrons of the Palestinian Jesus Movement (and also, most likely, in many synagogues), studied scripture (often searching for prophecies about the coming of the Messiah), taught (Acts 20:20), chanted psalms, hymns, and odes (Col. 3:15-16), and celebrated the Eucharist (Acts 2:46; 1 Cor. 11:17-34).

Ancient traditions in the Old Testament and in other early Jewish documents stressed the Temple as "the House," or "the House of YHWH." Developing these ancient traditions, Jesus' followers, especially in the Diaspora, developed the concept of the household of God and the church in the house (cf. 2 Tim. 4:19; Philem. 2; cf. 2 John 10). From one House to many houses, and from Jerusalem and Caesarea Maritima to Antioch and Corinth, entire households accepted Jesus as the One-who-was-to come (cf. Acts 16:34; 1 Cor. 1:16). The "house-church" provided the sacred space for worship once conceived as appropriate only in the Temple. Jews, in a parallel development, created sacred spaces in synagogues for worship, transforming an institution that had been the Jewish social center of civil and religious life.

Scholars who follow Jesus' life and teaching only according to Matthew and Mark and conclude that Jesus had no interest in Judea and Jerusalem misrepresent not only the variegated thoughts in the first three Gospels but miss the significance of the Fourth Gospel in historical research.[99] The Fourth Evangelist alone names many sites familiar to Christians everywhere; two parade examples are Bethesda and Siloam. One site is north of the Temple and the other south; they not only frame the Temple but are *mikvaot* (Jewish ritual purification baths). Those who wished to enter the Temple could immerse themselves in "living water" in the *mikveh*. After this ritual cleansing, the worshipper was purified and qualified for admission to the Temple.

Those who claim that Jesus becomes eventually the *axis mundi* for his followers are correct; but that does not make the Temple obsolete. The author of Revelation does portray the New Jerusalem without a Temple, but that is not because the Temple is obsolete. It is because of the fulfillment of prophecy; God now is living among his faithful ones in an unprecedented imminence. The oft-repeated prophecy is depicted as fulfilled: "I shall be their God and they shall be my people" (2 Cor. 6:16; cf. Ezek. 37:27).

Hopefully, the deliberations and proceedings of this symposium will challenge Christians to re-examine their presuppositions and to rethink the assumptions about the Temple in the life of Jesus and in the lives of his followers. Jesus and his apostles loved and honored the Temple; it was God's House. Jesus is much closer to so-called mainstream Judaism than is often assumed.

If I have been intermittently too positive and definite, that alone moves a discussion forward and contributes to a better recreation of the past. I appreciate the admission of Jerome Murphy-O'Connor: "Only definiteness, however, can provoke the reactions that in dialogue lead to progress."[100]

EXCURSUS: ATTITUDES TO THE TEMPLE: JESUS AND THE ESSENES IN JERUSALEM.

One brief note may help us comprehend the social life in Jerusalem between the time of Herod (37–4 BCE) and the destruction of 70 CE. In the early phases of Qumran (or Essene) history, the Qumranites separated themselves from

---

99. See J.H. Charlesworth, "The Historical Jesus in the Fourth Gospel: A Paradigm Shift?" *Journal for the Historical Jesus* 8 (2010): 3–46.

100. J. Murphy-O'Connor, *Paul: A Critical Life*, v.

the Temple and its services, rejecting the officiating priests as illegitimate (cf. esp. 1QS, the Pesharim, and 4QMMT). They could not, however, divorce themselves from the symbolic power of the Temple and Zion, because these concepts were formative symbols deeply embedded in documents sacred to them.[101] After Herod defeated the Hasmoneans in 37 BCE and replaced the Hasmonean high priests, the Essenes lost their main reason for rejecting the high priest, since their archenemies had been Hasmoneans priests and high priests.

They also were favored by Herod because an Essene had prophesied that he would become "king." It is conceivable, during the last phase in the history of the Essenes, that some entered the Holy City. If they lived in Jerusalem, but far from the Temple, and in the southwestern section, then one has to allow for the possibility of some contact between Jesus and the Essenes, because this is the section of Jerusalem in which Jesus celebrated his last supper, and it is precisely in this area that early sources report the followers of Jesus lived. This hypothesis would certainly help in ascertaining how Essene concepts may have been known to Jesus and his disciples or followers.

Are we to imagine that Jesus and the Essenes discussed God's Rule (which they both shared), apocalypticism (which shaped their thoughts), Sabbath rules and purity (in which there were often deep differences), and God's grace and loving forgiveness (in which much would be shared)? How would their views of the Temple compare? For Jesus and the Essenes, a faithful Jew could revere the Temple and some of its liturgy and yet despise some (or even all) of its ruling priests.

---

101. See the insightful reflections (in Hebrew) by Menahem Kister in "Jerusalem and the Temple in the Writings from Qumran," in *The Qumran Scrolls and Their World*, ed. Menaham Kister (Jerusalem: Yad Ben-Zavi, 2009) 2:477 –96. Kister does not sufficiently distinguish between "the Temple" and the cult in the Temple. One can love the Temple and even the cult but have problems with some ruling priests. That distinction is imperative in judging Jesus' and his followers' relation to the Temple.

8

The Temple and Jesus the High Priest in the New Testament

Harold W. Attridge

Early Christians display a variety of attitudes toward the Temple of Jerusalem and its priests, some taking it for granted, some using it as a multifaceted symbol, some considering it to be a relic of the past to be replaced by the new reality of the Christian community. Attitudes toward the Temple were no doubt affected by its destruction in 70 CE as well as by the tensions that developed between believers, both Jew and Gentile, in the Messianic status of Jesus, and traditional Jews who did not share that belief.

Our access to what early Christians thought about the Temple is provided mainly through the writings of the New Testament. Apocryphal materials and historical accounts add a few interesting tidbits, and we shall look at some of them here, but they generally reflect later realities. Using these writings requires some caution, since many tell stories about the past, including the life of Jesus or the experience of the early church. How much of that story is an accurate reflection of early belief and practice and how much is part of the theological imagination of the writer is not always clear. This paper will attempt to trace the attitudes of Jesus and his followers chronologically, from the earthly ministry of Jesus to the beginning of the second century, with some attention to later developments.

THE TEMPLE AND ITS PRIESTS IN THE WORDS AND DEEDS OF JESUS

The sayings of Jesus, though redacted and shaped by the imagination of later generations of Christians, contain tantalizing bits of information. Some of his sayings seem to take the Temple for granted as a holy place where certain kinds of religious transactions usually take place. Thus, Jesus admonishes one who is angry while on the way to bring a sacrifice to the altar, presumably in the Temple, to leave his sacrificial business aside until he resolves his personal relationship (Matt. 5:23-24). Similarly, in a story of the healing of a leper, Jesus tells the man healed to go, make the appropriate offering, and show himself to the priest (Matt. 8:4; Mark 1:44; Luke 5:14). In materials such as this, the Temple and its role in the life of Israel are assumed. It is, however, noteworthy how few of these sayings there are. Stories about Jesus and the Temple, especially in the last days of his ministry, are a prominent part of the Gospel tradition, but we need to assess those in the context of the narrative theology of the evangelists.

There is another saying about the Temple attributed to Jesus in several slightly different forms that merits special attention. All three of the Synoptic Gospels report that in his last week in Jerusalem Jesus predicted the destruction of the Temple, not one stone of which would stand on another (Matt. 24:2; Mark 13:2; Luke 21:6).

Scholars have long debated whether this saying, in some form or other, is an authentic prediction of the historical Jesus or a product of later Christian prophecy, perhaps uttered originally at the time when the Roman emperor Gaius attempted to have his statue placed in the Temple, or perhaps even later, at the time of the Jewish revolt against Rome.[1] We know from Josephus of the presence of at least one other prophet active at that time who predicted that the Temple would fall.[2] That Jesus of Nazareth, some years earlier, could have made a similar prophecy is not at all improbable.

In addition to the prediction of destruction, there is some evidence of a more direct threat against the Temple. Those who accused Jesus before the Sanhedrin alleged, according to the Gospel accounts, that he threatened to destroy the Temple and rebuild it in three days (Matt. 26:61; Mark 14:58). Luke's version of the trial scene (Luke 22:67-71) does not contain this detail, but a version of the charge appears in the narrative about the arrest of the protomartyr Stephen in Acts 6:14. One final saying of Jesus relating to the Temple and to the alleged threat appears in John 2:19, where Jesus tells the crowds in Jerusalem who have reacted to his driving the moneychangers from the Temple: "Destroy this Temple and in three days I shall raise it up again."

Some scholars, such as E.P. Sanders, have found in these sayings and in the action of "cleansing" the Temple an authentic reminiscence of the historical Jesus who, at least at the end of his career, pronounced a prophetic judgment on the Temple and the priestly leadership that governed it.[3] The traditions need

---

1. See, for example, Lloyd Gaston, *No Stone on Another: Studies in the Significance of the Fall of Jerusalem in the Synoptic Gospels*, Supplements to Novum Testamentum 23 (Leiden: Brill, 1970).

2. Josephus, *Jewish War*, 6.300-309, on the prophecies of another Jesus, son of Ananias.

careful sorting. Jesus almost certainly did say something about the destruction of the Temple, a remark that generated the prediction about the destruction of the Temple and the longer eschatological discourse of the Synoptic Gospels, with its various warnings about end-time events. The fact that Jesus said something about the destruction of the Temple does not, in and of itself, reveal his stance toward it.

The most primitive form of the saying threatening the Temple is that of the Gospel of John, despite the tendentious character of its placement early in the life of Jesus and a layer of interpretation that accompanies it. If that judgment is correct, we may get some sense of an attitude toward the Temple that will grow in importance as the post-resurrection movement of Jesus' followers develops.

A full treatment of the tradition of this saying would take more time and space than is allotted here. Let me simply point out the features that warrant my judgment about the Johannine version. The form of the saying, unlike that of the Synoptic Gospels, is a good Semitic idiom. A command functions as the equivalent of a conditional protasis. "Destroy this Temple" is the functional equivalent of "If you destroy this Temple." The apodosis, "I will build it up again in three days," might seem like a very pretentious claim; and so it was no doubt construed by many who heard it. Nonetheless, if there is a play on the various meanings of *bayit*, the saying would make excellent sense in a first-century Semitic milieu. In other words, it is easy to imagine Jesus saying, "If you destroy this House of God, I'll quickly rebuild God's House," that is, in the hearts and minds of the new "family" that his movement was creating. The fact that the Dead Sea Scrolls make a similar play on the community sense of the "house of God" indicates at least that such a claim was possible. There is, it should be noted, one other attestation of something like the saying in the Fourth Gospel. It appears in *Gospel of Thomas* 71, which reports an explicit threat: "Jesus said, 'Destroy this house and no one will be able to build it [...]." It remains unclear whether Jesus ever addressed the question of what kind of priests might serve in a "restored" or metaphorical temple.

The most primitive form of Jesus' remark about the Temple, then, is a kind of prophetic aphorism. In it, Jesus offers a challenge that many of his followers could not dismiss but had to interpret. Otherwise, particularly in light of the actual threat to the Temple in the time of the revolt against Rome, Jesus could all too easily be construed as another hotheaded insurrectionist. Matthew and Mark deal with the saying by denying that Jesus said anything of the sort.

3. See E.P. Sanders, *The Historical Figure of Jesus* (London: Penguin, 1993).

Claiming that it was a false accusation against him, they threw out the baby with the bathwater. Another option was to admit that Jesus said something but that he did not mean to say anything about the Temple itself. This is the path chosen by the Gospel of John, where the narrator tells us that Jesus was speaking not of the Temple but of his body (John 2:21).

My reading of the core of this tradition, found in the Johannine saying and also in the *Gospel of Thomas*, does not imply an implacable hostility toward the Temple on the part of Jesus. It is compatible with the other sayings attributed to Jesus that imply an acceptance of the presence of the Temple and its functions. What the saying aims to do, in good prophetic fashion, is to relativize the importance of the Temple. Yes, it is a place where lepers can show themselves to priests and make appropriate offerings, but if it were to be destroyed, God would still have a dwelling in humankind.

ATTITUDES TOWARD THE TEMPLE AND ITS PRIESTS AMONG EARLY FOLLOWERS OF JESUS

Whatever the attitude of Jesus toward the Temple, his immediate followers after his death and resurrection continued to frequent the holy place. The Book of Acts reports as much (Acts 2:46-47), while it also notes tensions between the followers of Jesus and contemporary Jews. Lukan theology may play a role here and it will be necessary to reexamine Luke's purposes. It is possible, however, to have some confidence that his report about at least some of the early Christians in Jerusalem is not simply a matter of his imagination or part of a theological construct. The historian Josephus, in his brief mention of James, the brother of Jesus (*Ant.* 20.200), notes that he was executed by the High Priest Ananus for having transgressed the Law. At the very least, this report indicates that followers of Jesus remained in Jerusalem until the outbreak of the Jewish revolt and were known to the priestly leadership. Later reports of the martyrdom of James, particularly the report attributed to the second-century author Hegesippus cited by Eusebius, associate him with the Temple.

> He alone was allowed to enter into the sanctuary (εἰς τὰ ἅγια εἰσιέναι). For he did not wear wool but linen, and he used to enter alone into the temple and be found kneeling and praying for the forgiveness for the people. (*HE* 2.23.6)

Although the account of Hegesippus has many legendary components, the association of James with the Temple and his martyrdom[4] is probably historical. Some of the followers of Jesus therefore continued to revere the Temple and use it as a place of prayer. Unfortunately, they have not left a record of that prayer life or belief, and those prayers and beliefs probably closely resembled those of their fellow Jews, except for their identification of Jesus as the Messiah.

The major source for the life of Christians in the decades after the death of Jesus and before the composition of the Gospels is the apostle Paul. His generally acknowledged letters do not say much about the Jerusalem Temple itself. They do use Temple imagery to make points about the life of believers, both collectively and individually. Particularly, in 1 Corinthians, where he wrestles with issues in a new community largely composed of Gentiles, Paul reminds his followers that, as a community constructed through the efforts of apostles like himself and Apollos, they were built as a "Temple of God" to stand the test of eschatological judgment (1 Cor. 3:10-17). Again, as individual Temples of the Holy Spirit, the Corinthians should not give themselves to prostitutes (1 Cor. 6:19). They are called to be holy, like the sacred space to which they are likened.

The attitude implicit in Paul's remarks recalls important features of the teachings of Jesus and, for that matter, the sectarians of Qumran. The Temple is not disparaged, but the reality that it embodies, the sanctity of the divine presence, is available in the communal life of believers. One implication of the image that will play a role in later Christian authors is that the ritual life of the community stands in relationship to the ritual activity of the Temple. Paul does devote attention to the sacred meal of the community, its relationship to the death of Jesus and the hope for his return (1 Cor. 11:23-26). He contrasts all of that with the sacrificial table of demons in Greco-Roman cults, but he does not draw the inference that the table of believers is a new sacrificial activity that somehow corresponds to or supplants the sacrifices of the Temple. Hints of that thinking will later appear in other authors.

If the account in the Acts of the Apostles is to be trusted, Paul's last visit to Jerusalem before his arrest and removal to Rome involved a visit to the Temple. As Acts describes it, the visit was cloaked in traditional Jewish piety, with Paul having taken the vow of a Nazarite (Acts 21:28-29). One can imagine that the man who tried to be a Greek to the Greeks and a Jew to the Jews (1 Cor. 9:20) did indeed do something like this in his efforts to bind Gentile and Jewish elements of the Jesus movement into closer harmony.

Acts also reports that Paul was accused on this visit of bringing a Gentile into the sacred space, presumably into the Court of the Israelites, breaking

---

4. *HE* 2.26.11-18; cf. *HE* 2.1.2-5, citing Clement of Alexandria. A similar account of the martyrdom of James is found in the Nag Hammadi text, *The Second Apocalypse of James*, Nag Hammadi Codices V, 4:61, 23-62, 15.

a taboo known through historical and epigraphical sources.[5] While it is not possible to confirm this report in Acts, and Luke hints that Paul was falsely accused, there is an element of plausibility to the story. If, that is, Paul was fundamentally inspired by the prophetic vision (Isa. 56:6-7; 60:3; 61:6; 66:23) that God would bring Gentiles to worship with Jews in his holy place, he may well have brought a Gentile, circumcised or uncircumcised, with him to Jerusalem and its Temple, leading to a negative reaction from fellow Jews and finally his arrest. If this reading of the evidence is correct, then Paul remained committed to the significance of the Temple for the new Messianic community as well as for traditional Jews. His understanding of that significance was, however, controversial.

The Temple and its Priests in the Theology of the Evangelists

As Acts reports, Paul continued his evangelistic career from the position of a prisoner in Rome, where later tradition reports he was martyred under Nero.[6] Within a decade of his death, the first of the surviving narrative accounts of the life and death of Jesus, the Gospel according to Mark, appeared on the scene, either just before or just after the Jewish revolt against Rome.[7] In another ten to fifteen years, Mark was rewritten by Matthew, who expanded the account of the teaching of Jesus. Both preserve the teachings of Jesus already discussed, and both emphasize the prediction of the destruction of the Temple. Matthew at least does so with a sense that prophecy has been fulfilled. He has, moreover, a theory about the cause of the destruction of the city and the Temple, based on a traditional Deuteronomistic theology. If the Jewish people and its sacred space have suffered, it is because the people have sinned. Their primary sin was to reject the Messiah sent to them by God and to call for his death. The sickening cry, "Let his blood be upon our heads and the heads of our children"

---

5. The prohibition is mentioned by Josephus, *War* 6.124-28. On the inscription, see Elias J. Bickermann, "The Warning Inscriptions from Herod's Temple," *Jewish Quarterly Review* 37 (1946–47), 387–405; Richard Pervo, *Acts* Hermeneia (Minneapolis: Fortress Press, 2009), 550, and most recently S.R. Llewelyn and D. van Beek, "The Temple Warning," in *New Documents Illustrating Early Christianity*, ed. S. R. Llewelyn and J. R. Harrison, with E. J. Bridge, New Documents 10 (Grand Rapids, MI: Eerdmans, 2012), 136–39.

6. *1 Clement* 5.4-7, written toward the end of the first or beginning of the second century, records the tradition about the martyrdom of Peter and Paul in his own generation. Cf. also Eusebius, *HE* 2.25.5-6; 3.1.1.

7. For discussion of the dating of the gospel, see Adela Yarbro Collins, *Mark* Hermeneia (Minneapolis: Fortress Press, 2007),11–14. She dates the gospel to the years of the Jewish revolt but before the destruction of the Temple.

(Matt. 27:25), which has worked its evil way in the history of Christian anti-Judaism, was probably meant by Matthew to be a dramatic explanation for the destruction of the Temple. But beyond that rather startling move, neither Mark nor Matthew make much of the Temple.

Luke makes much more of the Temple, both in the Gospel and in the Book of Acts, which is a companion volume to the Gospel, however closely related it may have been in time. The synoptic evangelists wrestle in various ways with the continuities and discontinuities between the past history of God's people and what they take to be its latest chapter, the life of Jesus and his followers. Luke does so dramatically by focusing on the Temple as a pivotal point. The initial annunciation of the birth of John the Baptist takes place when his priestly father, Zechariah, ministers in the Temple (Luke 1:5-20). After his birth, Jesus is brought to the Temple by his parents to fulfill the requirements of the Law. There they encounter prophetic voices of Simeon and Anna who greet them and their special son (Luke 2:22-38). The holy family returns to the Temple for a pilgrimage feast when Jesus is twelve and there he remains, in earnest discourse with the learned teachers, quite at home in his Father's house (Luke 2:44-52). The family of Jesus is, according to Luke, clearly rooted in the piety of ancient Israel and Jesus is fully a part of that scene and its most sacred space. At the same time, the note that Jesus can refer to his Father's business (Luke 2:49) foreshadows his special role in salvation history as Luke presents it. How that engagement will relate to the Temple remains to be seen.

The narrative of the third gospel also preserves the sayings of Jesus discussed above. Like Matthew, it takes the prophecy of destruction of the Temple found in Mark to have been fulfilled in the history of the Jewish revolt against Rome, but unlike Matthew and Mark, Luke is quite careful to distinguish between that horrific event and the final trials and tribulations of the end time, when the Son of Man will return (Luke 21:20).

The second volume of Luke's account of early Christianity, the Acts of the Apostles, continues the story begun in his Gospel, although some time may have elapsed since the first volume appeared. There are elements of continuity as well as discontinuity between the two books. Like the first volume, the Temple is a focal point for the beginning of the story of the expansion of the new movement. As Luke reports the story, the disciples, gathered in Jerusalem after the experience of Pentecost, begin to win adherents to their Messianic movement. Those converts come presumably from Jews, both from the Land of Israel and from the Diaspora, but they do not separate themselves from traditional Jewish observances. Instead, "Day by day, as they spent much time together in the temple, they broke bread at home and ate their food with glad and generous hearts, praising God and having the goodwill of all the people" (Acts 2:46-47). Later, Acts will report that a large number of new believers were priests (Acts 6:7). The account that follows throughout Acts records growing tensions between the followers of Jesus and leaders of the Jewish people, but the Temple remains a focal point of attention.

The Temple is the site of healing actions by the apostles (Acts 3:1-2). Luke recalls specific portions of the Temple: the "Beautiful Gate" (Acts 3:2, 10), where Peter and John encounter a lame beggar, or "Solomon's Portico," where Peter addresses the crowds astonished by the healing power of the apostles (3:11). That speech by Peter contains, *in nuce,* Luke's understanding of the relationship between the community of believers and the Jewish people, an understanding that will be worked out throughout Acts. Peter tells of the prophesied suffering Messiah appointed for a "time of universal restoration" (3:21), and hints at the ingathering of the Gentiles, the inauguration of which Acts will recount. This Messiah is the "prophet like me" foreseen by Moses (3:22, alluding to Deut. 18:15-16), whose message must be obeyed. Those who do not "will be utterly rooted out from the people" (Acts 3:23). That word of potential judgment will be echoed at the end of Acts in the words of Isa. 6:9-10 (Acts 28:26-27). The story of Acts is, in other words, a tragic tale of the working out of the divine will. That tale will confirm the promise of Torah that, through the descendants of Abraham, all the nations of the earth will be blessed (Gen. 22:18; 26:4), but not all of descendants of Abraham will choose to be part of the divine plan. The accounts of Paul's missionary activity, in particular, repeat that story time and again. According to Acts, wherever Paul went, he began his preaching in the synagogue, but while some accepted his message, he usually met with rejection, prompting him to turn to the Gentiles. Luke's attitude toward the Temple must be seen within the context of that larger vision of salvation history.

A crucial passage for Luke's understanding of the Temple is Stephen's speech in Acts 7. The account of the appointment of the seven "deacons" to minister to the needs of the widows of the "Hellenist" community in Jerusalem (Acts 6:1-6) has been the occasion of considerable speculation about the composition of the early community of believers. Luke's version of their appointment and responsibilities emphasizes their subordinate role in the community's leadership structure. It is the apostles who are in charge and who are responsible for the most important functions (Acts 6:2); deacons are supposed to be service providers. What Luke reports about the activity of leading deacons, especially Stephen (Acts 6–7) and Philip (Acts 8), suggests that these individuals played a much more prominent role in the community's life and development.

All that we know about the deacons is what we can infer from the pages of Acts. Their Greek names (Acts 6:5) suggest that they were Jews with roots in the Diaspora, or, if Luke's schematic understanding of the development of the Gentile mission is too neat, they may have included proselytes to Judaism or even Gentile converts to the new Jesus movement. In any case, Luke takes pains to give these characters in his narrative a major voice through the speech that Stephen gives before his martyrdom (7:55). That lengthy speech (Acts 7:1-53) offers an account of salvation history, rich with scriptural allusions, that tells the story of divine election of Israel's ancestors, the captivity in Egypt, and the deliverance of the people under the leadership of Moses, who promised that there would be a prophet like himself to lead the people in the future (Acts 7:37, citing Deut. 18:15-16; cf. Acts 3:22). Stephen also tells of the disobedience of the desert generation (Acts 7:39-41), whom God abandoned to their idolatry (Acts 7:42-43, citing Jer. 7:18 lxx). These Israelites worshipped in the tabernacle, whose heavenly paradigm Moses had seen (Acts 7:44), but then, in the land of Israel, Solomon built a Temple, despite the fact that God does not dwell in a manufactured house (Acts 7:48). According to Stephen, the prophet Isaiah had it right: heaven is God's throne and the earth his footstool. God does not need a house made by human hands (Acts 7:49, citing Isa. 66:1-2[8]). On that note, Stephen turns to denounce his accusers and judges as following in the footsteps of their ancestors who resisted the work of the Spirit of God. His outburst leads, naturally, to his martyrdom.

Note the pattern of the speech: God's acts in favor of Israel are followed by rebellion, deliverance from Egypt by idolatry in the desert; the divinely authorized tabernacle[9] is followed by a Temple that stands opposed to a fundamental truth about God. Those to whom mercy is now being shown in the appointment of the Messianic Prophet simply follow in the footsteps of their sinful ancestors. Stephen's speech is obviously not a Temple-friendly exercise. The severe critique of the Temple and its sacrificial cult, articulated through the

---

8. The inability of a handmade structure to house the Divine is recognized in the account of the construction of the Temple. See Solomon's prayer at the dedication of the first Temple in 1 Kgs. 8:27: "But will God indeed dwell on the earth? Even heaven and the highest heaven cannot contain you, much less this house that I have built!" The recognition of this principle underlies the theme of the dwelling of the divine name in the Temple. See Deut. 12:11; 1 Kgs. 5:3, 5; 8:16-20; 9:3.

9. In general on the role of the desert tabernacle in Second Temple Judaism and the literature of early Christianity, see Craig Koester, *The Dwelling of God: The Tabernacle in the Old Testament, Intertestamental Jewish Literature and the New Testament*, Catholic Biblical Quarterly Monograph Series 22 (Washington, DC: Catholic Biblical Association, 1989).

words of Isaiah, virtually equates it with idolatry in the cyclic pattern of Israel's relations with its God.

There is little doubt about the intensity of the polemic against the Temple articulated in Stephen's speech. The position of that polemic, both in Luke's overarching theology and in the history of early Christianity, is open to further interpretation. Nowhere else in Acts does Luke present such a forceful case against the Temple as something that stands in opposition to God's will for Israel, but his critique of those Jews who reject the gospel of Jesus continues and grows through the book. It may be that he is simply including material from a historical source about a position adopted by some elements of the early Christian movement, a position close to one soon to be seen in the Epistle to the Hebrews. Alternatively, Luke's presentation of Stephen is part of his larger critical program, in which the emphasis is not so much on the Temple itself as on the attitude of those who hold authority in it. In their rejection of God's appointed Messiah and eschatological Prophet, they put themselves in opposition to God. Their attitude affects all the institutions with which they are in touch, even one that can serve as a legitimate locus for the activity of pious followers of Jesus.

A Theologian of a New Temple

The previous sections of this essay have treated some of the sayings attributed to Jesus in various gospel sources. The sayings served as evidence for what may have been the attitudes of Jesus and his immediate followers to the Temple and its leadership. Their stance, involving both affirmation and critique, is reflected in various ways in the theology of Paul and the evangelists. One evangelist, the author of the Fourth Gospel, stands out as having a special interest in the Temple. Like all of the witnesses examined so far, the Fourth Evangelist also has a profound respect for the Temple and the traditions associated with it, but, at the same time, a disdain for the Temple reconstructed by Herod. As is so often the case in this text, what this evangelist seeks to provide is a radical rethinking of early Christian affirmations. In the process, he appropriates imagery connected with the Temple as a way of affirming his understanding of the significance of Jesus.[10]

The theme of the Temple in the Fourth Gospel is foreshadowed, like many others, in the Prologue, where the Divine Word is said to "pitch its tent" (ἐσκήνωσεν) in human flesh (John 1:14). The image is a transparent evocation

---

10. I have treated John's appropriation of Temple imagery previously, in H.W. Attridge, "Temple, Tabernacle, Time, and Space in John and Hebrews," *Early Christianity* 1 (2010): 261–274.

of the imagery of Ben Sira's praise of Wisdom, which is said to "pitch its tent" in Israel, as Torah, but it also evokes the dwelling of the divine name in the Temple (Deut. 12:21; 1 Kgs. 5:5; 8:16-20, 29). The Gospel will present Jesus as, indeed, a new Torah, but he is more.

The saying about the destruction of the Temple (John 2:19), already treated as a witness to a tradition of the historical Jesus, moves beyond general evocation of the dwelling of God among God's people to a symbolic equation of the body of Jesus with the Temple. The remark of the evangelist that, in this saying, Jesus was referring not to the Herodian Temple but to his body, could be construed as a simple apology, evacuating the saying of Jesus of any hint of political threat. But things are seldom simple in this Gospel, and the equation of Jesus' body with the (true) Temple enunciates a motif that will be further developed as the Gospel progresses.[11]

The evangelist hints at the notion of a new Temple in the dialogue between Jesus and the Samaritan woman in John 4. When the woman recognizes Jesus as a prophet because he has described her complex marital history (vv. 18-19), she changes the subject and focuses on the major religious division between Judeans and Samaritans, the competing sacred places of Mt. Gerazim and Mt. Zion. Jesus suggests that the division is to be transcended:

> Woman, believe me, the hour is coming when you will worship the Father neither on this mountain nor in Jerusalem . . . The hour is coming, and is now here, when the true worshippers will worship the Father in spirit and truth. . . . God is spirit, and those who worship him must worship in spirit and truth. (4:23-24)

The Gospel does not yet specify where or how such worship will take place, but the reader who remembers the saying associating Jesus' body with the Temple might suspect that true worship will have something to do with Jesus.

A major vehicle for further connecting Jesus with the Temple is the evocation of Israel's sacred calendar,[12] invoked at key points in the first half of the Gospel. The allusions begin with the healing of the paralytic in chapter 5, which takes place on the Sabbath, the first day named in the roster of feast

11. Major treatments of the topic include: Ulrich Busse, "Die Tempelmetaphorik als ein Beispiel von implizitem Rekurs auf die biblische Tradition im Johannesevangelium", in *The Scriptures in the Gospels*, ed. C.M. Tuckett, BETL 131 (Leuven: Leuven University Press, 1997), 395–428; Mary Coloe, *God Dwells with Us: Temple Symbolism in the Fourth Gospel* (Collegeville, MN: Liturgical, 2001), and A.R. Kerr, *The Temple of Jesus' Body: The Temple Theme in the Gospel of John*, Journal for the Study of the New Testament Supplement Series 220 (London: Sheffield Academic Press, 2002).

12. Exod. 23:10-17; 34:18-23; Lev. 23:3-44; Deut. 16:1-17.

days in Exod. 23:12 and Lev. 23:3. Next comes Passover in John 6:4. Jesus does not celebrate this pilgrimage feast in Jerusalem, but on the shore of the Sea of Galilee, where, after the miraculous feeding and walking on water, he preaches a sermon identifying himself as the new "bread from heaven" (John 6:32-58). The complexities of the discourse and its possible redactional layers have long intrigued scholars and we need not explore these issues now.[13] The major point for our purposes is clear: Passover is no longer to be celebrated as a pilgrimage festival connected with Jerusalem but is celebrated wherever the new manna is consumed, whether that consumption be metaphorical (6:41-50) or physical (6:51-58).

Mention of the next pilgrimage festival, Succoth, at John 7:2, introduces a lengthy discourse where the festival's symbolic elements, water and light, are associated with Jesus. On the last day of the festival, Jesus dramatically promises to provide "living water" to all who thirst (7:37-39). Met by unbelief,[14] Jesus makes another declaration, that he is also the "light of the world" (8:12). The logic of these chapters is analogous to that of John 6. Symbolic elements associated with a major pilgrimage festival focused on the Temple are now associated with Jesus, who becomes the "locus" in which true connection with the divine is to be made.

The next festival in the cycle is not one from the Pentateuchal roster, but one that came into being in the second century BCE after the persecution of Antiochus IV Epiphanes and the restoration of the Temple by Judas Maccabeus. The reference to the festival that we know as Hanukkah appears at John 10:22 where it is referred to in Greek as The Renewal (τὰ ἐγκαίνια).[15] The narrator notes that "It was winter and Jesus was walking in the Temple, in the portico of Solomon" (10:23). "The Jews" gather around him and ask him to speak plainly about his Messianic claims. He replies that he has already done so, through the works that he has done, and alluding to the previous discourse in this chapter remarks that his sheep hear his voice; they know and follow him (10:27).

It is intriguing that, unlike the other references to festivals in John, no explicit symbolic elements of the day play a role in the dialogue. The focus is entirely on Jesus and the community that has been formed around the call to his

---

13. See Peder Borgen, *Bread from Heaven: An Exegetical Study of the Concept of Manna in the Gospel of John and the Writings of Philo*, Supplements to Novum Testamentum 10 (Leiden: Brill, 1965); Paul N. Anderson, *The Christology of the Fourth Gospel: Its Unity and Disunity in the Light of John 6*, WUNT 2.77 (Tübingen: Mohr Siebeck, 1995).

14. The sequence of the dialogue is interrupted by the "pericope of the adulteress," John 7:53—8:11, generally recognized to be a later insertion into the text of the Gospel.

15. The nrsv translates as "The Festival of the Dedication."

sheep. It is, however, precisely in that focus that the allusion to the renewal of the Temple makes sense. The festival celebrated the rededication of a physical structure almost two centuries previously, a structure that was still undergoing a reconstruction begun by Herod (2:20). What the Temple, around which the festival cycle revolved, was supposed to do, is now, the evangelist claims, being done by the presence of Jesus. In his life and ministry the true "Renewal" has taken place.

After the reference to Hanukkah at 10:22, the festival cycle recurs once more, in the references to the final Passover that brought Jesus to Jerusalem (11:55; 12:1, 12) for the final act in his drama. In that act another substitution will occur, when Jesus is slain at the time that the Passover lambs are sacrificed. A scriptural citation at John 12:36—"None of his bones shall be broken" (Exod. 12:46), which was part of the instructions for dealing with the paschal lamb—seals the connection to Passover, while it echoes the proclamation by John the Baptist (John 1:29) of Jesus as the Lamb who takes away the sins of the world.

According to the Fourth Gospel, the center of sacred space and time has been displaced. The rituals and symbols associated with it pointed to another reality, the life and death of Jesus around whom a new community has been formed. The major function of the Temple—to be a place where God or, more commonly God's name, dwells—has now been assumed by the community of believers in Jesus. The lengthy discourses of the latter half of the Gospel make this point forcefully. Two key motifs contribute to the development of the theme. The first is the theme of the divine indwelling or "abiding." As is the case with so many other elements of the Fourth Gospel, more than one issue is involved in the development of the "abiding" motif. It appears first at John 14:2-3, where Jesus talks about his departure "to prepare a place" for his disciples, an abode (μονή) in the Father's mansion.[16] The saying evokes a rather simple image of eschatological restoration, one not unparalleled in Jewish apocalyptic sources. Yet this opening gambit just sets the stage for further reflection on divine "abiding" (μενεῖν). As Jesus soon makes clear, the place where God, or more specifically, where he and the Father, will abide, is in those who love him and keep his word (John 14:23). The language of mysticism, rather than apocalypticism, pervades this part of the discourse as Jesus affirms both that the Spirit of Truth will "abide with you and be in you" (14:17) and that there will be a mutual indwelling of Father, Jesus, and the believer (14:20). The place where God dwells is where, in an echo of the words to the Samaritan

---

16. I suspect that the image involved here is one of a unit in a larger apartment building, the sort of construction that was widespread in Roman cities of the first century.

woman (4:23-24), God is worshipped in Spirit and in Truth, a place defined by the word of Jesus.

The final element of the complex motif of the New Temple in the Fourth Gospel appears at the end of the last supper discourses, when Jesus offers a lengthy prayer (17:1-26).[17] The frequent designation of this as Jesus' "High-Priestly" prayer,[18] makes three general petitions to the Father, for Jesus himself (17:1-5), for his disciples (17:6-19), and for others beyond the immediate circle of disciples (17:20-26).[19] The major reason for thinking of this chapter as, in some loose sense, a "high priestly" prayer is two motifs prominent in the second portion of the text. The first is the focus on the divine name that Jesus claims in his prayer to have revealed to his disciples (17:6).[20] Whatever else this claim does, it evokes the strand of reflection on the first Temple as the dwelling place of God's name.[21] The evangelist does not here elaborate on the ways in which Jesus has revealed the name. The claim to have done so encompasses the whole of the "work" of Jesus in the first half of the Gospel, in which he points to himself as the one who "exegetes" who God is (1:18). He does so, in part, by identifying himself with the name of the one who is the divine name, I AM (John 8:58, alluding to Exod. 3:14). In bearing the divine name in such an intimate way, Jesus also evokes the vestments of the High Priest, which prominently (but our evangelist would say superficially) displays the divine

17. On the general literary tradition associated with this chapter, see Carsten Claussen, "Das Gebet in Joh 17 im Kontext von Gebeten aus zeitgenössischen Pseudepigraphen," in *Kontexte des Johannesevangeliums: Das vierte Evangelium in religions- und traditionsgeschichtlicher Perspektive*, ed. Jörg Frey and Udo Schnelle (Tübingen: Mohr Siebeck, 2004), 205–22.

18. See Raymond Brown, *The Gospel According to John (xiii-xxi)*, Anchor Bible 29A (Garden City, NY: Doubleday, 1970), 747, who notes that the designation is attested as early as Cyril of Alexandria in the fifth century (*In Jo* 11.8; PG 74:505), and was popularized in the Reformation period by the Lutheran theologian David Chyträus. Brown himself suggests that if there is a priestly image involved it is not an image of one who is about to do sacrifice, but a heavenly intercessor, as at Rom. 8:34 or Heb. 7:25. See also Craig S. Keener, *The Gospel of John: A Commentary*, 2 vols. (Peabody, MA: Henrickson, 2003) 2:1050–52, who also notes the intercessory role of various kinds of figures in Israel's history. On the whole issue, see H.W. Attridge, "How Priestly is the 'High Priestly' Prayer of John 17," *Catholic Biblical Quarterly* 75 (2013): 1–15.

19. On the structure of the chapter, see Jürgen Becker, "Aufbau, Schichtung und theologiegeschichtliche Stellung des Gebetes in Johannes 17," *ZNW* 60 (1969): 56–83, and Edward Malatesta, "The Literary Structure of John 17," *Biblica* 52 (1971): 190–214.

20. On the background to the theme of the name, see Adelheid Ruck-Schröder, *Der Name Gottes und der Name Jesu: Eine neutestamentliche Studie*, WMANT 80 (Neukirchen-Vluyn: Neukirchener Verlag, 1999).

21. See n. 8 above.

name (Exod. 28:36-38), an allusion that will reappear in the Book of Revelation (Rev. 19:12-13).

The second element of Jesus' final prayer that evokes priestly traditions is the content of the prayer for the disciples, that they be "sanctified" (ἁγίασον αὐτούς) in the truth that is God's word (John 17:17-19). The call for sanctification recalls the heart of the "holiness code" of the Book of Leviticus, which calls upon the people of Israel to be holy as God is holy (Lev. 18:2). For the Fourth Gospel, true holiness comes from association with the place where God and God's name now dwell. As noted above, that sacred place is the community that follows Jesus and obeys his command to love. The prayer reinforces the motif in its final portion, which prays for a unity among believers, grounded in the love (John 17:26) that flows from their unity with the Father and Son (17:21).

The complex symbolic world of the Fourth Gospel plays with imagery and motifs of the Temple, and, to a lesser extent, its priests, in order to make its provocative and extravagant claims for the centrality of Jesus. In the Gospel's vision, it is Jesus where God is worshiped "in spirit and truth." Through his spirit, present as the Paraclete, his disciples form a new and living Temple.

A THEOLOGIAN OF A NEW PRIESTHOOD

The next early Christian theologian relevant to our subject does not actually say anything directly about the Temple, in any of the stages of its history, but does make a great deal of the rituals performed in the Tabernacle of the desert generation, which were the models for what was performed in the Temple. The Epistle to the Hebrews, a homily, written probably in the last third of the first century, encourages believers in Jesus to remain faithful to their commitment to him in the face of persecution and perhaps disillusionment with Christian eschatological expectations.[22] The overall strategy of Hebrews to achieve that

---

22. The literature on Hebrews has grown enormously in recent years. See H.W. Attridge, *A Commentary on the Epistle to the Hebrews*, Hermeneia (Philadelphia: Fortress Press, 1989). Other useful recent commentaries include, Craig Koester, *Hebrews: A New Translation with Introduction and Commentary*, Anchor Bible 36 (New York: Doubleday, 2001); Luke Timothy Johnson, *Hebrews: A Commentary*, New Testament Library (Louisville: Westminster John Knox, 2006); Alan C. Mitchell, *Hebrews*, Sacra Pagina (Collegeville, MN: Liturgical, 2007). Several collections of essays provide a useful window onto contemporary scholarship on the text. See Gabriella Gelardini, *Hebrews: Contemporary Methods, New Insights*, Biblical Interpretation Series 75 (Leiden: Brill, 2005); Richard Bauckham et al., eds., *A Cloud of Witnesses: The Theology of Hebrews in its Ancient Contexts*, Library of New Testament Studies 387 (London: T&T Clark, 2009); and Eric F. Mason and Kevin B. McCruden, eds., *Reading the Epistle to the Hebrews: A Resource for Students* (Atlanta: SBL, 2011).

desired revitalization of faith is to draw a picture of the significance of Jesus and his relevance for the life of his followers using categories that had not before been systematically exploited. In doing so, Hebrews builds on traditional affirmations about the significance of Jesus and his death on the cross, but the text clothes those affirmations in new garb and, in a dazzling rhetorical exercise, invites its audience to participate in the reality that Christ's death, resurrection, and exaltation have made possible for them.

The central image of the text is of Christ as a High Priest, the unique high priest, systematically distinguished from high priests of flesh and blood. It was their responsibility to mediate between God and humankind (Heb. 5:1-4), but their sacrifices of bulls and goats had no power to cleanse the conscience of human beings (9:9-10; 10:1-4). This construal of Jesus as a priest may be seen as a kind of logical extension of traditional affirmations about his death, that it was a sacrifice of some sort (Rom. 3:25-27) providing for the forgiveness of sins or the redemption of his followers (Mark 10:45), an act of vicarious suffering by which, in the words of Isaiah, others were healed (1 Pet. 2:24, alluding to Isa. 53:5). If the death of Jesus was a sacrifice, it must have required a priest to perform it and the one who functioned in this capacity was none other than Jesus himself, who willingly offered himself. Furthermore, if that death is a sacrifice that effectively and for all time dealt with the reality of human sin, it is analogous to the sacrifice performed once a year on the Day of Atonement, not by ordinary priests, but by the High Priest.

Something like this logic probably generated the fundamental conceptual scheme at work in Hebrews. Much of the text's argument deals with obstacles to working out the fundamental insight. Among those obstacles is the fact that Jesus, according to early Christian tradition, was a descendant of David, therefore a member of the tribe of Judah, not eligible to be a priest (7:13), that is, a member of the tribe of Levi. Therefore, argues our creative homilist, he must be a priest of a different type, a type found in the mysterious reference in Ps. 110:4 to an "order of Melchizedek."[23] Perhaps inspired by the abundant speculation on this mysterious biblical figure circulating among Jews of the Second Temple period,[24] our author develops his rather spare midrash on the

<hr/>

23. On the importance of this verse, see James Kurianal, *Jesus Our High Priest: Psalm 110,4 as the Substructure of Heb 5,1-7,28* (Frankfurt: Peter Lang, 1999).

24. For recent efforts to trace the background of Hebrews in Second Temple Judaism, see Hugh Anderson, "The Jewish Antecedents of the Christology of Hebrews," in *The Messiah: Developments in Earliest Judaism and Christianity*, ed. James H. Charlesworth (Minneapolis: Fortress Press, 1992), 512–35; Eric Mason, "Cosmology, Messianism, and Melchizedek: Apocalyptic Jewish Traditions and Hebrews," in *Reading the Epistle to the Hebrews*, 53–76.

two Biblical passages mentioning Melchizedek (Ps. 110:4 and Gen. 14:17-24) in order to portray Jesus as an eschatological priest of an eternal, that is, divine order.

A second obstacle is the lack of anything in the death of Jesus like the ritual of Yom Kippur, in which the High Priest, before sending out the "scapegoat," manipulates the sacrificial blood to provide cleansing for the altar and thereby the people (Lev. 16:11-19). In order to find the parallel at least to the latter action—Hebrews ignores the scapegoat (Lev. 16:20-22)—our homilist then puts the parallel action of Christ on something of a Platonic plane,[25] having him enter not any earthly sanctuary, but the heavenly archetype of the holy space, where he offers his blood to God, thereby cleansing the "heavenly realities," which are finally identified as the consciences of his followers.

A further complication renders all of this elaborate conceit relevant for the lives of the faithful. The sacrifice of Christ is not simply a counterpart to the sacrifice of Yom Kippur; it also replicates the sacrifice that Moses offered when he inaugurated the first covenant. Christ's sacrifice also inaugurates a covenant, the new one promised by Jeremiah 31, written not on stone tablets but on human hearts. It does so because, as a "covenant" (διαθήκη in Greek, Heb. 9:15-17) it is also a "testament" (also διαθήκη in Greek), in which one leaves a legacy for one's heirs. By his death, Christ has bequeathed to his followers an example of life lived in conformity to God's will (10:1-10). That example is written on their hearts (8:10; 10:16). The life of fidelity to God's will that Christ lived in an exemplary fashion is a "new and living way" (10:19) that his disciples can follow to their promised inheritance, following in the footsteps of Christ, the "initiator and perfecter" of the life of faith (12:2).

What does all of this have to do with the Temple? Whatever knowledge of the Temple and its rituals may lie behind the text, the elaborate analogy of the death of Christ to (part of) the ritual of Yom Kippur (9:1-14) does not mention the Temple itself.[26] Hebrews relies instead on the Biblical description of the desert tabernacle (Exod. 25–26; Lev. 16) for its imagery. By and large the description in Hebrews mimics the biblical text, although there are some

---

25. The relationship of Hebrews to the Platonic tradition is a subject of continuing debate. For a vigorous defense of the relevance of "Middle Platonism" to the homily, see James M. Thompson, "What Has Middle Platonism to do with Hebrews?" in *Reading the Epistle to the Hebrews*, 31–52. My own position is that Hebrews plays ironically with a Platonic scheme. Ultimate reality for him is in the "body" of Jesus (Heb. 10:10).

26. For a treatment of the relationship of Hebrews to the Temple, see Barnabas Lindars, "Hebrews and the Second Temple," in *Templum Amicitiae*, ed. William Horbury, Journal for the Study of the New Testament Supplement Series 48 (Sheffield: Sheffield Academic Press, 1991), 410–33.

jarring elements. The most significant of these is no doubt the placement of the altar of incense, which Hebrews locates "within the veil" of the outer sanctuary (Heb. 9:2-4). Associated with that odd placement of a ritual item is the counterintuitive designation of the major spaces of the tabernacle in some manuscripts. In these the inner sanctuary is designated the "holy" and the outer the "holy of holies."[27] Whether this is a deliberate rhetorical move on the part of our homilist or a confusion in the manuscript tradition remains a matter of debate.[28] The description of the desert tabernacle is, in any case, a preliminary stage in the exposition of the ultimate high-priestly act that is Jesus' death. Where the implications for the Temple become a bit more clear is in the lessons that Hebrews draws from its elaborate exposition.

Two passages are particularly important. In Hebrews 7, when our homilist has finished with his explanation of how Melchizedek provides a clue to the character of the priesthood of Christ, he argues that Christ's office is a new priesthood, different from that of Aaron (7:11) and "when there is a change in the priesthood, there is necessarily a change in the law as well" (7:12). From the homilist's perspective, the institutional apparatus for dealing with sin has decisively changed. Hebrews hints at the same notion when, before launching into the Yom Kippur typology, the text cites the prophecy of a new covenant in Jeremiah (8:7-12) and then comments on the antithesis between new and old: "In speaking of a 'new covenant' he (scil. the Divine speaker of the prophecy) has made the first one obsolete. And what is obsolete and growing old will soon disappear" (8:13). Whether that last remark expresses an expectation or is a veiled comment about the destruction of the Temple in 70 CE, it articulates, in connection with the disparaging comment on the Law in 7:12, an early form of "supercessionist" thinking. The movement of believers in Christ has something better than the Temple and its rituals at its disposal.

A similar stance appears at the conclusion of the work, when the homilist summarizes the thrust of his exposition and exhortation (13:9-13):

> Do not be carried away by all kinds of strange teachings; for it is well for the heart to be strengthened by grace, not by regulations about food, which have not benefitted those who observe the. We have an altar from which those who officiate in the tent have no right to eat. . . . Let us then go to him outside the camp and bear the abuse he

27. The *outer* portion of the tabernacle is called ἅγια ἁγίων at Heb. 9:2 in P46 A D* vg ms, the *inner* portion is probably named in P46, though the actual reading is ANA a simple corruption of ΑΓΙΑ.

28. For discussion of the issue, see Attridge, *Hebrews*, 236–38.

endured. . . . Through him, then, let us continually offer a sacrifice of praise to God, that is, the fruit of lips that confess his name.

The allusive quality of this exhortation has generated many questions. Are the regulations about food *halakhoth* relating to *kashrut*? Probably. Is the "altar" that "we" have the Eucharistic table? Possibly. Whatever "we" have, it is not for those who participate in the traditional cult. The worship of this community is to take place "outside the camp,"[29] which may concretely be Jerusalem, but is certainly whatever stands in the tradition of the Israelites of the Exodus generation. The action of true worship does not involve animal sacrifice, but, in the words of the Psalmist, it consists of "a sacrifice of praise . . . the fruit of lips that confess his name."[30] The whole exhortation envisions worship in a covenant community where "priesthood" and "law" have changed and where the traditional forms of worship associated with the Temple no longer have value. The true sacrifices are performed by "priests," who like Jesus are not in a traditional Levitical lineage, but who offer metaphorical sacrifices in their life of prayerful worship,[31] while their heavenly high priest continues his priestly task of interceding for them before God (7:24-25). The irony, of course, is that the movement away from the Temple and its rituals depends on an argument that, in its form and much of its content is very Jewish indeed and relies on the Biblical passages that undergirded the ritual life of the Temple.[32]

29. On this motif, see Richard Johnson, *Going Outside the Camp: The Sociological Function of the Levitical Critique in the Epistle to the Hebrews*, Journal for the Study of the New Testament Supplement Series 209 (Sheffield: Sheffield Academic Press, 2001).

30. The language of "sacrifice of praise" appears in many psalms. In some, such as Ps. 27:6 and 116:17 it may refer to actual bloody sacrifices that served the purpose of offering praise. In others, such as Ps. 50:14, 23 and 107:22, the language seems to be more metaphorical, that is, prayers function as sacrifice.

31. On the possible notion of priesthood in Hebrews, see John M. Scholar, *Proleptic Priests: Priesthood in the Epistle to the Hebrews*, Journal for the Study of the New Testament Supplement Series 49 (Sheffield: JSOT, 1991).

32. Note the efforts to wrestle with the relationship of Hebrews to "supercessionism," by Richard B. Hays, "'Here We Have No Lasting City': New Covenantalism in Hebrews," in Bauckham et al., *The Epistle to the Hebrews*, 151–73; Oskar Sakrsaune, "Does the Letter to the Hebrews Articulate a Supercessionist Theology? A Response to Richard Hays," ibid., 174–81; Mark D. Nanos, "New or Renewed Covenantalism? A Response to Richard Hays," ibid., 183–88; and Morna D. Hooker, "Christ, the 'End' of the Cult," ibid., 189–212.

A Theologian of Radical Substitution: A Kingdom of Priests without a Temple

Reflections on, and appropriations of imagery related to, the Temple and its priests appear in other writings of the New Testament. Like the Fourth Gospel and the Epistle to the Hebrews, these other witnesses also display mixed feelings toward Israel's place of worship and its officiants. The symbolic value of the Temple and its priests remains vital, but the referent of the symbol has shifted. Where John and Hebrews had hinted at the substitution of the community of believers for the physical Temple, these texts make the move explicitly, and at the same time, draw out its implications in more detail.

The homily known as 1 Peter,[33] which displays many similarities to the language and motifs of Hebrews, calls its recipients to a life of faithful and holy discipleship. In doing so, it reflects on the divine action that provides a foundation and framework for that life. Echoing motifs in Paul's first letter to Corinth, the writer of 1 Peter reminds his addressees of the social reality that has been created by their adhesion to the gospel message. If they confess that Jesus is the Christ (1 Pet. 2:4), they acknowledge the "stone" on which their social edifice is based. That "stone" is the one mentioned by a prophet (Isa. 8:14; 1 Pet. 2:6). The builders rejected it (Ps. 118:22; 1 Pet. 2:7), but it has become the cornerstone of a new, metaphorical Temple, the community of believers. The believers themselves are the stones of which this sacred edifice (ἱεράτευμα ἅγιον) is constructed (1 Pet. 2:5).

As the author of 1 Peter develops this riff on the motif of the "stone," he shifts gears and the living stones become the functionaries who inhabit the edifice. After telling them they are the new spiritual edifice, the author, evoking language of Exod. 19:6 and Isa. 43:20, tells his addressees that they are an "elect people, a royal kingdom, a holy nation, a people set apart" (1 Pet. 2:9). They, the "elect of the diaspora" of Pontos, Galatia, Cappadocia, Asia and Bythinia (1 Pet. 1:1), whatever their ethnic heritage, are now, quite surprisingly, priests. The author of 1 Peter recognizes the radical claim that he is making at the end of this reflection on the Temple and its priesthood when, at 1 Pet. 2:10, he affirms that "those who were not a people are now God's people."

The basis for the remarkable claim of 1 Peter and related texts is no doubt the prophetic book that probably inspired so much of the Christian outreach to non-Jews. In its vision of the universal implications of Yahweh's rule over his people Israel, Isaiah makes some startling declarations—that foreigners who join themselves to the Lord will come to his holy mountain, make their joyful noise

---

33. In general, see Paul J. Achtemeier, *1 Peter*, Hermeneia (Minneapolis: Fortress Press, 1996).

of prayer in his house as their burnt offerings and sacrifices are accepted on his altar (Isa. 56:6-7).[34] Or, more succinctly, "nations shall come to your light and kings to the brightness of your dawn" (60:3). In this time of gathering in all who acknowledge Yahweh, the boundaries of traditional priesthood seem to be dissolved. After telling his addressees that "strangers shall stand and feed your flocks; foreigners shall till your land and dress your vines (61:5), the prophet tells his audience that "you shall be called priests of the Lord; you shall be named ministers of our God" (62:6). The expansive vision of who will be priests reaches its climax in the final oracle of trito-Isaiah. After describing yet again the influx of the "kindred from all the nations" (6:20)[35] to the Holy Mountain, the prophet, speaking for Yahweh, says "And I will also take some of them as priests and as Levites" (66:21). The passage may refer not to Gentiles, but to Jews scattered among the nations. However, for a reader caught up in the universal vision of the rest of the prophecy, the promise could well be taken to apply to all who have come to worship.

All the precise scriptural warrants for the claim of 1 Peter are not clearly displayed, but enough of them are to suggest that the vision of the final chapters of Isaiah may undergird this author's appeal to his community of believers in Jesus. These believers, in their corporate identity, have become the very place where God now dwells and they, in their worship, are the continuation of the priestly lineage that served in the Temple of Jerusalem.

The final book of the New Testament contains a similar play on the themes of Temple and priesthood. Much of the Book of Revelation works through a juxtaposition of the calamities of the persecuted community on earth and the heavenly realm of peace where the elect perpetually worship God. The initial vision after the messages to the Churches of Asia Minor evokes that heavenly scene (Rev. 4:1-11), where the visionary sees the living creatures familiar from prophetic visions of Isaiah and Ezekiel and hears them recite the Trishagion, which Isaiah heard in similar circumstances (Isa. 6:3). The message of consolation and encouragement that this text tries to convey to the believers in Jesus in Asia Minor is that they are already part of that heavenly scene.

The ground of the confidence that the visionary preaches is what he takes to be the result of the death of the messianic Lamb. Following the vision of the worship of God with its very traditional elements in chapter 4 is a

---

34. The passage is evoked in the Markan narrative of the "cleansing" of the Temple, when Jesus says, in the words of Isa. 56:7, that God's house will be "called a house of prayer for all peoples" (Mark 11:17).

35. The lxx of Isa. 66:20 reads "your brethren from all nations" (τοὺς ἀδελφοὺς ὑμῶν). For a reader attuned to the metaphorical use of "brethren," the verse would be easily read as a reference to Gentile converts.

complementary vision of the worship of Lamb, "with seven horns and seven eyes, which are the seven spirits of God sent out into all the earth" (Rev. 5:6). This slain lamb with the spiritual reach is praised by the creatures and elders around the throne, who "sing a new song," hymning what the Lamb has accomplished:

> You are worthy to take the scroll and to open its seals, for you were slaughtered and by your blood you ransomed for God saints from every tribe and language and people and nation; you have made them to be a kingdom and priests serving our God and they will reign on earth. (Rev. 5:9-10)

The hymn echoes the theme already encountered in our discussion of 1 Peter: people from the nations have been assembled to worship God and they constitute a "royal priesthood."

The image is repeated in the next vision of the saints in heaven, who consist of two groups: the 144,000 "sealed out of every tribe of the people of Israel" (Rev. 6:4) and "a great multitude that no one could count, from every nation, from all tribes and peoples and languages" (6:9). These have "washed their robes and made them white in the blood of the Lamb" and therefore "worship him day and night within his temple" (7:14-15), as one might expect a royal, priestly people to do.

Allusions to the worship in the heavenly Temple recur in later chapters (11:15-19; 14:1-5), as well as calls to those on earth to worship God properly (14:7). These allusions culminate in the final vision of a New Jerusalem that comes to earth "as a bride adorned for her husband" (21:2). A voice declares the meaning of the vision:

> See the home of God is among mortals. He will dwell with them and they will be his peoples and God himself will be with them; he will wipe every tear from their eyes [cf. 7:17]. Death will be no more; mourning and crying and pain will be no more, for the first things have passed away. (21:3-4)

This vision of eschatological bliss expands in a final vision that offers a new interpretation of the traditional apocalyptic image (21:9-22:7). The heavenly city expected for the end time is now depicted as a perfectly square structure with twelve towers, whose foundations bear "the names of the twelve apostles of the Lamb" (21:14). A prominent characteristic of this city is that in it "there is no temple, for the temple is the Lord God the Almighty and the Lamb" (21:22).

This city is a pure and light-filled space in which the nations of the earth walk (21:23-27). God's presence provides the light and in that light all his servants will worship him, bearing his name on their foreheads (22:3-5), like the high priests of old (Exod. 28:36-38, noted in connection with the "name" motif in John 17).

The final vision of the book of Revelation interprets the reality of the community of messianic believers. The interpretation bears a family resemblance to the vision sketched by Hebrews and particularly to 1 Peter. The place in which God is now present to humankind is not a temple of stone, but a community of those faithful to him. The members of that community, coming both from the people of Israel and from the nations has been ordained as priests, obviating the need for the mediators of old.

LATER EARLY CHRISTIAN APPROPRIATIONS OF TEMPLE AND PRIESTHOOD

A review of the ways in which early Christian literature outside of the canon of the New Testament treated themes of Temple and Priesthood would far surpass the bounds set for this essay. In conclusion, it will be useful to note the existence of two trajectories that develop the heritage of the first century of Christian literature. The dominant strand appropriates the themes of Temple and priesthood with enthusiasm, finding in Christian practice a substantive continuation of the traditions of the Hebrew Bible.

The tendency is evident by the end of the first century, in the letter known as *1 Clement*, written by Roman Christians to help mediate a dispute in the Christian community at Corinth. The text knows the motif prominent in Hebrews of Christ as the "high priest" of the believing community (*1 Clem.* 64.1), and it probably knows Hebrews itself, although it does not explicitly cite it.[36] Yet, *1 Clement* does not dwell on the role of Christ. The author also knows about and can recommend metaphorical sacrifices of praise (52.1), but his interest is not the details of ritual practice.

The presenting issue has apparently been the dismissal of leaders of the Church at Corinth. Our author wants to reverse the situation and restore the expelled elders to their former role. In arguing for that restoration, the author invokes the precedent of the sacerdotal structures of ancient Israel.

For special liturgical rites have been assigned to the high priest, and a special place has been designated for the regular priests, and special

---

36. For discussion of the relationship of *1 Clement* and Hebrews, see Attridge, *Hebrews*, 6–7.

ministries are established for the Levites. The lay person is assigned to matters enjoined on the laity (40.5).[37]

Those who act contrary to the divine plan for the priestly hierarchy "bear the penalty of death" (41.3). The sacred order and divine authorization that obtained for the priests of old also applies to the ministers of the Christian community, to the apostles and the bishops and deacons who have succeeded them (42.1-5).

Clement's typology evidences a new principle at work in some Christian circles at the turn of the century. The appropriation of the language of Temple and priesthood by the followers of Jesus is now no longer an egalitarian alternative to the traditional priesthood of Jerusalem. The old categories have been revived to support a new structure of authority. The Church is indeed the new Temple and its bishops and deacons are its priests and Levites.

The instinct of *1 Clement* continues in the later life of the Church, which increasingly thought of its leaders as priests and the liturgical work that they did as the non-bloody continuation of the sacrifices of the Old Covenant. A minority opinion resisted too close an assimilation of old and new models of priesthood. The recent discovery of the *Gospel of Judas*, a Gnostic text probably from the third century, has let that voice be heard again.

Much of the initial literature on the *Gospel of Judas* was highly sensational and focused on the figure of Judas.[38] Such concern, however engaging, misses the major feature of this text, which is to mount a severe criticism of the leadership of the Church and its practices. The main vehicle for that is a vision of the disciples interpreted by Jesus. In that vision, the disciples see a group of twelve priests standing around an altar in the Temple. These priests do horrible things like sacrificing their own wives and children, sleeping with other men, all the while deferring to one another (*Gos. Jud.* 38).[39] Jesus then offers an

---

37. The translation is that of Bart Ehrman, *The Apostolic Fathers*, 2 vols., Loeb Classical Library 24, 25 (Cambridge, MA: Harvard University Press, 2003), 107.

38. See Rodolphe Kasser, Marvin Meyer, and Gregor Wurst, *The Gospel of Judas* (Washington, DC: National Geographic Society, 2006); Herbert Krosney, *The Lost Gospel: The Quest for the Gospel of Judas Iscariot* (Washington, DC: National Geographic Society, 2006); Bart D. Ehrman, *The Lost Gospel of Judas Iscariot: A New Look at Betrayer and Betrayed* (New York: Oxford, 2006); Elaine Pagels and Karen L. King, *Rereading Judas: The Gospel of Judas and the Shaping of Christianity* (New York: Viking, 2007); and now Lance Jenott, *The Gospel of Judas: Coptic Text, Translation and Historical Interpretation*, Studien und Text zu Antike und Christentum 64 (Tübingen: Mohr Siebeck, 2011).

39. See Kasser et al., *Gospel*, 26.

allegorical interpretation of the vision that identifies the priests with his disciples and the sacrificial victims as the people whom they lead astray.

Whatever the precise complaint of the author against the hierarchy,[40] the polemic of this text stands on its head the kind of symbolism that *1 Clement* begins to exploit. Christian leaders, it protests, too closely assimilate themselves to ancient models of priesthood and the sacrificial function of the Temple. The perspective of the *Gospel of Judas* reminds us that not all followers of Jesus were happy with the appropriation of imagery of Temple and priesthood that came to dominate the orthodox Church.

CONCLUSION

This brief survey of first-century Christian literature reveals a tensive relationship between followers of Jesus and the realities at the center of Jewish ritual life before 70 CE. Different impulses were at work in the period. One, evident in the reports of Acts, continued adherence to the Temple and its leadership, based on the hope that Christians shared with Isaiah that the Temple would be a house of prayer for all nations. Another found in the Temple and its priests symbols of realities that were now experienced in the life of the community of believers. Rejection of the vision of "neither Jew nor Greek" (Gal. 3:28) by more traditional Jews and eventually the destruction of the Temple itself fostered the second impulse and fueled the tendency of Christians to think that they had replaced the ancient realities. Most of the major witnesses to a theological reflection on Temple and priesthood (Hebrews, Acts, 1 Peter, Revelation) attest to versions of this second impulse. A final impulse, evident in *1 Clement*, attests a new symbolic appropriation of the language of priestly hierarchy to undergird a new social reality. Although that third impulse came to dominate the Christian scene, it did not do so without protest.

Enshrined in its various symbolic ways in the canonical texts of Christian scripture and tradition, the Temple and those who served in it have continued to influence Christian thought and practice for two millennia.

---

40. Pagels and King (see n. 37) suggest that the theology of and encouragement for martyrdom by leaders of the church was the key issue. Hence the "sacrificing" of those led astray would have a meaning for this author.

9

An Unperceived Early Jewish-Christian Temple Source

George T. Zervos

The *Protoevangelium of James* (*Prot. Jas.*) is one of the oldest and most important of the Christian Apocrypha, but its full significance for the study of early Judaism and Christianity has not been fully appreciated by modern scholarship.[1] The *Prot. Jas.* generated considerable excitement when it was found in the East and reintroduced to Western Europe in the sixteenth century. The early western scholars who studied and published the *Prot. Jas.* were not equipped with the critical evaluative processes by which they could ascertain the authenticity of this new and unfamiliar text, which had every appearance of being a genuine early Gospel. The French humanist Guillaume Postel discovered the *Prot. Jas.* on a 1549–51 expedition to the Near East and first published the work in a Latin translation in 1552.[2] Postel named his newfound Gospel the *Protevangelion*—or first gospel—indicating his belief that the *Prot. Jas.* contains primary gospel material rivaling the antiquity and authenticity of the canonical Gospels themselves.[3] The first printed Greek text of the *Prot. Jas.* was published in 1564 by Michael Neander in a volume that contains various

---

1. See the discussion below on pp. 3–5 (of 25).

2. Theodor Bibliander, *Protevangelion, siue De natalibus Iesu Christi, et ipsius matris uirginis Mariae, sermo historicus diui Iacobi minoris, consobrini et fratris Domini Iesu, apostoli primarii, et episcopi Christianorum primi Hierosolymis. Euangelica historia, quam scripsit beatus Marcus, Petri apostolorum principis discipulus et filius, primus episcopus Alexandriae, collecta ex probatioribus autoribus, per Theodorum Bibliandrum* (Basel: ex officina Ioannis Oporini, 1552).

3. William J. Bouwsma, *Concordia mundi: the career and thought of Guillaume Postel, 1510–1581* (Cambridge, MA: Harvard University Press, 1957). Irena Backus, "Guillaume Postel, Théodore Bibliander et le Protévangile de Jacques: Introduction historique, édition et traduction française du MS. Londres, British Library, Sloane 1411, 260r–67r," Apocrypha 6 (1995).

religious, historical, and philological works in Greek and Latin, foremost among which was the *Small Catechism* of Martin Luther.[4]

After this prestigious first edition, the Greek text of the *Prot. Jas.* found its way into a variety of published collections of early non-canonical Christian documents.[5] Constantin von Tischendorf awarded the primacy of position to the *Prot. Jas.* in his classic 1853 collection of the apocryphal Gospels.[6] And it has more recently come to light that some sixteen centuries before Tischendorf, the *Prot. Jas.* was likewise given the first position in a series of four early Christian writings that were copied on sixty-eight consecutive pages of a small, self-contained papyrus codex that has been labeled by this writer "the *Prot. Jas.* complex."[7] This codex has been so called because the first forty-nine pages of

4. Martin Luther and Michael Neander, *Katēchēsis Marteinou tou Loutherou, hē mikra kaloumenē, hellēnikolatinē Catechesis Martini Lvtheri parua, græcolatina, postremùm recognita. Ad eam verò accesserunt sententiæ aliquot patrum selectiores græcolatinæ: narrationes item Apocryphæ de Christo, Maria, &c. cognatione ac familia Christi, extra Biblia: sed tamen apud ueteres probatos autores, patres, historicos, philologos, & multos alios scriptores græcos repertæ. Omnia græcolatina, descripta, exposita & edita studio & opera Michaelis Neandri Sorauiensis.* (Basileae: Per Ioannem Oporinum, 1564).

5. Johann Jacob Grynaeus, *Monumenta S. Patrum orthodoxographa, hoc est, Theologiae sacrosanctae ac synceriorus fidei doctores, numero circiter LXXXV, ecclesiae columina luminaq[ue] clarissima, authores partim Graeci partim Latini, ob uetustatem & eruditionem uenerandi, quoru[m] quidam hactenus non aediti latuerunt: uerbis breves, Diuini verò Spiritus doctrina multoru[m] scriptorum quantumuis prolixa uolumina superantes, ut uerè possint appellari Theologica bibliotheca* (Basileae: Ex officina Henricpetrina, 1569); Johann Albert Fabricius, *Codex apocryphus Novi Testamenti, collectus, castigatus, testimoniisque, censuris & animadversionibus illustr. a J.A. Fabricio* (Hamburgi, 1703); Andreas Birch and Johann Albert Fabricius, *Auctarium Codicis apocryphi N.T. Fabriciani, continens plura inedita, alia ad fidem codd. mss. emendatius expressa. Congessit, disposuit, edidit Andreas Birch, Fasciculus primus* (Copenhagen: Arntzen et Hartier, 1804); Johann Karl Thilo, *Codex Apocryphus Novi Testamenti, Tomus Primus: e libris editis et manuscriptis, maxime Gallicanis, Germanicis et Italicis, collectus, recensitus notisque et prologomenis illustratus* (Leipzig: Vogel, 1832).

6. Constantin von Tischendorf, *Evangelia Apocrypha adhibitis plurimis codicibus Graecis et Latinis maximam partem nunc primum consultis atque ineditorum copia insignibus* (Lipsiae: Avenarius et Mendelssohn, 1853). In later, more expanded editions of the Christian Apocrypha, the *Prot. Jas.* was relegated to first place within the subcategory of Birth or Infancy Narratives, cf. J.K. Elliott, *The Apocryphal New Testament: A Collection of Apocryphal Christian Literature in an English Translation* (New York: Oxford University Press, 2005); Wilhelm Schneemelcher and Robert Wilson, *New Testament Apocrypha*, 2 vols. (Cambridge: James Clark, 1991); James, *The Apocryphal New Testament: Being the Apocryphal Gospels, Acts, Epistles, and Apocalypses, with Other Narratives and Fragments* (Oxford: Clarendon, 1955).

7. The first four documents contained in the Bodmer Miscellaneous Codex, characterized as the "ProtoJames Complex," are: P.Bodm V, the Protevangelium of James; P.Bodm X, the Apocryphal Corinthian Correspondence; P.Bodm XI, Odes of Solomon 11; and P.Bodm VII, the canonical epistle of Jude, cf. Zervos, "The Protevangelium of James and the Composition of the Bodmer Miscellaneous

this four-document complex are occupied by the exceptionally well preserved *Papyrus Bodmer V* (*P Bodm V*), which contains a complete text of the *Prot. Jas.* that can be dated paleographically at least as early as the third century CE. To this original complex were subsequently added other smaller groups of texts to form what is known as the *Bodmer Miscellaneous Codex*.[8] Contained within this important larger codex are also the earliest extant copies of the canonical epistles of Jude as well as First and Second Peter; these three letters are otherwise known collectively as P^{72}.[9]

In addition to this remarkable early evidence, the *Prot. Jas.* was preserved in at least 168 Greek manuscripts (157 of them completely or partially extant) beginning with *Papyrus Bodmer V* in the third century CE and ending with a nineteenth-century manuscript that this writer photographed on the island of Paros. The latter manuscript was proved to be a handwritten copy of Neander's 1564 first edition of the *Prot. Jas.*;[10] such is the continuing influence of this apocryphal gospel on the catholicizing Christians. [11] Thus, the historical journey of the *Prot. Jas.* did not begin with Postel, but had already endured centuries of copying and revision, as witnessed by the relatively large number of extant manuscripts containing this document. Many of these texts of the *Prot. Jas.* were incorporated into some liturgical manuscripts, various collections of religious and spiritual texts, and commentaries on particular liturgical events in the life of Jesus and his mother Mary; they were secondary and supplementary to the canonical Gospels and epistles. The canonical writings were bound

Codex: Chronology, Theology, and Liturgy," in *"Non-canonical" Religious Texts in Early Judaism and Early Christianity*, ed. James Charlesworth, vol. 14 of *Jewish and Christian Text* (Edinburgh: T&T Clark, 2012).

8. Cf. E.G. Turner, *The Typology of the Early Codex* (Philadelphia: University of Pennsylvania Press, 1977).

9. These include the Epistle of Jude (*P.Bodm VII*) and the First and Second Epistles of Peter (*P.Bodm VIII*).

10. The nineteenth-century manuscript designated Paros Longovard. 679 in my 1986 doctoral dissertation contains the only known copy of the Greek *Prot. Jas.* text that has the actual word "Protoevangelium" in its title; Zervos, *Prolegomena to a Critical Edition of the Genesis Marias (Protevangelium Jacobi): The Greek Manuscripts* (PhD diss., Duke University, 1986).

11. We must be diligent not to misuse later, political, labels such as "Catholic," "Roman Catholic," "Orthodox," and "Eastern Orthodox," when speaking of the earliest "Christian" communities. In this paper I refer to the ancient undivided "Catholic" Church as the "One, Holy, Catholic, and Apostolic Church" of the Nicene Creed, which split in 1054 CE into two equally catholicizing churches, the Western Roman Catholic Church and the Eastern Orthodox Catholic Church. The earliest historical use of the term "Catholic Church" was in the early second century by Bishop Ignatius of Antioch in his letter to the Smyrnaeans 8, 2: "Wherever Jesus Christ is, there is the Catholic Church."

together in their own official liturgical volumes that were used universally in church services and in the monasteries;[12] apocryphal works, like the *Prot. Jas.*, were scattered in a variety of bound formats.

The ultimate irony is that a writing such as the *Prot. Jas.* could be almost completely shunned in the early New Testament canon discussions and condemned in the entire Western Church, and yet be considered so believable a source of early Christian tradition, that some of its themes were incorporated into the catechetical program of the catholicizing churches on various levels. For example, the *Prot. Jas.* is the earliest witness to the fundamental Catholic doctrine of the perpetual virginity of Mary. The original author of the *Prot. Jas.* could be the first writer to report Mary's descent—and therefore Jesus'—from the royal tribe of Judah. If this is the case, he is in all likelihood the originator of these teachings.[13] Furthermore, he portrays Jesus' brothers—who are listed by name in Mark and Matthew—as the sons of Joseph by a previous marriage. Such rationalizations of Jesus' questionable messianic credentials became stock church teaching in the following centuries.[14] Other stories unique to the *Prot. Jas.* continue to play a central role in the liturgical life, hymnology, and iconography of the church, especially the Eastern Church. A number of the major and lesser feast days of the church relating to Jesus and his mother Mary derive specifically and directly from the *Prot. Jas.* and not from the canonical Gospels.[15]

More recently, the *Prot. Jas.* has been the subject of dedicated scholarly monographs with full introductions and critical texts.[16] As the Greek text of

---

12. Euangelion, Euangelistarion, Apostolos.

13. See Zervos, "Seeking the Source of the Marian Myth: Have We Found the Missing Link?" in *Which Mary?: The Marys of Early Christian Tradition*, ed. F. Stanley Jones (Atlanta: Society of Biblical Literature, 2002). This article supports the priority of the *Prot. Jas.* over the *Ascension of Isaiah*, the other early Christian Apocryphon that contains teachings similar to those regarded as distinctive in the *Prot. Jas.*

14. For Jesus to be a bona fide Messiah (anointed as King of Judea by the High Priest of the Temple), he would have had to have been of the tribe of Judah. Both Matthew and Luke provide genealogies of Jesus in their Gospels, but both give Joseph's genealogy, and, paradoxically, both depict Mary as being a virgin when she conceived Jesus. The problem is that Mary is generally considered to have been from the vicinity of Nazareth in the Galilee, and not from Judea. The *Prot. Jas.* seems to have been written, at least in part, to support Jesus' Davidic descent by declaring Mary to be of the tribe of David.

15. For example, the Birthday of the Virgin Mary on September 8; the commemoration of her parents Saints Joachim and Anna (first named in the *Prot. Jas.*) on September 9; the Eisodia (Entrance) of the Birth-giver of God into the Temple on November 21. The birth of Jesus in a cave, as is described in the *Prot. Jas*, is still the standard depiction of the Nativity of Christ in Orthodox Catholic (Byzantine) iconography and hymnography. One also could argue that the roots of the specifically Roman Catholic doctrine of the Immaculate Conception are found in the *Prot. Jas.*

the *Prot. Jas.* was being published in increasingly more comprehensive editions, scholars were also conducting penetrating studies in order to determine the authorship, date, provenance, and other characteristics of this apocryphon. The discussions on the compositional history of the *Prot. Jas.* were particularly vigorous. By the early part of the twentieth century, Adolf von Harnack's 1897 compositional theory of the *Prot. Jas.* had gained general acceptance among scholars.[17] According to Harnack, the *Prot. Jas.* is a combination of three originally separate, independent parts: 1) chapters 1–17, which he named the *Nativity of Mary*, a history of the conception, birth, and life of Mary up to her own conception of Jesus; 2) chapters 18–20, Harnack's *Apocryphon of Joseph*, concerning the nativity of Jesus and the virginity of Mary "*in partu et post partum*"; and 3) chapters 22–24, his *Apocryphon of Zacharias*.[18] Harnack dated the various parts of the *Prot. Jas.* between the second and fourth centuries CE. Although subsequent scholars disagreed on the dates of the individual sources of the *Prot. Jas.*, most of them assigned significant parts of this document to the second century.

But the attention of the scholarly world was turned away from earlier theories of the composite nature of the *Prot. Jas.* by the Belgian Jesuit priest-scholar Émile de Strycker, who published what has been perhaps the most influential scholarly work on this document to date, *La Forme la plus ancienne du Protévangile de Jacques*.[19] In this landmark study of the *Prot. Jas.*, de Strycker rejected Harnack's three-source compositional theory and judged this apocryphon to be a unitary composition, a secondary writing of the latter part of the second century CE that was heavily influenced by the canonical Gospels of Luke and Matthew. Furthermore, de Strycker relegated *Papyrus Bodmer V* to a diminished status as a later fourth-century product, and characterized it as a "hasty and unintelligent abridgement" of the original text of the *Prot. Jas.*[20]

16. C.A Suckow, *Protevangelium Jacobi, ex cod. MS. Venetiano descripsit prolegomenis, varietate lectionum, notis criticis instructum*, ed. C.A. Suckow (Vratislaviae: Apud Grassium, Barthium et Socium, 1840); Émile Amann, *Le Protévangile de Jacques et ses remaniements latins introduction, textes, traduction et commentaire* (Paris: Letouzey et Ané, 1910).

17. Adolf von Harnack, *Die Chronologie der altchristlichen Literatur bis Eusebius* 2 vols. (Leipzig: Hinrichs, 1897): 1:598–603.

18. Harnack, *Chronologie*, 600. " *1) die Geschichte der Empfängniss, Geburt und des Lebens der Maria bis zu dem Moment, wo die kanonischen Texte einsetzen. 2) Geschichte der Geburt Jesu, erzählt von Joseph, also ein Apocryphum Josephi, 3) ein Apocryphum Zachariae.*"

19. Émile de Strycker, *La Forme la plus ancienne du Protévangile de Jacques: Recherches sur le Papyrus Bodmer 5, avec une édition critique du texte grec et une traduction annotée* (Bruxelles: Société des Bollandistes, 1961).

He thought the original text was better represented in the later manuscripts. It was largely through the influence of de Strycker's impressively complex, though flawed, publication that the *Prot. Jas.* was demoted from its former more prestigious position among the early Christian writings and is now usually dismissed as having been written too late to have any relevance as a source of early Christian thought.[21]

This writer's investigations into the *Prot. Jas.*, published as a series of articles from 1994 to the present,[22] have revealed what seem to be serious weaknesses in fundamental aspects of de Strycker's treatment of this important early writing and its most ancient witness, *Papyrus Bodmer V*. The fourth-century date assigned to *Papyrus Bodmer V* by de Strycker was found to have been based arbitrarily on a miscommunication between him and other scholars;[23] this unique papyrus may prove to be significantly older. These studies also uncovered evidence indicating the possible existence of an underlying document that served as a source in the composition of the *Prot. Jas.* This evidence calls for a re-examination of the pre-de Strycker compositional theories of the *Prot. Jas.* and a comprehensive reassessment of de Strycker's overall interpretation of this work. His erroneous position favoring a later date for *P.Bodm V* and his model of the unitary composition of the *Prot. Jas.* seem to have predisposed his conclusions regarding its late date and authorship. With the principle sustaining pillars of de Strycker's position thus compromised, and his entire interpretation of the *Prot. Jas.* in doubt, a new approach to this important early document is clearly indicated. The essential first step in such a process is the establishment of a reliable Greek text of the *Prot. Jas.* with appropriate emphasis on the primary material witness of *Papyrus .Bodmer V*. It is on this foundation that the discussion may be renewed regarding the sources of the *Prot. Jas.* and the compositional and redactional process that produced this apocryphon in its present form.

The research presented in this essay stems from a study of the original text of *Papyrus Bodmer V* that was based on the working hypothesis that a very early copy of the *Prot. Jas.*, one produced within a century—or less—of the composition of the apocryphon itself, could possibly preserve traces of

---

20. Ibid., 391.

21. See the discussion on the influence of de Strycker's work in Zervos, "Dating the Protevangelium of James: The Justin Martyr Connection," in *Society of Biblical Literature Seminar Papers* 33 (Atlanta: Scholars, 1994).

22. See nn. 6, 9, 12, and 20 above, also nn. 24 and 25 below.

23. Zervos, "The Protevangelium of James."

redactional activity that is characteristic of an evolving text. Without access to the papyrus or to photographs of its pages, its original text initially had to be reconstructed from the printed editions of Michel Testuz and de Strycker. The text of *Papyrus Bodmer V* was purified by the elimination of the layers of corrections and revisions placed on the text by ancient scribes and supplemented by modern editors. This task is now facilitated by photographs of *Papyrus Bodmer V*, published under the auspices of the Bodmer Library.[24] It remains for further investigation to determine the value of *Papyrus Bodmer V* as a witness to the original text of the *Prot. Jas.*, as well as the great significance of this gospel for our understanding of the thought and literature of the early followers of Jesus.

The section of the *Prot. Jas.* that immediately concerns the present conference on Jesus and the Jerusalem Temple is the annunciation story found in chapters 10–12, a passage that is also particularly well suited to illustrate the composite nature of our document. In an article published in 1997, this writer described what appear to be traces of an original, underlying, idiosyncratic annunciation story that may have formed part of a larger underlying source document that was revised and incorporated into what is known today as the *Prot. Jas.*[25] It is perhaps appropriate to name this source the *Genesis Marias* (*GenMar*), which is the first half of the title of the *Prot. Jas.* written on *Papyrus Bodmer V*—and only on *Papyrus Bodmer V*—of all the known manuscripts of this text.[26] The *GenMar* annunciation story thus reconstructed differs substantially from that found in the present, redacted form of the *Prot. Jas.*, which has been harmonized by a later editor with the nativity stories occurring in the canonical Gospels of Matthew and Luke.

The story of Mary's annunciation in *Prot. Jas.* 11, 1-3 occurs within the larger context of an initiative by the temple priests (*Prot. Jas.* 10, 1-2 and 12, 1) to replace the temple veil with a new veil made from a variety of colored threads spun by undefiled Jewish virgins, one of whom was Mary. This story is followed by a brief narrative describing Mary's visit to her relative Elizabeth and return to her own home in *Prot. Jas.* 12, 2-3.[27] During this time Joseph had left

24. M. Bircher, *Bibliotheca Bodmeriana. La collection des papyrus Bodmer* (Munich: K. G. Saur, 2000). Unfortunately these images are of such inferior quality as to make it difficult to discern important diacritical marks in the papyrus.

25. Zervos, "An Early Non-canonical Annunciation Story," in *SBLSP* 36 (Atlanta: Scholars, 1997).

26. Γένεσις Μαρίας Ἀποκάλυψις Ἰακώβ. A number of later manuscripts have the similar word *gennesis* in their title, which means more specifically "birth" or "nativity."

27. These citations from the text of the *Prot. Jas.* and *P.Bodm V* are based on the versification system in de Strycker's *La Forme*. A new edition of the text of the *Prot. Jas.*, which is based on the text of the

Mary in his home at the end of *Prot. Jas.* 9 and departed on a business trip. Upon returning from his trip in *Prot. Jas.* 13, he finds Mary pregnant. Joseph assumes that Mary has been sexually defiled and interrogates her about her pregnancy. Mary insists upon her innocence and swears that she does not know how she became pregnant.

The following outline and text of *Prot. Jas.* 10–12 will exhibit what have been identified as the elements of the original *GenMar* annunciation story and will distinguish them from the additions of the later editor. The versification system employed in this outline is unique to this publication; the standard chapter/verse structure found in previous editions of the *Prot. Jas.* has been retained and augmented with additional subdivisions within the verses indicated by lower case letters. The texts below are presented according to these formatting guidelines:

1. The original Annunciation Story of the *GenMar* is written in regular text:

1a And there was a council of the priests saying:
"Let us make a veil for the Temple of the Lord."

2. All textual material inserted by the later *Prot. Jas.* editor is indented and italicized.

This material falls into three categories, which are distinguished from each other thus:

Verses from canonical Luke's and Matthew's annunciation stories are underlined, with the citations from Luke and Matthew noted in angle brackets:

2e   *At that time Zacharias went silent*. <Luke 1:20-21>
His place was taken by Samuel until Zacharias spoke.

Verses intended to locate the Annunciation in Mary's house are simply underlined:

1d   *and becoming afraid she entered into her house*

Bodmer papyrus, would require a new versification. This is also called for by the confusion in the various versification systems present in previous editions.

Editorial glosses are indicated by bold:

2c *But Mary forgot the mysteries which Gabriel the angel spoke.*

AN EARLY NON-CANONICAL ANNUNCIATION STORY: *PROTOEVANGELIUM OF JAMES* 10-12

CHAPTER 10

1a And there was a council of the priests saying:
"Let us make a veil for the Temple of the Lord."
1b And the priest said: "Call the undefiled virgins from the tribe of David."
1c And the servants went out and sought and found seven

1d *And the priest remembered the child Mary, that*
     She was of the tribe of David and undefiled to God.
1e *And the servants went out and brought her.*

2a and led them into the Temple of the Lord.
2b And the priest said: "Cast lots for me here.
Who will spin the gold and the white and the fine linen
and the silk and the blue and the scarlet and the true purple?"
2c And to Mary's lot fell the true purple and the scarlet.

2d *And taking the scarlet she was spinning in her house.*
2e *At that time Zacharias went silent.* <Luke 1:20-21>
     His place was taken by Samuel until Zacharias spoke.

2f And Mary, taking up the scarlet, was spinning.

CHAPTER 11

1a And she <<<*put down the scarlet and* (see 12, 2b below)>>>
picked up the pitcher and went out to fill it with water.
1b And behold, a voice saying to her:
"Hail, you have received grace among women." <Luke 1:28>
1c And Mary looked around to the right and left
from where might be that voice. <Luke 1:29>

1d   *and becoming afraid she entered into her house*

1e And putting down the pitcher
she picked up the purple and sat on the throne and spun the purple.

2a   *And behold an angel stood before her saying*: <Luke 1:26>
      "Do not be afraid, Mary,
      for you have found grace before the master of all. <Luke 1:30–31>

2b   *You will conceive from the Logos."*

2c   *Mary, hearing, considered in herself saying*: <Luke 1:34>
      "Will I conceive from the living Lord God as every woman gives
      birth?"

3a   *And behold an angel stood before her saying to her*: <Luke 1:26>
      "Not thus, Mary. For the power of God will overshadow you,
      <Luke 1:31–32; 35>
      so that which is born will be called holy, the son of the most high.

3b   *And you will call his name Jesus. For he will save his people from*
      their sins. <Matt 1:21>

3c   *And Mary said: "Behold,the servant of the Lord before him.*<Luke
      1:38>
      Let it be to me according to your word."

CHAPTER 12

1a And she finished the purple and the scarlet and took them to the
priest.
1b And, taking them, the priest blessed her and said:
"Mary, the Lord God blessed your name,
and you will be blessed in all the generations of the earth."

2a   *Receiving joy, Mary went out to her relative Elizabeth* <Luke
      1:39–40>
      and knocked on the door.

2b   *And hearing, Elizabeth* <Luke 1:41>
      <<<*put down the scarlet and* (see 11, 1a above)>>>
      ran to the door and opened to her and blessed her and said: <Luke
      1:42–43>

"Whence is it to me that the mother of the Lord comes to me?
For behold, that in me leaped and blessed you." <Luke 1:44>

2c   *But Mary forgot the mysteries which Gabriel the angel spoke.*

2d And she sighed to heaven and said:

"Who am I that, behold, all the **women (generations?)** of the earth will bless me?"

3a   *And she stayed for three months with Elizabeth* <Luke 1:56>

3b And day by day her womb swelled.

3c   *Being afraid, Mary came into her house* <Luke 1:56>
    And hid herself from the sons of Israel.

3d   **And she was sixteen when those mysteries happened to her.**

COMMENTARY

THE FIRST INTERPOLATION: PROT. JAS. 10, 1A-2A

Chapter 10

1a And there was a council of the priests saying:
"Let us make a veil for the Temple of the Lord."

    1b And the priest said: "Call the undefiled virgins from the tribe of David."
    1c And the servants went out and sought and found seven

1d   *And the priest remembered the child Mary, that*
        She was of the tribe of David and undefiled to God.
1e   *And the servants went out and brought her.*

    2a and led them into the Temple of the Lord.

According to the *Prot. Jas.*, Mary had been living in the Jerusalem Temple for nine years, since her dedication to the Temple by her parents at the age of three.

A council of priests decided to make a new veil for the Holy of Holies and sent servants out to gather the undefiled virgins of the tribe of David to spin the thread. The servants went out and found seven virgins and led them back to the priests. In the source document, the *GenMar*, line 10, 1c originally ended with "and found seven" which flows seamlessly into "and led them" at 10, 2a. The original mission of the Temple servants was to go out, seek, and find "the undefiled virgins from the tribe of David." This first mission was completed when the servants in 10, 1c and 10, 2a "went out and sought and found seven and led them into the Temple of the Lord."

The inserted material 10, 1d-e, relating the priest remembering Mary and the servants going out a second time to bring Mary to the Temple, interrupts the servants' first mission in which "the servants went out and sought [undefiled Davidic virgins] and found seven . . . and led them into the Temple of the Lord." How can the servants go out a second time when they have not yet returned from their first outing to gather the seven undefiled virgins? And in the original story, they would not have had to go out from the Temple a second time in the original *GenMar* story to retrieve Mary since she is already present in the Temple, where she has been living for the past nine years. This is the first of four editorial revisions in the *Prot. Jas.* annunciation story whose purpose is to relocate the coming angelic annunciation to Mary's house. It should be noted that the explicit reference to Mary's Davidic descent is also found in the interpolation; this may be implied, although not emphasized, in the underlying *GenMar* line 10, 1b, where the priest is calling for virgins specifically from the "tribe of David."

THE SECOND INTERPOLATION: PROT. JAS. 10, 2

Chapter 10

2b And the priest said: "Cast lots for me here.
Who will spin the gold and the white and the fine linen
and the silk and the blue and the scarlet and the true
purple?"
2c And to Mary's lot fell the true purple and the scarlet.

2d   *And taking the scarlet she was spinning in her house.*
2e   *At that time Zacharias went silent.* <Luke 1:20-22>
     His place was taken by Samuel until Zacharias spoke.

2f And Mary, taking up the scarlet, was spinning.

Prot. Jas. 10, 2b-c describes a lottery held by the priests to determine which of the virgins will spin the various colored threads (gold, white, linen, silk, blue, scarlet, and purple); to Mary's lot fell the scarlet and purple thread, and she began to spin the scarlet in 10, 2d and again in 10, 2f. The presence of an interpolation in this passage is indicated by three separate elements: 1) the redundancy between the first line of the inserted material, 10, 2d, "And taking the scarlet she was spinning in her house," and line 10, 2f from the original underlying *GenMar* story, "And Mary, taking up the scarlet, was spinning"; 2) the second instance of an editorial revision in 10, 2d, this time using inserted material to place Mary "in her house" for the annunciation, and not in the Temple as in the original *GenMar* story; and 3) the presence of Lukan annunciation material in 2e in the reference to Zechariah becoming silent (Luke 1:5-25, 57-64, NRSV).

As was the case with the first interpolation above, the tension caused by the inserted material in 10, 2d-e between the immediately preceding and succeeding lines is resolved by the removal of this second interpolation as well. The remaining text in 10, 2c and 2f reads seamlessly: "And to Mary's lot fell the true purple and the scarlet. And Mary, taking up the scarlet, was spinning." Excising this second interpolation from the *Prot. Jas.* annunciation story not only eliminates the offending redundant second reference to Mary "spinning in her house," but also removes the second attempt by the redactor, in 10, 2d, to relocate the *GenMar* annunciation from the Temple to Mary's house. The reference in the interpolated material to the Lukan story of the silence of Zechariah, the father of John the Baptist, appears within this context to serve the redactor's purpose of bringing the *GenMar* annunciation story further into conformity with that of canonical Luke.

THE THIRD INTERPOLATION: PROT. JAS. 11, 1

Chapter 11

1a And she <<*put down the scarlet and* (see 12, 2)>>
picked up the pitcher and went out to fill it with water.
1b And behold, a voice saying to her:
"Hail, you have received grace among women." <Luke 1:28>
1c And Mary looked around to the right and left
from where might be that voice. <Luke 1:29>

1d   *and becoming afraid she entered into her house*

> 1e And putting down the pitcher
> <u>she picked up the purple and sat on the throne and spun</u>
> <u>the purple.</u>

The third in this series of revisions of the *GenMar* is found in *Prot. Jas.* 11, 1, which, apart from this one element in 11, 1d was in all probability the original annunciation story of the *GenMar*. According to the *GenMar* account Mary receives a relatively short annunciation in the Temple from a mysterious unidentified voice. Mary is spinning the scarlet thread (from 10, 2f above). She hears an unidentified voice telling her that she among women has received grace. Mary puts down the scarlet thread then picks up the purple thread, sits on the throne, and spins the purple thread. This very significant passage contains three indications of redactional activity: 1) the presence of a dislocated verse in *Prot. Jas.* 12, 2b that originally seems to have been situated in *Prot. Jas.* 11, 1a; 2) the third consecutive instance in which the redactor attempts to relocate the *GenMar* annunciation event from the Temple to Mary's house; 3) the enigmatic reference to Mary sitting on "the throne" after entering "her house" to spin the purple thread.

Textual critics have long noticed the problematic statement in the story of Mary's visit to her relative Elizabeth in *Prot. Jas.* 12, 2b, after Mary's double angelic annunciation in *Prot. Jas.* 11, 2 and 3 (see the Fourth and Fifth Interpolations below). In *Prot. Jas.* 12, 2b, upon hearing Mary knocking at her door, Elizabeth "*put down the scarlet* [thread] *and*" ran to open her door. Why would Elizabeth be holding scarlet thread in 12, 2b, when it was Mary who was spinning scarlet thread previously in 10, 2d and 2f? Being six months pregnant, according to the Lukan source of this material (see below), Elizabeth is certainly not one of the virgins participating in weaving the new Temple veil. A reasonable solution to this long-standing paradox may be found in the intense redactional activity in *Prot. Jas.* 10–12 that has been revealed in this investigation. The radical revision of the *GenMar* annunciation story occurring in these chapters—including the insertion of extensive Lukan textual material at the very point at which Mary is spinning the scarlet thread—provides a realistic scenario in which the words "put down the scarlet [thread] and" could have been dislodged from their original location in *Prot. Jas.* 11, 1a, where they would have referred to Mary, and embedded in the extraneous material from Luke's story of Mary's visit to Elizabeth (Luke 1:39-44), where they now refer to Elizabeth.

It was shown above that both the First and Second Interpolations contain material inserted by the redactor specifically for the purpose of changing the location of the annunciation story from the Temple to Mary's house; the Third Interpolation in *Prot. Jas.* 11, 1d adds yet another such instance. But in this case, the words "and becoming afraid she entered into her house" do not interrupt the flow of the narrative in 11, 1a in which Mary puts down the scarlet thread that she has been spinning, picks up a pitcher, and goes out to fill it with water. Still outside, Mary hears the voice telling her that she among women has received grace (11, 1b) and looks around for the source of the voice (11, 1c). It is at this point (11, 1d) that one finds the insertion containing the words "she entered into her house" which at first seem necessary to relate how Mary returned inside, where she picks up the purple thread, sits on the throne, and spins the purple. However, Mary's entry "into her house," causes considerable tension with the immediately following text, which states that Mary "sat on the throne and spun the purple." Would Mary have had a throne in her private residence? It seems likely in this scenario that the redactor either modified or replaced the original words in the *GenMar* story that would have recounted Mary's reentry into the Holy of Holies—her location throughout the story—where she put down the pitcher of water, picked up the purple thread, sat on the throne *of God*, and commenced to spin the purple thread. Mary is now worthy to sit on the very throne of God in the Holy of Holies and spin the royal purple thread because she has conceived in her womb a significant royal and religious figure in Israel.

THE FOURTH INTERPOLATION: PROT. JAS. 11, 2 AND 3

Chapter 11

2a   *And behold an angel stood before her saying*: <Luke 1:26>
   "Do not be afraid, Mary,
   for you have found grace before the master of all.
   <Luke 1:30-31>

2b   *You will conceive from* the Logos."

2c   *Mary, hearing, considered in herself saying*: <Luke 1:34>
    "Will I conceive from the living Lord God as every
    woman gives birth?"

3a   *And behold an angel stood before her saying to her*:
   <Luke 1:26>

"Not thus, Mary. For the power of God will
overshadow you, <Luke 1:31-32; 35>
so that which is born will be called holy, the son of the
most high.

3b   *And you will call his name Jesus,*
       for he will save his people from their sins <Matt 1:21>
3c   *And Mary said: "Behold, the servant of the Lord before him.*
       <Luke 1:38>
       Let it be to me according to your word."

Prot. Jas., 11, 2 and 3, in their entirety, occupy about two thirds of the text of chapter 11 and constitute the most extensive interpolation of external material into the original *GenMar* annunciation story. These lines are replete with references to the canonical annunciation story of Luke, and in one instance, to the corresponding story of Matthew. As was the case with the other interpolations noted above, this material interrupts the text into which it was inserted. If *Prot. Jas.* 11, 2 and 3 are removed from the text, the narrative flows seamlessly from 11, 1e, where Mary is sitting on the throne in the Holy of Holies spinning the purple thread, to 12, 1a, where Mary finishes spinning the purple and the scarlet thread and takes them to the priest. The original text without the insertion would have read as follows: 11, 1e, "she picked up the purple and sat on the throne and spun the purple, 12, 1a, and she finished the purple and the scarlet and took them to the priest."

The redactor attempted to bring the *GenMar* annunciation story into conformity with that of Luke by appending to the original story of the unidentified voice in *Prot. Jas.* 11, 1 a relatively long tract recounting two consecutive angelic visitations to Mary. The inserted material in *Prot. Jas.* 11, 2 and 3 was positioned to follow immediately after, and thus to supplement, the unidentified voice episode. Within the context of the present form of the *Prot. Jas.*, the purpose of the messengers was to elucidate for Mary the significance of the words of the unidentified voice. The contrived dialogue between Mary and the two angels contains a number of verbal parallels with the vocabulary of Luke 1:26-38. With the addition of this copious Lukan material, the *GenMar* story appears to be highly reminiscent of the account of Mary's interaction with the archangel Gabriel in Luke 1. The redactor has accomplished his purpose; the idiosyncratic *GenMar* annunciation story has been made more orthodox and consequently the *Prot. Jas.* has been considered by most modern researchers to be a later secondary writing that was dependent upon canonical Luke and Matthew.

THE FIFTH INTERPOLATION: PROT. JAS., 12, 2

Chapter 12

1a And she finished the purple and the scarlet and took them to the priest.
1b And, taking them, the priest blessed her and said:
"Mary, the Lord God blessed your name,
and you will be blessed in all the generations of the earth."

2a   *Receiving joy, Mary went out to her relative Elizabeth*
      <Luke 1:39–40>
      and knocked on the door.

2b   *And hearing Elizabeth* <Luke 1:41>
         <<*put down the scarlet and* (see 11, 1a above)>>
         ran to the door and opened to her and blessed her and
         said: <Luke 1:42–43>
         "Whence is it to me that the mother of the Lord comes to
         me?
         For behold, that in me leaped and blessed you." <Luke
         1:44>

2c   *But Mary forgot the mysteries which Gabriel the angel spoke.*

2d And she sighed to heaven and said:
"Who am I that, behold, all the **women (generations?)**
of the earth will bless me?"

The Fifth Interpolation is inserted into a dialogue in the *GenMar* between Mary and the priest to whom she is returning the thread she has spun; the priest blesses Mary and she responds as if perplexed by his blessing. The redactor has inserted elements from Luke 1:39-44 between the priest's blessing in *Prot. Jas.* 12, 1b and Mary's response in *Prot. Jas.* 12, 2d. The interpolation is a shorter version of the story of Mary's visit to Elizabeth in Luke's annunciation narrative (Luke 1:39-56). The alien nature of the inserted text within the context of the *GenMar* annunciation story is attested strongly by four elements: 1) the occurrence of texts with a strongly Lukan character closely resembling those in the Fourth Interpolation above, 2) the presence of the line "put down the scarlet and" which here refers to Elizabeth putting down the scarlet thread, but which fits more naturally in the Third Interpolation above (*Prot. Jas.* 11, 1a) where Mary was spinning the scarlet thread and would have put it down before going out to fill her pitcher with water, 3) the obvious editorial gloss placed by the redactor in 12, 2c to explain why Mary was perplexed by the priest's blessing; she simply "forgot the mysteries which Gabriel the angel spoke" to her in the preceding Fourth Interpolation, and 4) a possible editorial adjustment to the text "all the women of the earth will bless me" in 12, 2d for the purpose of accommodating the interpolation to the preceding and following texts in the underlying *GenMar* story.

The verbal parallels between the inserted text in *Prot. Jas.* 2a-c and Luke 1:39-44 are obvious; both describe Mary's visit to Elizabeth after her annunciation. The *Prot. Jas.* version provides less detail but cites parts of Luke 1:43-44 almost verbatim. Part of the phrase from Luke 1:42 ("Blessed are you among women") has already appeared in *Prot. Jas.* 11, 1b. But apart from the manifest Lukan character of the interpolated text, there are additional, and even more blatant, indications of the secondary nature of this material. It is in this interpolation also that is found the dislocated phrase "put down the scarlet and" (set off by double angle brackets), which was discussed above in the Third Interpolation regarding *Prot. Jas.* 11, 1a. This displaced phrase can be excised from its present context with no effect on the preceding and following lines; as we have seen this is a telltale sign of editorial activity. Without this interruption Mary's encounter with Elizabeth flows smoothly in 12, 2a-b, "Mary went out to her relative Elizabeth and knocked on the door. And hearing, Elizabeth ran to the door and opened to her . . ."

The redactor was acutely aware of the tension caused by his introduction of a Lukan story of Mary's visit to Elizabeth into the *GenMar* account of Mary's dialogue with the priest. In the original *GenMar* story the dialogue would have passed seamlessly from the priest's blessing upon Mary in *Prot. Jas.* 12, 1b, "you will be blessed in all the generations of the earth," to what without the insertion would have been Mary's response to the priest's words in *Prot. Jas.* 12, 2d, "who am I that, behold, all the generations of the earth will bless me?" The redactor endeavors to alleviate the incongruity caused by his insertions into the original text by making at least one, possibly two adjustments. First he adds an obvious editorial comment at 12, 2c that "Mary forgot the mysteries which Gabriel the angel spoke." With these words the redactor attempts to explain why Mary is baffled by the successive blessings she has just received from the priest in 12, 1b (in the *GenMar* story) and from Elizabeth in 12, 2b (in the interpolated Lukan text), much less by the even more astonishing messages she just received in her previous dialogues from the two angels in the Fourth Interpolation above.

A second possible editorial adjustment to this passage regards the word "women" in 12, 2d. The redactor appears to have altered what would have been Mary's original response to the priest's blessing in the *GenMar* story, in order to harmonize the wording of her response to that of Elizabeth's blessing in the inserted text. Since the priest's statement in 12, 1b was that Mary "will be blessed in all the *generations* of the earth," Mary's original response to him in 12, 2d would have been to question why "all the *generations* of the earth" will bless her. But with the interpolation now separating Mary's response from the priest's blessing, the redactor has now caused Mary's response to be directed to Elizabeth's blessing in the intervening material at 12, 2b, according to which Elizabeth "ran to the door and opened to her [Mary] and blessed her." It is reasonable to assume that the redactor would have substituted the word "women" (*gynaikes*) in 12, 2d for the word "generations" (*geneai*)[28] from the priest's blessing in 12, 1b, to reflect the new context of Mary's response to being blessed by a woman, Elizabeth, in 12, 2b.

THE SIXTH INTERPOLATION : PROT. JAS. 12, 3.

Chapter 12

3a   *And she stayed for three months with Elizabeth* <Luke 1:56>

3b And day by day her womb swelled.

3c   *Being afraid, Mary came into her house* <Luke 1:56>
        and hid herself from the sons of Israel.

3d   **And she was sixteen when those mysteries happened to her.**

The Sixth Interpolation closes the redacted *GenMar* annunciation story in the same manner that Luke's annunciation story is closed, in fact by the addition of elements from the concluding verse of Luke's story, Luke 1:56: "And Mariam remained with her [Elizabeth] for three months and returned to her home." In 12, 3a the redactor adopts the Lukan three-month duration of Mary's stay with

28. The Greek word γενεαι resembles γυναικες.

Elizabeth, and in 12, 3b repeats his own statement implanted in 11, 1d that Mary became afraid and entered into her house. This is the fourth and final occasion in the *Prot. Jas.* annunciation story that the redactor reiterates what is obviously an important issue for him, that the events of Mary's annunciation must occur in Mary's "house" instead of in the Temple (*Prot. Jas.* 10, 1e, 2d; 11, 1d; 12, 3c). In the original *GenMar* story, Mary is still in the Temple where all the events of the annunciation by the unidentified voice take place. The only element from the original story that has survived in *Prot. Jas.* 12, 3 is the statement in 3b that "day by day her [Mary's] womb swelled." This line originally followed immediately after the dialogue between Mary and the priest to whom she has brought the thread she has spun in *Prot. Jas.* 12, 1a–b and 12, 2d, without all the Lukan materials inserted by the redactor.

The *Prot. Jas.* redactor concludes his editorial work on the annunciation story by the addition of another flagrant gloss in 12, 3d stating that Mary "was sixteen when those mysteries happened to her." At the beginning of the annunciation story in *Prot. Jas.* 8, 2 Mary was twelve years old. The successive events described in *Prot. Jas.* 9–12 would hardly have taken four years to unfold. Why must the redactor make her sixteen now? Perhaps he was performing his editorial work in a cultural milieu that would have found it offensive for a twelve-year-old girl to have been impregnated by the voice of God.

The Original Annunciation Story of the *Genesis Marias*

10 And there was a council of the priests saying:
"Let us make a veil for the Temple of the Lord."
And the priest said: "Call the undefiled virgins from the tribe of David."
And the servants went out and sought and found seven,
And led them into the Temple of the Lord.
And the priest said: "Cast lots for me here.
Who will spin the gold and the white and the fine linen
and the silk and the blue and the scarlet and the true purple?"
And to Mary's lot fell the true purple and the scarlet.
And Mary, taking up the scarlet, was spinning.

11 And she put down the scarlet and picked up the pitcher
and went out to fill it with water.
And behold, a voice saying to her:
"Hail, you have received grace among women."
And Mary looked around to the right and left from where might be

that voice.
And putting down the pitcher she picked up the purple
and sat on the throne and spun the purple.

12 And she finished the purple and the scarlet and took them to the
priest.
And, taking them, the priest blessed her and said:
"Mary, the Lord God blessed your name,
and you will be blessed in all the generations of the earth."
And she sighed to heaven and said: "Who am I that, behold,
all the generations of the earth will bless me?"
And day by day her womb swelled.

Conclusions

Previous research seems to have detected the presence of a pre-existing source
document, the *GenMar*, which is preserved in the apocryphal gospel known
today as the *Prot. Jas.* This study presents certain portions of the *GenMar* that
pertain to the topic of this conference on Jesus and the Temple. The texts in
question occur in the original annunciation story of the *GenMar*, which appears
to have been altered substantially by the later editor of the *Prot. Jas.* in order
to conform the earlier story to the canonical Gospel tradition. Two important
elements appear to have been modified purposely by the editor of the *Prot. Jas.*:

> 1. the original location of the annunciation—which in the *GenMar*
> took place in the Jerusalem temple—was changed to Mary's home in
> accordance with the infancy stories in Luke and Matthew;
> 2. the agent of the annunciation—which in the *GenMar* story was a
> mysterious and unidentified voice—was transformed into a double
> angelic annunciation to Mary modeled after, and using materials
> from, the Lukan annunciation story.

Both of these elements are in agreement with one of the central features of
this apocryphal gospel, its strongly pro-Jewish character. In the *GenMar*, many
of the customary roles of the Jews, as portrayed in the New Testament, are
reversed; the high priests, priests, and scribes are respected and revered figures,
and the Pharisees are not even mentioned. Although the author of the *GenMar*
does not appear to have had direct knowledge of the religious practice of the
Temple, he is concerned to present the Jewish Temple cult in a most positive
light. The Temple is indeed the Holy Place and God's throne is in the Holy

of Holies. The rites and rituals carried out by the priests of the Temple are effective in discerning the divine will and in dispensing justice. The events that occur in the *GenMar* do so within an atmosphere that is saturated with a natural, comfortable Jewishness.

A strongly pro-Jewish document with a positive focus on the Jerusalem Temple and its cult is an oddity among the early writings attributed to the followers of Jesus. The idiosyncratic nature of the *GenMar* raises questions regarding the time and place of its origins. When, where, and by whom could such a text have been written? When and where were Jews and Jesus-believers so closely identified with each other? Why would this apocryphon contain an annunciation story that differed so radically from the parallel stories in canonical Matthew and Luke, and yet stand beside these Gospels as a third primary source for Mary's virginal conception? In what scenario would a later editor have modified the text in ways that betray a proto-Orthodox Catholic bent? And what is the identity of the mysterious voice that spoke to Mary in the Temple and, in effect, impregnated her with a person so holy that holding him in her womb made Mary worthy to sit on the throne of God in the Holies of Holies?

The *Prot. Jas.* and its source document, the *GenMar*, raise many questions that potentially may have a considerable impact on our understanding of the early Palestinian Jesus Movement. But the mysteries contained in these texts can be interpreted and evaluated fully only on the basis of a reliable text of the original document (insofar as that is possible) and an understanding of its textual and compositional history. This new information will enable scholars to integrate the *GenMar* into the fabric of its proper historical setting. The present writer is currently preparing a scholarly edition of the Greek text of the *Prot. Jas.* with an introduction that will address these critical issues.[29]

---

29. Forthcoming from T&T Clark.

Selected Bibliography

Brady Alan Beard

This bibliography includes the most pertinent works cited in the preceding chapters as well as additional publications. They are organized here into five major sections: 1) The Jerusalem Temple: Its Description and Archaeological Evidence; 2) Worship in the Temple; 3) Jesus and the Temple; 4) Jesus' Followers and the Temple; and 5) General Materials.

JERUSALEM TEMPLE: ITS DESCRIPTION AND ARCHAEOLOGICAL EVIDENCE

Adan Bayewitz D., F. Asaro, M. Wieder, and R. Giauque. "Preferential Distribution of Lamps from the Jerusalem Area in the Late Second Temple Period (Late First Century BCE–70 CE)." *Bulletin of the American Schools of Oriental Research* 350 (2008): 37–85.

Adler, Yonatan. "The Archaeology of Purity." PhD diss., Bar Ilan University, 2011.

Amar, Z. "The Showbread Table on the Coins of Mattathias Antigonus: A Reconsideration." *INJ* 17 (2010): 48–58.

Aviam, M. *The New Encyclopedia of Archaeological Excavations in the Holy Land.* Jerusalem: Israel Exploration Society & Carta, 2008.

Avigad, Nahman. *Discovering Jerusalem.* Oxford: Basil Blackwell, 1984.

Bachmann, Michael. *Jerusalem und der Tempel: Die geographish-theologischen Elemente in der lukanischen Sicht des jüdischen Kultzentrums.* BWANT 109. Stuttgart: Kohlkammer, 1980.

Bauckham, Richard. "Josephus' Account of the Temple in *Contra Apionem* 2.102-109." In *Josephus' Contra Apionem: Studies in its Character and Context With Latin Concordance to the Portion Missing in Greek*, 327–47. Edited by Louis H. Feldman and John R. Levison. Leiden: Brill, 1996.

Berman, Joshua. *The Temple: Its Symbolism and Meaning Then and Now.* Northvale, NJ: Aronson, 1995.

Day, John, ed. *Temple and Worship in Biblical Israel.* London: T&T Clark, 2005.

Gibson, Shimon. *The Final Days of Jesus: The Archaeological Evidence.* New York: HarperOne, 2009.

————. "New Excavations on Mount Zion in Jerusalem and an Inscribed Stone Cup/Mug from the Second Temple Period." In *New Studies in the Archaeology of Jerusalem and its Region Collected Papers*. Edited by D. Amit, O. Peleg-Barkat, and G.D. Stiebel. Jerusalem: Israel Antiquities Authority, 2010.

Goodman, Martin. "The Pilgrimage Economy of Jerusalem in the Second Temple Period." In *Jerusalem: Its Sanctity and Centrality to Judaism, Christianity and Islam*. Edited by Lee I. Levine. New York: Continuum, 1999.

————. "The Temple in First Century CE Judaism." In *Temple and Worship in Biblical Israel*, 459–68. Edited by John Day. London: T&T Clark, 2007.

Gunewag, J. and I. Perlman. "The Origin of the Herodian Lamps." *Bulletin of the Anglo-Israel Archaeological Society 1984–5* (1984): 79–83.

Habas, L. "An Incised Depiction of the Temple Menorah and Other Cult Objects of the Second Temple Period." In *Jewish Quarter Excavations in the Old City of Jerusalem*, 329–342. Ed. H. Geva. Vol. 2. Jerusalem: Israel Exploration Society, 2003.

Hachlili, R. *Ancient Mosaic Pavements: Themes, Issues, and Trends*. Leiden: Brill, 2009.

Hamblin, William J. and David Rolph Seeley, *Solomon's Temple: Myth and History*. London: Thames & Hudson, 2007.

Hirschfeld, Y. *Ramat Hanadiv Excavations*. Jerusalem: Israel Exploration Society, 2000.

Küchler, Max. *Jerusalem: Ein Handbuch und Studienreiseführer zur Heiligen Stadt*. Orte und Lanschaften der Bibel 4.2. Göttingen: Vandenhoeck & Ruprecht, 2007.

Levine, Lee I. "Josephus' Description of the Jerusalem Temple." In *Josephus and the History of the Greco-Roman Period: Essay in Memory of Morton Smith*, 233–46. Edited by Fausto Parente and Joseph Sievers. Studia Post-Biblica 41. Leiden: Brill, 1994.

Lundquist, John M. *The Temple of Jerusalem: Past, Present, and Future*. Westport, CT: Praeger, 2008.

Magen, Y. *The Stone Vessel Industry in the Second Temple Period*. Jerusalem: Israel Exploration Society, 2002.

Magen, Y. D.T. Ariel, G. Bijovsky, Y. Tzionit, and O. Sirkis. *The Land of Benjamin*. Jerusalem: Israel Antiquities Authority, 2004.

Mazar, Benjamin. "The Temple Mount." In *Biblical Archaeology Today, Proceedings of the International Congress on Biblical Archaeology, Jerusalem,*

April 1984, 463–68. Edited by Avraham Biran. Jerusalem: Israel Exploration Society, 1985.

Mazar, Eilat. *The Temple Mount Excavations in Jerusalem 1968–1978 directed by Benjamin Mazar*. Jerusalem: Institute of Archaeology, 2003. [authoritative]

———. *The Walls of the Temple Mount.* Jerusalem: Shoham Academic Research and Publication, 2011.

Netzer, E., Y. Kalman, and R. Loris. "A Hasmonaean Synagogue at Jericho." *Qadmoniot* 117 (1999): 17–24. [in Hebrew]

Netzer, Ehud. *The Architecture of Herod, the Great Builder*. Grand Rapids, MI: Baker Academic, 2008.

On, A. and S. Weksler-Bdolah. "Khirbet Um el-Umdan: A Jewish Village with a Synagogue from the Second Temple Period at Modiin." *Qadmoniot* 130 (2005): 107–116. [in Hebrew]

Parrot, André. *Le Temple de Jérusalem*. Neuchâtel: Delachaux & Niestlé, 1954. [ET: New York: Philosophical Library, 1957]. [dated]

———. *Le Temple lieu de conflit: Actes du colloque de Cartigny 1991*. Leuven: Peeters, 1994.

Patrich, Joseph. *Hidushim ba-arkhe'ologyah shel Yerushalayim u-sevivoteha: Kovets mehkarim.* Jerusalem: Rashut ha'atikot, Merhav Yerushalayim, 2007. [in Hebrew]

Rahmani, L.Y. *A Catalogue of Jewish Ossuaries*. Jerusalem: Israel Antiquities Authority, 1994.

Reich, R. "Jewish Ritual Baths at the Second Temple Period, Mishnah and Talmud." PhD diss., Hebrew University, 1990.

Ritmeyer, Kathleen and Leen Ritmeyer. "Reconstructing Herod's Temple Mount." *Biblical Archaeology Review* 15, no. 6 (1989): 3–42.

Ritmeyer, Leen. *The Quest: Revealing the Temple Mount in Jerusalem*. Jerusalem: Carta, 2006.

Rosenau, Helen. *Vision of the Temple*. London: Oresko Books, 1979.

Safrai, Shmuel. *Pilgrimage at the Time of the Second Temple*. 2nd ed. Jerusalem: Akademon, 1985. [in Hebrew]

Schiffman, Lawrence H. "Architecture and Law: The Temple and its Courtyards in the *Temple Scroll*." In *From Ancient Israel to Modern Judaism*, 1.267–84. Edited by Jacob Neusner, Ernest S. Frerichs, and Nahum M. Sarna. Brown Judaic Studes 159. 4 vols. Atlanta: Scholars, 1989.

Schmidt, Francis. *How the Temple Thinks*. Translated by J.E. Crowley. The Biblical Seminar 78. Sheffield: Sheffield Academic Press, 2001. See esp. ch. 3: "The Temple."

Syon, D. "Tyre and Gamla." PhD diss., Hebrew University, 2004.

————. "Yet Again on the Bronze Coins Minted at Gamla." *INR* 2 (2007): 117–122.

Syon, D. and Z. Yavor, eds. *Gamla II. The Architecture*. Israel Antiquities Authority Reports 44. Jerusalem: Israel Antiquities Authority, 2010.

Trudinger, Peter L. *The Psalms of the Tamid Service: A Liturgical Text from the Second Temple*. Supplements to Vestum Testamentum 98. Leiden: Brill, 2004.

Viollet-le-Duc and Eugene Emmanuel. "Appendix 1: On Restoration." In *Our Architectural Heritage: From Consciousness to Conservation*. Paris: Cevat Erder, 1986.

Vogüé, Melchior de. *Le Temple de Jérusalem. Monographie du Haram ech-cherif, suivie d'un essai sur la topographie de la Ville Sainte*. Paris: Noblet & Baudry, 1864.

Warren, Charles. *Plans, Elevations, Sections, etc., Showing the Results of the Excavations at Jerusalem, 1867–1870, Executed for the Committee of the Palestine Exploration Fund*. London: V. Brooks, Day & Son, 1884.

Weinfeld, Moshe. "Instructions for Temple Visitors in the Bible and in Ancient Egypt." In *Egyptological Studies*. Edited by Sarah Israelit-Groll. Scripta Hierosolymitana 28. Jerusalem: Magnes, 1982.

Weiss, Z. *The Sepphoris Synagogue*. Jerusalem: Israel Exploration Society, 2005.

Wilson, Charles. *Ordinance Survey of Jerusalem*. London, 1865.

WORSHIP IN THE TEMPLE

Barré, Michael L. *The Lord Has Saved Me: A Study of the Psalm of Hezekiah (Isaiah 38:9-20)*. Catholic Biblical Quarterly Monograph Series 39. Washington, DC: Catholic Biblical Association of America, 2005.

Barucq, André and François Daumas. *Hymnes et prières de l'Égypte ancienne*. Littératures anciennes du Proche-Orient. Paris: Cerf, 1980.

Charlesworth, James H. "A Prolegomenon to a New Study of the Jewish Background of the Hymns and Prayers in the New Testament." In *Essays in Honour of Yigael Yadin*, 265–85. Edited by Geza Vermes and Jacob Neusner. *Journal of Jewish Studies* 33, no. 1–2 (1982).

Charlesworth, James H., ed. "Psalms and Psalters in the Dead Sea Scrolls." In *The Bible and the Dead Sea Scrolls*, vol. 1: Scripture and the Scrolls. Waco, TX: Baylor University Press, 2006.

Dimant, Devorah. "The Qumran Manuscripts: Contents and Significance." In *Time to Prepare the Way in the Wilderness: Papers on the Qumran Scrolls by Fellows of the Institute for Advanced Studies of the Hebrew University, Jerusalem, 1989–90*. Edited by Devorah Dimant and Lawrence H. Schiffman. Studies on the Texts of the Desert of Judah 16. Leiden: Brill, 1995.

Eliav, Yaron Z. *God's Mountain: The Temple Mount in Time, Place, and Memory*. Baltimore: Johns Hopkins University Press, 2005.

Flint, Peter. "Psalms and Psalters in the Dead Sea Scrolls." In *The Bible and the Dead Sea Scrolls*. Vol. 1: *Scripture and the Scrolls*, 233–72. Edited by James H. Charlesworth. Waco, TX: Baylor University Press, 2006.

Hallo, William W., ed. *The Context of Scripture: Canonical Compositions*. Vol. 1. Leiden: Brill, 1997.

Hayward, C.T.R. *The Jewish Temple: A Non-biblical Sourcebook*. London: Routledge, 1996.

Henshaw, Richard. *Female and Male: The Cultic Personnel: The Bible and Rest of the Ancient Near East*. Allison Park, PA: Pickwick, 1994.

Jacobsen, Thorkild. *The Harps that Once...: Sumerian Poetry in Translation*. New Haven, CT: Yale University Press, 1987.

Kaufmann, Yehezkel. *The Religion of Israel: From Its Beginnings to the Babylonian Exile*. Translated by Moshe Greenberg. Chicago: University of Chicago Press, 1960.

———. *Toledot ha-'Emuna ha-Yisra'elit*. 8 vols. Tel-Aviv: Bialik/Devir, 1937. [in Hebrew]

Kilmer, Anne D., Richard L. Crocker, and Robert R. Brown. *Sounds from Silence: Recent Discoveries in Ancient Near Eastern Music*. Bit Enki Records, 1976. http://www.amaranthpublishing.com/hurrian.htm or http://www.bellaromamusic.com.

Knohl, Israel. *The Sanctuary of Silence*. Minneapolis: Fortress Press, 1995.

Koester, Craig. *The Dwelling of God: The Tabernacle in the Old Testament, Intertestamental Jewish Literature, and the New Testament*. Catholic Biblical Quarterly Monograph Series 22. Washington, DC: Catholic Biblical Association, 1989.

Langer, Ruth. *To Worship God Properly: Tensions Between Liturgical Custom and Halakhah in Judaism*. Cincinnati: Hebrew Union College Press, 1998.

Peters, John J. *The Psalms as Liturgies*. New York: Macmillan, 1922.

Roberts, Jimmy Jack McBee. "Temple, Jerusalem." In *New Interpreter's Dictionary of the Bible* 5.507–8. 5 vols. Edited by Kathrine Doob Sakenfeld. Nashville: Abingdon, 2009.

Rowland, Christopher. "The Temple in the New Testament." In *Temple and Worship in Biblical Israel: Proceedings of the Oxford Old Testament Seminar*, 469–83. Edited by John Day. London: T&T Clark, 2007.

Sarna, Nahum M. "The Psalms Superscriptions and the Guilds." In *Studies in Jewish Religious and Intellectual History: Presented to Alexander Altmann on the Occasion of his Seventieth Birthday*, 281–300. Edited by Siegfried Stein and Raphael Loewe. Tuscaloosa: University of Alabama Press, 1979.

Schiffman, Lawrence H. *The Courtyards of the House of the Lord: Studies on the Temple Scroll*. Edited by Florentino García Martínez. Studies on the Texts of the Desert of Judah 75. Leiden: Brill, 2008.

———. *Reclaiming the Dead Sea Scrolls: The History of Judaism, the Background of Christianity, the Lost Library of Qumran*. Philadelphia: Jewish Publication Society, 1994.

Jesus and the Temple

Bruce, F.F. "New Wine in Old Wine Skins: III. The Corner Stone." *Expository Times* 84 (1972–73): 231–35.

Charlesworth, James H. *The Historical Jesus: An Essential Guide*. Nashville: Abingdon, 2008.

———. "The Historical Jesus in the Fourth Gospel: A Paradigm Shift?" *Journal for the Historical Jesus* 8 (2010): 3–46.

———. "The Historical Jesus: How to Ask Questions and Remain Inquisitive." In *Handbook for the Study of the Historical Jesus*, 1:91–128. Edited by Tom Holmén and Stanley E. Porter. Leiden: Brill, 2010.

———, ed. *Jesus and Archaeology*. Grand Rapids, MI: Eerdmans, 2006.

———, ed. *Jesus Research: New Methodologies and Perceptions*. Grand Rapids, MI: Eerdmans, 2013.

———, ed. *The Messiah: Developments in Earliest Judaism and Christianity* Minneapolis: Fortress Press, 1992.

———. "The Temple, Purity, and the Background to Jesus' Death." *Revista Catalana de Teologia* 38, no. 2 (2008): 395–442.

Crossan, John Dominic. *The Historical Jesus: The Life of a Mediterranean Jewish Peasant*. New York: HarperOne, 1991.

Edersheim, Alfred. *The Temple: Its Ministry and Services as They Were at the Time of Jesus Christ*. London: Religious Tract Society, 1874; reprinted in 1989.

Evans, Craig A. *Jesus and His World: The Archaeological Evidence*. Louisville: Westminster John Knox, 2012.

Gray, Timothy C. *The Temple in the Gospel of Mark: A Study in its Narrative Role*. Tübingen: Mohr Siebeck, 2008.

Goodman, Martin. *Judaism in the Roman World: Collected Studies*. Leiden: Brill, 2007.

Juel, Donald H. *The Messiah and Temple: A Study of Jesus' Trial before the Sanhedrin in the Gospel of Mark*. Missoula, MT: Scholars, 1977; republished 1984.

Kerr, Alan R. *The Temple of Jesus' Body: The Temple Theme in the Gospel of John*. London: Sheffield Academic Press, 2002.

Liebi, Roger. *The Messiah in the Temple: The Symbolism and Significance of the Second Temple in Light of the New Testament*. Christlicher Medien Vertrieg, 2012.

Mathew, S.P. *Temple-criticism in Mark's Gospel: The Economic Role of the Jerusalem Temple During the First Century CE*. Foreword by G. Theissen. Delhi: ISPCK, 1999.

Perrin, Nicholas. *Jesus the Temple*. Grand Rapids, MI: Baker Academic, 2010.

Sanders, E.P. "Common Judaism and the Temple." In *Judaism: Practice and Belief 63 BCE–66 CE*. Philadelphia: Trinity Press International, 1992.

———. *Jesus and Judaism*. Philadelphia: Fortress Press, 1985.

Schürer, Emil, Geza Vermes, Fergus Millar, and Matthew Blacks, eds. *The History of the Jewish People in the Age of Jesus Christ*. 3 vols. Edinburgh: T&T Clark, 1973.

Tabor, James. *The Jesus Dynasty*. New York: Simon & Schuster, 2006.

Walker, P.W.L. *Jesus and the Holy City: New Testament Perspectives on Jerusalem*. Grand Rapids, MI: Eerdmans, 1996.

Wright, N.T. *Jesus and the Victory of God*. London: Society for Promoting Christian Knowledge, 1996.

Jesus' Followers and the Temple

Attridge, Harold W. *A Commentary on the Epistle to the Hebrews*. Hermeneia. Philadelphia: Fortress Press, 1989.

Barker, Margaret. *The Great High Priest: The Temple Roots of Christian Liturgy*. Edinburgh: T&T Clark, 2003.

Barrett, Charles Kingsley. "Attitudes to the Temple in the Acts of the Apostles." In *Templum Amicitiae: Essays on the Second Temple Presented to Ernst Bammel*, 345–67. Edited by W. Horbury. Journal for the Study of the New Testament Supplement Series 48. Sheffield: JSOT, 1991.

Bauckham, Richard, ed. "James and the Jerusalem Church." In *The Book of Acts in its Palestinian Setting*. Grand Rapids, MI: Eerdmans, 1995.

———. *Jude and the Relatives of Jesus in the Early Church*. Edinburgh: T&T Clark, 1990.

Ben-Daniel, John and Gloria Ben-Daniel. *The Apocalypse in the Light of the Temple*. Jerusalem: Beit Yochanan, 2003.

Bissoli, Giovanni. *Il tempio: nella letteratura giudaica e neotestamenaria*. Jerusalem: Franciscan Printing Press, 1994.

Briggs, Robert A. *Jewish Temple Imagery in the Book of Revelation*. New York: Peter Lang, 1999.

Chester, A.N. "Hebrews: The Final Sacrifice." In *Sacrifice and Redemption: Durham Essays in Theology*, 57–72. Edited by S.W. Sykes. Cambridge: Cambridge University Press, 1991.

Davies, William David, ed. "Temple." In *The Gospel and the Land: Early Christianity and Jewish Territorial Doctrine*. Berkeley: University of California Press, 1974.

Dunn, James D.G. *The Parting of the Ways: Between Christianity and Judaism and Their Significance for the Character of Christianity*. London: SCM, 2006.

Ego, Beate, Armin Lange, and Peter Pilhofer, eds., *Gemeinde ohne Temple—Community Without Temple: Zur Substituierung und Transformation des Jerusalemer Tempels und seines Kults im Alten Testament, antiken Judentum und Frühen Christentum*. WUNT 118. Tübingen: Mohr Siebeck, 1999.

Evans, Craig A., ed. *The World of Jesus and the Early Church: Identity and Interpretation in Early Communities of Faith*. Peabody, MA: Hendrickson, 2011.

Gaston, Lloyd. *No Stone on Another: Studies in the Significance of the Fall of Jerusalem in the Synoptic Gospels*. Supplements to Novum Testamentum 23. Leiden: Brill, 1970.

Gärtner, Bertil E. *The Temple and the Community in Qumran and the New Testament*. Cambridge: Cambridge University Press, 1965.

Goodman, Martin. "The Temple in First Century Judaism." In *Temple and Worship in Biblical Israel*. Edited by John Day. London: T&T Clark, 2007.

Green, Joel B. "The Demise of the Temple as 'Culture Center' in Luke-Acts: An Exploration of the Rending of the Temple Veil." *Revue Biblique* 101 (1994): 495–515.

Han, Kyu Sam. *Jerusalem and the Early Jesus Movement: The Q Community's Attitude Toward the Temple*. Journal for the Study of the New Testament Supplement Series 207. London: Sheffield Academic Press, 2002.

Hofius, Otfried. *Katapausis: Die Vorstellung vom endzeitlichen Ruheort im Hebräerbrief*. WUNT 11. Tübingen: Mohr Siebeck, 1970.

Horbury, William, ed. *Templum Amicitiae: Essays on the Second Temple Presented to Ernst Bammel*. Journal for the Study of the New Testament Supplement Series 48. Sheffield: JSOT, 1991.

Kister, Menahem. "Jerusalem and the Temple in the Writings from Qumran." In *The Qumran Scrolls and Their World*, 477–96. Vol. 2. Jerusalem: Yad Yitshak Ben-Tsevi, 2009. [in Hebrew].

Lindars, Barnabas. "Hebrews and the Second Temple." In *Templum Amicitiae*, 410–33. Edited by William Horbury, Journal for the Study of the New Testament Supplement Series 48. Sheffield: Sheffield Academic Press, 1991.

Marcus, Joel. *The Way of the Lord*. Louisville: Westminster John Knox, 1992.

McKelvey, R.J. *The New Temple:The Church in the New Testament*. Oxford Theological Monographs. Oxford: Oxford University Press, 1969.

Rosenau, Helen. *Vision of the Temple: The Image of the Temple of Jerusalem in Judaism and Christianity*. London: Oresko Books, 1979.

Schiffman, Lawerence H. "Temple, Sacrifice and Priesthood in the Epistles of the Hebrews and the Dead Sea Scrolls." In *Echoes from the Caves: Qumran and the New Testament*, 165–76. Edited by Florentino García Martínez. Leiden: Brill, 2009.

Schüssler Fiorenza, Elizabeth. "Cultic Language in Qumran and in the NT." *Catholic Biblical Quarterly* 38 (1976): 159–77.

Spatafora, Andrea. *From the "Temple of God" to God as the Temple: A Biblical Theological Study of the Temple in the Book of Revelation.* Tesi Gregoriana serie teologia 27. Rome: Editrice Pontificia Università Gregoriana, 1997.

Walton, Steve. "A Tale of Two Perspectives? The Place of the Temple in Acts." In *Heaven on Earth: The Temple in Biblical Theology*, 135–49. Edited by Simon Gathercole and T. Desmond Alexander. Carlisle, UK: Paternoster, 2004.

Wardle, Timothy. *The Jerusalem Temple and Early Christian Identity.* WUNT 2.291. Tübingen: Mohr Siebeck, 2010.

GENERAL MATERIALS

Aviam, Mordechai. *Jews, Pagans, and Christians in Galilee.* Rochester, NY: University of Rochester Press, 2004.

Baumgarten, J. M. *Qumran Cave 4.XIII: The Damascus Document (4Q266-273).* Discoveries in the Judaean Desert 18. Oxford: Clarendon, 1996.

———. "Invented Traditions of the Maccabean." In *Geschichte–Tradition–Reflexion: Festschrift für Martin Hengel zum 70 Geburtstag*, 197–210. Ed. P. Schäfer Vol. 1. Tübingen: Mohr-Siebeck, 1996.

Brown, J.R. *Temple and Sacrifice in Rabbinic Judaism.* Winslow Lectures. Evanston, IL: Seabury-Western Theological Seminary, 1963.

Charlesworth, James H. with Lawrence Schiffman et al., eds., *The Temple Scroll and Related Documents.* Princeton Theological Seminary Dead Sea Scrolls Project 7. Tübingen: Mohr Siebeck, 2011.

Cohn, Steve J.D. *The Beginning of Jewishness: Boundaries, Varieties, Uncertainties.* Berkeley: University of California Press, 1999.

Congar, Yves. *The Mystery of the Temple.* London: Burns & Oates, 1962.

Cross, Frank M. *Canaanite Myth and Hebrew Epic.* Cambridge, MA: Harvard University Press, 1973.

Elliott, J.K., ed. *The Apocryphal New Testament A Collection of Apocryphal Christian Literature in an English Translation.* New York: Oxford University Press, 2005.

Ginsberg, H.L. *The Israelian Heritage of Judaism.* New York: Jewish Theological Seminary, 1982.

Gordon, Cyrus H. and Gary A. Rendsburg. *The Bible and the Ancient Near East.* New York: Norton, 1997.

Goulder, Michael D. *The Psalms of the Sons of Korah*. Journal for the Study of the Old Testament Supplement Series 20. Sheffield: JSOT Press, 1982.

Kugel, James L. *How to Read the Bible: A Guide to Scripture Then and Now*. New York: Free Press, 2007.

Levanoni, Y.D. *HaMikdash: A Description of the Second Temple According to the Rambam*. Jerusalem: Berit Shalom, 1995.

Levine, Lee I. *The Ancient Synagogue: the First Thousand Years*. New Haven, CT: Yale University Press, 2000.

Qimron, Elisha. *The Temple Scroll: A Critical Edition with Extensive Reconstructions*. Beersheva: Ben-Gurion University of the Negev and Israel Exploration Society, 1996.

Rendsburg, Gary A. *Linguistic Evidence for the Northern Origin of Selected Psalms*. Society of Biblical Literature Monograph Series 43. Atlanta: Scholars, 1990.

Schneemelcher, Wilhelm and Robert McLachlan Wilson, eds. *New Testament Apocrypha*. Rev. ed. 2 vols. Louisville: Westminster John Knox, 1991.

Schwartz, Daniel R. and Zeev Weiss with Ruth A. Clements. *Was 70 CE a Watershed in Jewish History? On Jews and Judaism Before and After the Destruction of the Second Temple*. Leiden: Brill, 2012.

Stieglitz, Robert R. "The Hebrew Names of the Seven Planets." *Journal of Near Eastern Studies* 40 (1981): 135–37.

Sukenik, Eleazar L. *Naḥamu, Naḥamu ʿAmi*. Jerusalem: Mosad Bialik, 1948. [in Hebrew]

Urbach, Ephraim E. *The Sages: Their Concepts and Beliefs*. Jerusalem: Magnes, 1987.

Yadin, Yigael. *The Temple Scroll*. 3 vols. Jerusalem: Israel Exploration Society, 1983.

Zervos, George T. "The Protevangelium of James and the Composition of the Bodmer Miscellaneous Codex: Chronology, Theology, and Liturgy." In *"Non-canonical" Religious Texts in Early Judaism and Early Christianity*. Vol. 14 of *Jewish and Christian Text*, 177–95. Edited by James H. Charlesworth. London: T&T Clark, 2012.

Index of Biblical and Ancient Literature References

EARLY JEWISH AND CHRISTIAN LITERATURE

CPSIA information can be obtained at www.ICGtesting.com
Printed in the USA
LVOW10s0503300414

383816LV00007B/10/P

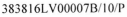

3 4711 00219 8960

9 781451 480368